P9-CRN-021

Accounting Ethics

Foundations of Business Ethics
Series editors: W. Michael Hoffman and Robert E. Frederick

Written by an assembly of the most distinguished figures in business ethics, the Foundations of Business Ethics series aims to explain and assess the fundamental issues that motivate interest in each of the main subjects of contemporary research. In addition to a general introduction to business ethics, individual volumes cover key ethical issues in management, marketing, finance, accounting, and computing. The books, which are complementary yet complete in themselves, allow instructors maximum flexibility in the design and presentation of course materials without sacrificing either depth of coverage or the discipline-based focus of many business courses. The volumes can be used separately or in combination with anthologies and case studies, depending on the needs and interests of the instructors and students.

1   John R. Boatright, *Ethics in Finance*, second edition
2   Ronald Duska, Brenda Shay Duska, and Julie Ragatz, *Accounting Ethics*, second edition
3   Richard T. De George, *The Ethics of Information Technology and Business*
4   Patricia H. Werhane and Tara J. Radin with Norman E. Bowie, *Employment and Employee Rights*
5   Norman E. Bowie with Patricia H. Werhane, *Management Ethics*
6   Lisa H. Newton, *Business Ethics and the Natural Environment*
7   Kenneth E. Goodpaster, *Conscience and Corporate Culture*
8   George G. Brenkert, *Marketing Ethics*

Forthcoming

Denis Arnold, *Ethics of Global Business*

Accounting Ethics

SECOND EDITION

Ronald Duska

The Center for Ethics in Financial Services
The American College

Brenda Shay Duska

Del Pizzo & Associates

Julie Ragatz

The Center for Ethics in Financial Services
The American College

WILEY-BLACKWELL

A John Wiley & Sons, Ltd., Publication

This edition first published 2011
© 2011 Ronald Duska, Brenda Shay Duska, and Julie Ragatz

Blackwell Publishing was acquired by John Wiley & Sons in February 2007. Blackwell's publishing program has been merged with Wiley's global Scientific, Technical, and Medical business to form Wiley-Blackwell.

Registered Office
John Wiley & Sons Ltd, The Atrium, Southern Gate, Chichester, West Sussex, PO19 8SQ, United Kingdom

Editorial Offices
350 Main Street, Malden, MA 02148-5020, USA
9600 Garsington Road, Oxford, OX4 2DQ, UK
The Atrium, Southern Gate, Chichester, West Sussex, PO19 8SQ, UK

For details of our global editorial offices, for customer services, and for information about how to apply for permission to reuse the copyright material in this book please see our website at www.wiley.com/wiley-blackwell.

The right of Ronald Duska, Brenda Shay Duska, and Julie Ragatz to be identified as the authors of this has been asserted in accordance with the UK Copyright, Designs and Patents Act 1988.

All rights reserved. No part of this publication may be reproduced, stored in a retrieval system, or transmitted, in any form or by any means, electronic, mechanical, photocopying, recording or otherwise, except as permitted by the UK Copyright, Designs and Patents Act 1988, without the prior permission of the publisher.

Wiley also publishes its books in a variety of electronic formats. Some content that appears in print may not be available in electronic books.

Designations used by companies to distinguish their products are often claimed as trademarks. All brand names and product names used in this book are trade names, service marks, trademarks or registered trademarks of their respective owners. The publisher is not associated with any product or vendor mentioned in this book. This publication is designed to provide accurate and authoritative information in regard to the subject matter covered. It is sold on the understanding that the publisher is not engaged in rendering professional services. If professional advice or other expert assistance is required, the services of a competent professional should be sought.

Library of Congress Cataloging-in-Publication Data

Duska, Ronald F., 1937-
    Accounting ethics / Ronald Duska, Brenda Shay Duska, Julie Ragatz. – 2nd ed.
        p. cm. – (Foundations of business ethics)
    Includes bibliographical references and index.
    ISBN 978-1-4051-9613-0 (pbk. : alk. paper)
    1. Accountants–Professional ethics.   2. Accounting–Moral and ethical aspects.
    I. Duska, Brenda Shay.   II. Ragatz, Julie.   III. Title.
    HF5625.15.D87 2011
    174'.9657–dc22
                                        2010042189

A catalogue record for this book is available from the British Library.

This book is published in the following electronic formats: ePDFs 9781444395884; Wiley Online Library 9781444395907; ePub 9781444395891

Set in 10.5/12.5 pt Minion by Toppan Best-set Premedia Limited
Printed and bound in Singapore by Fabulous Printers Pte Ltd

1   2011

To:
Elizabeth Catherine Duska
and
Catherine Shay

**A daughter and mother who put up with tax seasons
and manuscript deadlines, and whose Irish eyes and smiles bring
joy and love to our lives without ever holding us to account
for the cost to them of our writing this book.**

Table of Contents

Acknowledgments

First Edition

When Mike Hoffman and Bob Frederick first suggested a book on accounting ethics the names of all the people more qualified came to mind. However, what better challenge for a business ethicist than to tackle the field his wife dealt with in her day to day work, and who better to work with than an accountant with integrity who has no time for cutting corners. Against the advice of those who counseled against spouses writing a book together, we plunged in where angels fear to tread. It has been a fruitful opportunity, both of us learning more and more about the other's enterprises. So we are grateful to both Mike and Bob for the opportunity, and trust the endeavor has worthwhile fruit.

We would also like to thank Beth Remmes for her constant attention, not to mention gentle prodding, which helped us get on with the work when the tedium got the better of us. Thanks also to Patricia Werhane, Norm Bowie and Jim Mitchell for their input and encouragement. They should not in any way be held accountable for the shortcomings of this book. Gratitude is also called for toward the American College, Sam Weese its president, and Gary Stone and Walt Woerheide, who allowed us to use some of my time in the completion of this work. Finally we are grateful to Jack Del Pizzo of Del Pizzo & Associates for his insights, encouragement and general knowledge of accounting practices, which he was happy to share during the making of this book.

Second Edition

First and foremost we want to express special gratitude to Sara Taylor, the assistant director of the American College Center for Ethics in the Financial Services, for all the help in editing, reading, advising and sorting out the various details of the book. Without her immense help this task would not have been accomplished. We are grateful to Wiley-Blackwell for the opportunity to publish a second edition *Accounting Ethics*. The first edition was well received. We are grateful for the prodding of Jeff Dean and Tiffany Mok, for keeping us on track. Special thanks are due to Lynn Hayes, who has edited this second edition extensively, which has made it eminently more readable. Thanks are also due to Adam Scavette, our intern, who helped us update cases as well as work laboriously on checking and correcting citations. Thanks are also due to the numerous reviewers of the first edition, in particular Jim Gaa, and Ellen L. Landgraf whose comments have been especially helpful.

Thanks are in order to the American College, and its current president and CEO, Larry Barton, who along with Walt Woerheide, have given us encouragement and opportunity to complete this task. We would also like to thank Jim and Linda Mitchell who help in numerous ways to support the American College Center for Ethics in Financial Services and for encouraging our work during this project. We are also grateful to Dr Anthony Catanach, the Cary Maguire Fellow of the Center, and our colleague Charles DiLullo, both of whom as accountants have been of great help.

Thanks are also due to Norman Bowie, Ed Freeman and Pat Werhane – our colleagues in business ethics whose encouragement and friendship have been a constant over the years. Final thanks are due to one person, who over the years has given us encouragement in our endeavors, and who passed away recently - Tom Dunfee. Tom was a leader in business ethics and served on the Independence Standards Board. Tom also initiated the program for a doctorate in business ethics at the Wharton School of the University of Pennsylvania.

Preface

Much has happened in the accounting profession since we completed the first edition of this book in 2002. The Sarbanes–Oxley Act has altered the approaches to ethical problems, resulting in the replacement of the Independence Standards Board with the Financial Accounting Standards Board (FASB) and the Public Company Accounting Oversight Board. The financial crisis of 2008 put more pressure on accountants, specifically relating to the pros and cons of mark-to-market and fair-value accounting. Add to that the push to move to principles-based accounting as part of the impetus to adopt the International Financial Reporting Standards (IFRS) instead of Generally Accepted Accounting Principles (GAAP), and we have a whole new set of problems to explore.

To address these new topics, we have added an Afterword, in which we highlight the debates over the use of fair-value accounting and principles-versus rules-based standards. We have also reduced radically the amount of space the first edition devoted to the Enron debacle, including the elimination of the chronology of *The Wall Street Journal* articles on the Enron/Andersen story. We have preserved the section on the responsibilities of accounting firms, because although firms now face new challenges, the responsibilities have not changed.

Finally, we have added Julie Anne Ragatz, a doctoral fellow at The American College Center for Ethics in the Financial Services, as a co-author. Julie has been researching new developments in accounting ethics and teaching accounting ethics to executive MBAs for the past several years.

Introduction

"To preserve the integrity of his reports, the accountant must insist upon **absolute independence of judgment and action**. The necessity of preserving this position of independence indicates certain standards of conduct. If the confidence of the public in the integrity of accountants' reports is shaken, their value is gone." (Arthur Andersen in a 1932 Lecture on Business Ethics.)

Rosemarie is the controller for a small construction company, Acme builders. She is new on the job and grateful to the CEO, Peter, for allowing her to work flex-time so that she can take care of her young daughter, who is in day care. Rosemarie is concerned about the collectability of receivables from Fergus Motel, for whom Acme has done extensive work. Rosemarie thinks that the allowance for these receivables should be adjusted. When she expresses her concern to Peter, she learns that adjusting for the receivables might put the approval of a much-needed loan in jeopardy. It seems clear to Rosemarie that when Peter said, "Well, do what you think is right," he was really saying that he expected her to look out for the company and fudge the figures. Should she be a team player and go along with what Peter obviously wants but didn't specifically ask for?

John is a young accountant at a local CPA firm. He is wrestling with a problem: trying to decide whether to cover up a mistake made in not attaching an irrevocable election to a key client's recently submitted tax return. If he does not report the mistake, he can relieve a significant portion of the client's tax burden. John thinks taxes are unfair anyway and believes that his obligation is to look out for the client's best interests and save him from paying as much tax as possible. John also knows that keeping the client is important for the company's financial health. Do you think most accountants would cover up such a mistake? Would they be justified in doing so?

Accounting Ethics, Second Edition. Ronald Duska, Brenda Shay Duska, and Julie Ragatz.
© 2011 John Wiley & Sons, Ltd. Published 2011 by John Wiley & Sons, Ltd.

Leo is a senior accountant assigned to audit CHC, a closely held corporation. Leo discovers that CHC's income has been materially misstated, probably because of a cutoff error, but possibly deliberately. The managing partner, who is negotiating a consulting contract with CHC, is pressuring Leo to get the files to him as soon as possible. The audit has already taken significantly longer than was projected in the budget, and an investigation into the misstatement would involve a lot of time. Leo talks to Adele, the audit manager, who tells him not to mention the adjustment in the working papers, because she sees no tax implications – no harm, no foul. Should Leo follow Adele's "advice," or does he have a responsibility beyond that to work for the benefit of the client?[1]

Situations like the ones in these scenarios happen every day. They typify the ethical concerns that accountants face, whether they are management accountants, tax accountants, auditors, valuation specialists, or accountants performing any number of other accounting activities.

Such situations occurred long before the now infamous Enron bankruptcy case, in which the auditors and consultants from the accounting firm of Arthur Andersen came under criticism for not appropriately carrying out their responsibilities as accountants. In one instance, Arthur Andersen, functioning in the role of outside auditor, failed to detect and/or disclose financial transactions wherein Enron shifted assets to a special purpose entity, which made the value of the company appear to be significantly more than it was. While Andersen defenders declared that such activity was within the law and generally accepted accounting principles, critics maintain that accountants are obliged to do more.

We have seen the outcome of the Enron/Andersen case with the demise of both Enron and Andersen, passage of the Sarbanes–Oxley Act, and the institution of the Public Company Accounting Oversight Board, but it is important to remember that the Enron/Andersen case did not present new ethical difficulties. It simply brought to light ethical questions that had been simmering for well over a quarter of a century, and unfortunately continue to simmer. Enron/Andersen, because it involved billions of dollars and affected so many people's lives, illustrated dramatically the ethical difficulties accountants face. The Enron/Andersen case, and each of the scenarios above raise these ethical questions: What is the appropriate behavior for accountants? What are accountants supposed to do? What are their responsibilities?

The scenarios given above, ironically, raise another important point. If you look at the citation, you will see that the scenarios were developed for a business ethics program sponsored by none other than Arthur Andersen.

---

[1] These scenarios are adapted from Arthur Andersen and Co.'s *Business Ethics Program: Minicase Indexes*, 1992.

It was a project that brought together leading thinkers of the business ethics community to develop teaching tools for use in college courses on business ethics. Arthur Andersen had the reputation from his earliest days in Chicago for being a person of impeccable integrity, and from its inception, the company was dedicated to doing the right thing.

What went wrong with his company is a story told many times from many perspectives. From our perspective, there are two main reasons. One is on the individual level. Accountants, at least in the Houston offices of Andersen, did not do what they were supposed to do. They made the common mistake of many auditors who think their main obligation is to please the client who hires them. Rather, as we will try to show, accounting has a public purpose. It needs to serve the public good first. We will discuss this purpose at length in the book. The second reason is that Arthur Andersen succumbed to the systemic temptations that regularly beset the accounting firms, particularly the large firms. Firms, or the human beings who run them, are susceptible to the pressures of incentives; we get what we reward. As an auditor, Arthur Andersen had a clear mission – to attest that the financial statements it was auditing reflected what was really going on in the company. However, Andersen eschewed that mission in favor of fees.

A venerable firm like Andersen had prided itself on its role as auditor; as an auditing firm, it filled an important public function. Along with other large accounting firms, however, Andersen apparently forgot its main function as it began to expand. What was the purpose of the expansion? To do consulting. Why? To bring in more profits. There was little reflection on the effect of this consulting on an auditing firm's primary function and responsibility. There was little speculation about the reliance on consulting fees' impact on auditing.

An auditor's responsibilities are clear. If, however, consulting brings in more profit than auditing does, there will be pressure to do even more consulting. Some might say, if that results in soft auditing, so be it. It's simply human nature to follow pursuits that enhance our income stream. But how can we reconcile giving in to such pressure with accounting ethics?

Individuals and systems are much alike. They both give in to temptations. Hence, any serious treatise on ethics must look at the pressures the system exerts on individual accountants and their firms, and examine the rewards of the system to determine whether they align with its purposes. These are the major issues we will address in this book on accounting ethics.

Ethics is an overarching concern in all areas of life; it is involved in all human activity. Human activity is an activity for which an individual is responsible, one that he or she does deliberately and can control, one that helps or harms the individual or others, and one that is deemed to be either just or unjust, right or wrong. In this book, we will examine the ethical dimensions of the human activity of accounting. To understand it fully, we must first consider where and how the activity of accounting fits into the larger scheme of human activities.

We will look into how accounting is both an essential practice and a vital profession. It is an essential practice because today's economically developed system could not exist without accounting. Business and the financial market, as we know it, would grind to a halt if there were no way to account for the existence and disposition of the world's wealth and goods. For markets to function efficiently, it is necessary to have transactions based on accurate portraits of the financial worth of any entity being traded. Those portraits are painted by accountants. Power relationships, property rights, ownership claims, valuations, receivables, and debts are all social constructs that define who owns what and owes what to whom. All of these constructs are identified and tracked by accountants and bookkeepers.

Because of its essential role in tracking the complicated financial relationships in today's world, accounting has developed into a service profession. There are general ethical responsibilities that accrue to professionals and specific responsibilities that arise from being a professional accountant. Covering all areas and activities that have an ethical dimension would require an inordinately large book. This book, therefore, will concentrate on what we perceive as major areas of concern for the ethics of accounting.

Determining, examining, and evaluating the purposes of activities or practices is one of the major tasks of ethics. This approach to ethics is a functional one, as it involves an evaluation of a function or purpose. For example, if we take a functional approach to a knife, we see that a knife has a basic purpose or function – to cut. It is considered a good knife, with respect to its basic function, if it cuts well; if it is a dull knife that does not cut sharply, it is considered a poor knife. But we can also analyze whether the function itself is a worthwhile activity. Whether cutting is worthwhile depends on what is being cut and why – that is, the purpose for which the activity is engaged.

Every activity is done either for its own sake, in which case it is intrinsically worthwhile, or for the sake of something else, in which case it is instrumentally worthwhile. Cutting is an activity for the sake of something else, and it is judged as worthwhile or not depending on the purpose for which it is performed. A good knife can be used to cut up food, or it can be used to kill human beings.

Accounting, because it is a practice and an activity, is done for some purpose. Thus, we can determine whether an accountant is acting well to fulfill the purpose of rendering accurate portraits of a financial entity. It is important in this context to remember that the cunning accountant can hide assets as well as disclose them. But we can ask the larger questions: Why is this activity of creating financial portraits being performed? What does it accomplish?

Therefore, accounting as an instrumental activity can also be judged on the basis of the purpose for which it is used.

Providing accurate financial pictures of business activities – the primary activity of an accountant – is an instrumental activity, because it offers an indispensable service to those who need that information to engage in financial decision making. While instrumental activities can provide great benefits to human beings (and thus be viewed as noble), they can also bring about great harm. Accounting and the skills of the accountant can be utilized to do great harm to society if the purposes for which the information is used are harmful or illegal. For example, an accountant for organized crime or an accountant for the Nazi Party is providing a useful service for his clients, but the clients corrupt that service by exploiting it for evil purposes or ends.

Furthermore, accounting is not limited to business activities. The Congressional Budget Office utilizes accounting principles to determine the costs of pending legislation. The members of Congress need accurate pictures of true costs.

Hence, we judge the purpose of accounting, which is to provide information of economic affairs, as laudable. Having done so, though, we still need to judge the skilled accountant from the perspective of the use to which his or her accounting skills are put. If it is a noble purpose – to keep a worthwhile business or social entity functioning well – it will be lauded. If it is a malicious purpose – to cheat the public out of legitimate tax dollars – it will be condemned.

With those goals in mind, we begin the book by briefly explaining the history, nature, and purpose of accounting. Because it is the invention of human beings and, consequently, the result of human conventions, it will be helpful to review how accounting has evolved. Financial activities are necessary for survival in our present world, and when accounting helps to facilitate these activities, it is usually beneficial. Yet, accounting can be misused to benefit some at the expense of others, to deceive and to defraud others. At such times, the accounting itself might be performed well, but the accountant's practice and skills are denigrated by their unethical use.

Next, we will turn our attention to this question: What is ethics? We will explore current ethical theories to see how they can be applied to accounting today, focusing on both the ethics of purpose and the ethics of relationships. Ethics is more than simply the pursuit of good; it is also about fidelity to ethically acceptable relationships. A crucial relationship is that of a professional toward his or her clients. Because accounting is a skill that demands expertise, and because accountants have clients who depend on that expertise, accounting can be included among the professions. We will demonstrate why that invests accounting with an ethical dimension. We will also look at the characteristics of professionalism and the concept of agency inherent in any profession. We will show that being a professional obligates the accountant to act in the best interests of various constituencies, from the client to the company to the general public.

Accountants, as professionals, have developed various codes of ethics that mandate the rules accountants must follow to be accepted members of a profession. In this book, we will examine the American Institute of Certified Public Accountants' code of ethics, as it is the most extensive code and probably representative of most other codes. We will illustrate the ethics and ethical standards that code embodies.

Then we will examine specific ethical issues involved in three major functions of the accountant today: auditing, management accounting, and tax accounting.

Auditing. In the aftermath of the Enron/Andersen scandal, public policy debates raged on what sorts of limits should be imposed on auditors to ensure that they perform their auditing function well. What are the ethical issues involved in auditing? What responsibilities does that function entail? What conflict-of-interest problems arise for public auditors in particular?

Management Accounting. What are the responsibilities and limits of the individual who performs internal audits or prepares financial statements for companies to be used by management and perhaps by other external constituencies? Is the management accountant's primary responsibility to the company or to the general public?

Tax Accounting. What are the tax accountant 's responsibilities? How aggressive should the tax accountant be as his or her client's advocate in the face of legitimate government tax requirements?

We could address consulting, since consulting is the newest growth area for accounting firms. We could ask how it works. Usually accountants who consult rest their work on the firm's knowledge of financial situations. Their intimate knowledge of those situations makes them knowledgeable of the client's business and has led to many accounting firms acting as consultants for the firms they audited. However, this led to a huge conflict of interest with the audit function, which led to legislation like Sarbanes–Oxley. We could ask whether the Sarbanes–Oxley act did the correct thing in prohibiting accounting firms from consulting for firms that they audit? Does this consulting function jeopardize the independence of auditors? However, consulting is a generically a different activity to accounting activities, so we will pass over considerations of the ethics of consulting and focus on the major areas of auditing, managerial accounting, and tax accounting.

After examining those three major functions of the accountant, we will look at the social responsibilities of accounting firms. Specifically, we will explore how the changing world of financial services and increased competition have altered the nature of the accounting profession.

Finally, we will look at some current issues being debated in the accounting community. We will also explain the use and role of fair value accounting, and we will discuss whether or not it was a contributing factor to the financial crisis of 2008 and 2009. We will also discuss the use of principled-based versus rule-based accounting. Which is better public policy? It is our hope that this book will facilitate, at least in some small way, the understanding of accountants' ethical responsibilities and will improve accounting behavior.

Chapter One

The Nature of Accounting and the Chief Ethical Difficulty: True Disclosure

In October 2001 Enron began to collapse as a company. On October 16, 2001, Enron took a $1.01 billion charge related to write-downs of investments. Of this, $35 million was attributed to partnerships run by CFO Andrew Fastow. According to *The Wall Street Journal,* Enron disclosed that it shrank shareholder equity by $1.2 billion as a result of several transactions, including ones undertaken with Mr Fastow's investment vehicle. Arthur Andersen was Enron's auditing firm. On June 15, 2002, Andersen was convicted of obstruction of justice for shredding documents related to its audit of Enron, resulting in the Enron scandal. The United States Securities and Exchange Commission (SEC) does not allow convicted felons to audit public companies. The accounting firm agreed to surrender its CPA licenses and its right to practice before the SEC on August 31, 2002, putting Arthur Andersen out of business in the United States. These two companies will be tied together in financial history as an illustration of scandalous ethical behavior.

Although the Enron/Arthur Andersen collapse in 2001–2002 was a watershed moment in the history of accounting, the problems, practices, conflicts, and issues that led to the collapse were not new and have still not been overcome. Even before Enron, there were problems and shoddy practices. In an article from *The Washington Post* in 1998, then SEC chairman Arthur Levitt, Jr, called attention to what he dubbed a "numbers game" in which companies manipulate accounting data to produce desired results. These results range from "making one's numbers" – meeting Wall Street projections – to smoothing out quarterly results to produce a steady run of increases. According to Levitt, "This process has evolved over the years into what can best be characterized as a game among market participants."

Accounting Ethics, Second Edition. Ronald Duska, Brenda Shay Duska, and Julie Ragatz.
© 2011 John Wiley & Sons, Ltd. Published 2011 by John Wiley & Sons, Ltd.

How could this happen? We would claim that either the accountants did not understand their purpose in society, or that they deliberately avoided fulfilling that purpose. The purpose of accounting is fairly simple – to make sure that the portrait the company's accountants paint in the financial statements is as accurate as possible. According to Albert B. Crenshaw in an October 1999 article in *The Washington Post*, companies were trying to "game the numbers" in order to meet the pressures of quarterly earnings projections.[1] But what is the primary job of the accountant? It is our contention throughout this book that the fundamental ethical obligation of the accountant is to do his or her job. But to get clearer about what that job is, we need to look at the nature of accounting. It should be noted that accounting is, in a sense, what ancient Greeks called an ethos, by which we mean a custom or convention. Accounting was a human convention developed to do certain things. To understand those activities we need to briefly talk about the nature of accounting.

I The Nature of Accounting

Accounting is a technique, and its practice is an art or craft developed to help people monitor their economic transactions. Accounting gives people a financial picture of their affairs. Its original – and enduring – fundamental purpose is to provide information about the economic dealings of a person or organization. Initially, only the person or organization needed the information. Then the government needed the information. As the economy became more complex and regulated, the number of those who needed the information – the number of users of economic statements – increased. The extent of the importance of the information to the user increases the ethical factors governing the development and disbursement of that information. Some people have a right to the information; others do not.

The accountant provides information that can be used in a number of ways. An organization's managers use it to help them plan and control the organization's operations. Owners, managers, and/or legislative bodies use it to help them appraise an organization's performance and make decisions about its future. Owners, managers, lenders, suppliers, employees, and others use it to help to decide how much time and/or money to devote to the organization. Finally, government uses it to determine how much tax the organization must

[1] Albert B. Crenshaw, "In the Red or in the Black? Pictures Painted by Company Statements, Audits Questioned," *The Washington Post*, October 24, 1999, Sunday Final Edition, Financial Section, p. H02.

pay.[2] Hence, the accountant's role is to furnish various entities that have a legitimate right to know about an organization's affairs with useful information about those economic affairs. Useful information is owed to those various entities, and the accountant has an obligation to provide as true a picture of those affairs as possible.

Thus, accountants issue financial statements that a range of constituencies – from company management, to tax agencies, to potential investors – need to access. Those statements, which are expected to give a reliable and useful picture of the organization's financial affairs, are made within the guidelines developed by the profession itself. The accounting practice rests on what the Financial Accounting Standards Board (FASB) of the Financial Accounting Foundation calls a conceptual framework:

> The conceptual framework is a coherent system of interrelated objectives and fundamentals that is expected to lead to consistent standards and that prescribes the nature, function, and limits of financial accounting and reporting. It is expected *to serve the public interest* [italics added] by providing structure and direction to financial accounting and reporting to facilitate the provision of evenhanded financial and related information that helps promote the efficient allocation of scarce resources in the economy and society, including assisting capital and other markets to function efficiently.[3]

For financial markets to work well, stock analysts and investors need to get a "true picture" of a company. The very notion of a "true" picture, however, presents some problems, for there are any number of ways to look at the economic status of an organization, and in reality several pictures of a company can be developed. Often, the picture an accountant develops may serve the interest of the party who hires the accountant more than other need-to-know parties. Depending on the techniques used, a corporate accountant can make an organization look better or worse. For loan purposes, it can be made to look better. For tax purposes it can be made to look worse. We will return to the issue of the true picture later. For now we ask, what kinds of pictures are there? What kinds of financial statements do accountants produce?

There generally are four components of financial statements:

---

[2] cf. *Encyclopedia Britannica Micropaedia*, Accounting. [www.britannica.co.uk]
[3] "Proposed Statement of Financial Accounting Concepts; Using Cash Flow Information and Present Value in Accounting Measurements," Exposure Draft (Revised) from the Financial Accounting Standards Board of the Financial Accounting Foundation (FASB), March 13, 1999, Revision of Exposure Draft issued June 11, 1997.

- balance sheet
- income statement
- statement of changes in retained earnings
- statement of changes in cash flow

The balance sheet has three elements: (1) assets – the tangible and intangible items owned by the company; (2) liabilities – the organization's debts, involving money or services owed to others; and (3) owners' equity – funds provided by the organization's owners and the accumulated income or loss generated over years. The total assets, of course, equal the total liabilities plus the owners' equity. Owners' equity (net assets) equals the total assets minus the total liability (net assets). To put it another way, total assets equals liabilities plus owners' equity. This view of the equation indicates how assets were financed: by borrowing money (liability) or by using the owner's money (owner's equity).

Developing such statements is where the art and craft of accounting comes in, for it requires skill, judgment, use of the appropriate technique, and the application of principles to determine what counts as assets and liabilities. Sometimes, the assets and liabilities are clear; at other times, they depend on the accountant's judgment, which for better or worse, can be influenced by the pressures of the situation. As with all general principles, however, there are simply times when the principles used don't fit the situation and individual judgment is required.

For example, T. Rowe Price's manager, Richard P. Howard, says that many accountants' way of looking at companies is out of sync with modern markets, which focus on a company's earnings rather than its asset value:

> "One of the problems that accountants have is that they're still working on the theory that the balance sheet [the statement of assets and liabilities] is sacrosanct. So they err on the side of writing down assets. They think that they're being conservative, but that's wrong."[4]

Howard points out that writing down assets – reducing their value on the company's books – actually results in aggressive statements of profit:

> "For example, if you write down the value of a plant, you take a one-time hit, but in future years the depreciation that would be assigned to the plant, and

[4] Albert B. Crenshaw, "In the Red or in the Black? Pictures Painted By Company Statements, Audits Questioned." *The Washington Post*, October 24, 1999, Sunday Final Edition, Financial Section, p. H02.

that would be subtracted from earnings, is reduced or gone, so earnings are higher. And as equity is reduced, the same amount of income produces higher return on equity."[5]

Assets and liabilities can be classified as either current or noncurrent. Noncurrent assets are noncurrent receivables and fixed assets such as land, buildings, and long-term investments. Current assets include cash, amounts receivable, inventories, and other assets expected to be consumed or readily converted into cash in the next operating cycle. The owners' equity is divided between common or preferred stock, paid-in capital, and retained earnings, where common stock is the set dollar per share, paid-in capital is the premium paid for the stock (shares), and retained earnings is the amount earned/lost in the past and dividends distributed to owners. But what is "expected" to be consumed or converted into cash? Such items can be manipulated or at the least reported in any number of ways to determine what the owner's equity is.

The income statement shows net income (profit) when revenues exceed expenses and net loss when expenses exceed revenues. The statement of changes in retained earnings explains the changes in those earnings over a reporting period: assets minus liabilities equal paid-in capital and retained earnings. The statement of changes in financial position identifies existing relations and reveals operations that do or do not generate enough funds to cover an organization's dividends and capital investment requirement.

Because, as we noted, preparation of these statements allows great leeway in what to take account of and what not, as well as where to put things in presenting the statements, opportunities abound to paint different pictures of an organization's financial affairs. It takes little imagination to envision a manager who, for fear of his job and wanting to impress his board, puts pressure on the managerial accountant to "cook the books" so that retained earnings look much more substantial than they are. But cooking the books and "creative accounting," as the terms suggest, clearly have an unethical element and are activities that must be examined under the ethics of truth telling and disclosure. More recently, "aggressive accounting" and "pro-forma accounting" are euphemisms, at least in some cases, for presenting pictures of a company's financial situation that, while not deceptive, are less than candid.

[5] Albert B. Crenshaw, "In the Red or in the Black? Pictures Painted By Company Statements, Audits Questioned." *The Washington Post*, October 24, 1999, Sunday Final Edition, Financial Section, p. H02.

II Ethics of Disclosure

The ethics of truth telling and disclosure is a complicated issue for the accountant. *Why and to what extent is the accountant ethically obliged to disclose a true picture? Is there such a thing as a true picture?* To discern the principles that will help to answer the first question, we will reflect for a moment on three things: first, how accounting is involved in an exchange that encompasses selling; second, how exchange and selling are market transactions; and third, what lack of disclosure in market transactions has in common with lying.

Accounting is developing information that is going to be used. If the use of the information is benign and the information is truthful, no ethical problems arise. But if the information persuades people to act in one way or other, and their action either benefits or harms the persons giving or getting the information, this information giving takes on ethical importance. Depending on the use, giving out information can be very much like selling. For example, the CEO is "selling" the board or the stockholders on the soundness of the company's financial situation. His bonus might be tied to how rosy a picture he paints. The worth of the CEO's stock options rests on the financial picture. He may sell the Internal Revenue Service (IRS) a different picture of the company, and sell still a different picture to potential investors or lenders. Because accounting entails presenting the product to be sold, it enters into and influences market transactions.

In the ideal market transaction, two people decide to exchange goods because they hope the exchange will make both better off. In a market exchange, nothing new has been produced, but the exchange is beneficial to both people. Ideally, there is perfect information about the worth of what is being given and received in return. Such a trade, freely entered into with full information, should maximize satisfaction on both sides. That is the genius of the market and the defense of our free market system – freedom of exchange that leads to the overall improvement of the traders' lot.

If, however, one of the parties is misled into believing a product is what it is not, because the product is misrepresented, that misrepresentation undermines the effect of both sides being better off. Deception usually leads to the deceived party's getting something different and less valuable from what he or she expected. The deceived party most likely would not have *freely* entered into the exchange had that party known the full truth about it. The bank would not have made the loan, the public offering of stock would not have been so successful, the CEO's bonus would not have been so large, if the true picture of the company had been available.

Thus, the conditions for an ideal market transaction include the freedom or autonomy of the participants and full knowledge of the pertinent details of the product. Both conditions are required for what is often called *informed consent.* Consent cannot be presumed if a party is either forced into an exchange or lacks adequate knowledge of the bargained-for product. It might even be said that a choice based on inadequate information is not a choice at all.

It is important to note that lying is not synonymous with saying something false. Sometimes people simply make a mistake or inadvertently misspeak. In that case, they say something false, but their action can hardly be construed as lying. Telling a lie involves more than simply getting things wrong and not telling the truth. The essence of lying is found in its purpose, which is to alter another's behavior. Lying involves deliberately misrepresenting something to another person to get that person to act in a certain way, a way the liar suspects the person would not act if that person knew the truth. We can characterize lying, therefore, as an attempt by one person – usually through spoken or written words that are untrue (lying can also be accomplished with gestures or looks) – to get another person to act in a way that person would probably not act if he or she knew the truth. Misrepresentation or lying can thus be defined as a deceptive activity meant to evoke a certain response that would not have occurred if the truth were told. Simply put, we lie and deceive others to get our way. For example, if Enron officials misrepresented the company's financial health in order to persuade their employees to hold on to their stock so the value of the stock would not drop, the officials lied. In order to keep their own stock options at an inflated price the officials deceived the employees, who if they had known the truth probably would have sold their shares, thus deflating the value of the stock even more.

If we apply the notion of lying to an activity in which we paint a false picture of an organization's affairs to change a prospective investor's view of the company's financial health, we misrepresent the state of the organization to get the investor to do what we think he wouldn't do if the investor had a true picture. Viewed from this perspective, a deceptive sale is an activity whose goal is to induce the buyer to do what the seller thinks the buyer probably won't do if the buyer knew the truth. From an economic point of view, such behavior violates the ideal market principle of free exchange based on perfect information. But more important, from a moral point of view, in getting the buyer to do other than the buyer would, the seller takes away the buyer's *real* choice in the situation and thereby uses the buyer for the deceiver's own ends. Such use, as we will see in the next chapter, is unjust and immoral and often called exploitation or manipulation.

We recognize that we shouldn't lie because people will not trust us if we do. That is true, but it is a somewhat self-centered reason for not lying. From a moral perspective, the primary reason for you not to lie is that it subordinates another to your wishes without the other person's consent, for your benefit without concern for the other person. It violates the rule, a version of the Golden Rule, which says, "Don't do to others what you wouldn't have done to you." You want to know what you are getting when you buy something. So does everyone else.

Does failure to disclose fit these considerations? Some would say that not disclosing isn't lying; it's just not telling. But that misses the point. Any action of deliberately withholding information, or coloring information to get others to act contrary to the way they would if they had true information, has the same deceptive structure and consequence as an overt lie. It doesn't allow an informed choice.

But how much must the accountant disclose? Must the accountant disclose everything?

It is an accepted principle of effective salesmanship (not to be confused with ethical salesmanship) not to say anything negative about the product the salesperson is selling and certainly not to disclose shortcomings unnecessarily. A manager selling the worth of his company to a bank where he hopes to obtain a loan is in much the same situation. How many of the company's "warts" must the manager expose to the bank? What is the accountant's obligation in this situation? There are pictures, and there are pictures. Is the obligation in business more stringent that the obligation in private affairs?

As an example, if you are selling your home, is it necessary to point out all the little defects that only you know? There are, after all, laws that require disclosure of some things. Are you ethically obliged to go beyond the law? If you do, and disclose every small defect, you might succeed in discouraging every prospect from buying your home. Job applicants, as another example, need to sell themselves. Should they point out their flaws to their potential employers? No job counselor is likely to suggest that.

The questions arise, therefore, about how much a party needs to disclose and to what extent failure to disclose can be construed as market misconduct. Certainly, some failure to disclose is wrong, but how much must be disclosed? The above characterization of lying should help us decide. Whenever you are tempted not to disclose something, ask yourself why. If you are withholding information because you fear the person won't act as you wish that person would if he or she knew the whole story, you are manipulating.

Some might argue that if a person doesn't benefit from a nondisclosure, as in some social occasions, it is not lying. For example, when your friends ask how you are, you don't have to disclose that you feel miserable. They probably don't want to hear it. Or when your coworker asks you if she looks okay, you don't have to say, "You look terrible, like you just crawled out of bed."

That kind of social nondisclosure is acceptable because you are not trying to change another's behavior to benefit personally from it. Hence, if you shade the truth for some reason other than manipulating the behavior of the person to whom you are talking, it may not be wrong. This is what we call a "white lie."

Nevertheless, a caveat is in order. Paternalism – the desire to help, advise, or protect that may neglect individual choice and personal responsibility – may be involved in such social situations. There also may be many assumptions, perhaps false, about what the other person wants or needs. It is not clear that social nondisclosure is a totally harmless activity.

But to return to our main point: It may difficult in some situations to decide how much to disclose. The accountant must at least meet the disclosure requirements of governing authorities. What sort of disclosure and auditing requirements do accountants encounter?

III The Financial Statement

The Securities and Exchange Commission (SEC) oversees financial statements of corporations. The financial statements are prepared by the company's own accountants. Outside accountants audit the financial statements. (In the United States, certified public accountants (CPAs) execute the audits. In the United Kingdom and its affiliates, chartered accountants perform the audit function.) Accountants certify that the companies' financial statements are *complete* in all material aspects and the figures have been calculated through the *use of acceptable measurement principles.*

The most common measurement principles are generally accepted accounting principles. Those principles are supervised by the Financial Accounting Standards Board, not the SEC, which does have the statutory authority to set financial accounting and reporting standards for publicly held companies under the Securities Exchange Act of 1934. Throughout its history, SEC's policy has been to rely on the private sector to set standards. In the United States, much of this is now under review, given some of the shortcomings of the regulatory system that surfaced during the Enron/Andersen investigations, and self-regulation has been superseded by the Public Company Accounting Oversight Board.

But even with adherence to *Generally Accepted Accounting Principles* (GAAP), problems of disclosure arise. Take, for example, the problem of determining and disclosing asset value. (See the Afterword for more information on fair market value.) Asset measurement presents a problem because it can be based on what assets cost or on what assets could be sold for now. It can be manipulated in other ways, too. For example, Michael Schroeder wrote in *Business Week*, that Howard M. Schilit reported in 1994 that Heiling-Meyers Company's books showed that the company included installment sales in revenues before sales were final. Now such a practice is perfectly legal and in accordance with GAAP, but according to Schilit, such accounting policies "may distort the true financial condition" of the company.[6]

So what is asset value? Asset value is the value to the owners or what a buyer would be willing to pay the owners, which can be determined by what the company expects to be able to do with the asset. Asset value depends on three factors: the amount of anticipated future cash flows, the timing, and the interest rate.

Asset value can also be determined by the amount the company could obtain by selling its assets. This determination, however, is rarely used because continued ownership of an asset implies that its present value to the owner is greater than its market value, which is its apparent value to outsiders. (Such a formulation enters into values beyond monetary, even including possible ethical values.)

In addition to asset value, there is asset cost. Most assets are measured at cost because it is difficult to verify forecasts upon which a generalized value system would have to be based. The historical cost of an asset equals the sum of all the expenditures the company made to acquire it. This, obviously, is sometimes difficult to determine.

Consequently, with so much latitude in establishing the value of an organization's assets, the financial and economic picture can be skewed in any number of ways. Thus, it is important from an ethical standpoint to determine: (1) who the financial picture is being created for and for what purposes; (2) who has the right to the picture and for what purposes; and (3) what is to be done when different pictures benefit different parties at the expense of other parties entitled to those pictures.

For example, should the financial picture developed for the IRS show less in assets and earnings than the picture developed for a prospective financier? Should those two pictures be different from the one developed for the board or the stockholders? Further, should the 10K form (the annual report to the Securities and Exchange Commission) reflect merely the quantitative picture of the company, or should it point out the red flags and trends that will affect an organization's operations in the next business cycle?

Finally, to complete our discussion of the financial statement, we need to highlight some of the chief concepts and techniques that accountants utilize:

---

[6] Michael Schroeder, "The Sherlock Holmes of Accounting", *Business Week*, September 5, 1994.

- *Net income.* Net income indicates the change in a company's wealth, during a period of time, from all sources other than the injection or withdrawal of investment funds.
- *Transactions approach.* This approach recognizes as income only those increases in wealth (that can be substantiated) from data pertaining to actual transactions that have taken place with persons outside the company. The approach does not recognize, for example, the wealth that a service company gains by hiring a dynamic new employee who will produce salable commodities.[7]
- *Recognition of income.* This involves revenue estimates and expense estimates. The accountant needs to estimate the percentage of gross sales, recognizing that for some goods payment will never be received. Expense estimates are based on historical cost of resources consumed. Thus, net income equals the difference between value received from the use of resources and the cost of the resources consumed in the process.
- *Historical cost less depreciation.* To determine the value of assets, it is necessary to depreciate some items. There are several depreciation formulas, including but not limited to the modified accelerated cost recovery system, accelerated cost recovery system, straightline method, double declining balance method, and sum of the year's digits method. Which of these an accountant uses will certainly affect the picture of the company's financial affairs.
- *Cost of goods sold formulas.* To determine the cost of goods sold, the accountant can use one of several measurement methods:
  (a) FIFO (first in, first out). In FIFO, the cost of goods sold is equal to the total cost of various batches of goods available, starting with the oldest batch in the inventory.
  (b) LIFO (last in, first out). The opposite of FIFO, LIFO means that the most recently purchased items are recorded as sold first.
  (c) Average cost. In this method, it is assumed that the cost of inventory is based on the average cost of the goods available for sale during the reporting period. Average cost is determined by dividing the total cost of goods available for sale by the total units available for sale.

Once again, when we look at the multiple procedures that are acceptable to portray an organization's financial affairs, it clear that there are ample opportunities to present a picture that meets acceptable methods of accounting but, with clever manipulation, distorts the picture of the company.

---

[7]The problem of what counts as wealth is a perennial one for economists, dating back even before Adam Smith's argument with the monetarists.

IV Roles an Accountant can Fulfill

Although the accountant's primary purpose is to present a picture of an organization's financial affairs, accountants play many other roles. We will enumerate them here and discuss some of them more fully in later chapters:

- *Auditing.* The most important role is the role of the independent accountant (auditor). The auditor's function is to determine that the organization's estimates are based on formulas that seem reasonable in the light of whatever evidence is available and to see that those formulas are applied consistently from year to year – thus, to ensure reasonable application and consistent application. The role of the auditor is not to determine whether the formulas are justifiable. That, at least in the United States, is FASB's job.
- *Managerial accounting.* A second role for accountants is managerial accounting. Businesses need controllers and internal auditors. For example, they need in-house accountants whose role is to give the most accurate picture of the organization's economic state so that the company can flourish. The accountant's main responsibility is to the company, but if the company's board, managers, and shareholders are at cross-purposes, the accountant is conflicted. These conflicts form the grounds for many ethical problems.
- *Tax accounting.* A third role for accountants is the determination of tax liabilities for clients, either individual or corporate.
- *Financial planning.* More and more accountants are engaging in a fourth kind of activity, which springs from their knowledge of tax law and financial investment markets – financial planning. Some might argue this is not a role of an accountant as such, but rather a role the accountant may be well qualified to assume, given his or her areas of expertise.
- *Consulting.* Finally, there is the area of consulting. Because an accountant is exceedingly familiar with the financial status of the companies he/she serves, the accountant can become a valuable company consultant in money management, income distribution, and accounting and auditing functions. Here, too, some might argue that this is not the accountant's role, but rather one he or she can assume based on the accountant's expertise.

In later chapters we will examine the first three of these roles – auditing, managerial accounting, and tax accounting – along with the consequent ethical responsibilities that they create. We will also look at the role of consulting and the difficulties it brings with respect to conflict of interest and independence, particularly for accountants or firms that are fulfilling both an auditing and consulting role for a client.

The performance of all of these different functions has moved the accounting profession from the more traditional profession of auditor to the more entrepreneurial professions of consultant and planner. Many claim that the move has generated a crisis for accountants and contend that the dual roles have been circumscribed by the passage of the Sarbanes–Oxley Act.

Because of the events of the past several years, accounting is no longer viewed as a staid, reliable profession. It is now viewed as a profession in crisis, whose credibility is in question. The face of accounting is changing, if not accounting itself, which maintains the same functions – auditing, attesting, preparing taxes, and running the financials of a company – then at least in the makeup and orientation of accounting companies.

Long before the Enron/Andersen debacle, Rick Telberg made this pessimistic observation in *Accounting Today*:

> "In fact we are probably past the time when independence mattered. CPA firms long ago became more like insurance companies – complete with their focus on assurances and risk-managed audits – than attestors. Auditors are backed by malpractice insurance in the same way that an insurance company is backed by a re-insurer, so they have become less like judges of financial statements than underwriters weighing probabilities."

Some in the profession have even argued that auditors should function less like ultimate arbiters of fact and financial reality, and be allowed, instead, to function more like investment bankers, and provide only "due diligence." So that CPAs, who once valued fairness and truthfulness in financial reporting, would then promise little more than nods and winks, all beyond the reach of meaningful oversight.[8]

The danger in Telberg's scenario is that if every auditor or attestor acted in that way, audits and attestations would be worthless. There would still be a use for accountants as tax preparers and financial reporters, but the audit function – the heart of the accounting profession – would be excised from the practice, rendered virtually useless by its misuse.

If we take the stand that the function of the accountant is to do what is required for a company to flourish monetarily, that would not be ethics. Society needs audited reports. It needs truthful reports. If the delivery of these reports is not profitable, then accounting firms committed to maximizing their own profit will eschew the audit function. That will leave an enormous

[8]Rick Telberg, Editorial, *Accounting Today*, September 26, 1999.

accounting job still to be done. Someone will step into the gap and perform the service. That person will then be subject to the same ethical requirements as the professional auditor of today. The names may change, but the function will remain.

In an ideal world, the conventions developed in an ethos work for the common good. So in an ideal world accountants would do what they should do and fulfill their responsibilities. But that raises two questions. They might lack knowledge of what the best way to do things is, and they might be tempted to do things that are self-serving that violate these practices. To answer these problems societies develop standards that outline best practices and regulate behavior. When the ethos or ethics breaks down, we need legal constraints. Hence the development of regulatory bodies and standards. At this point it will be helpful to engage in a brief survey of the development of accounting standards.

V Development of Explicit Accounting Standards and Regulations

While much of the general public has become familiar with the breakdown of the accounting ethos because of the Enron/Andersen debacle, and with the consequent attempt to answer these breakdowns with the Sarbanes–Oxley Act, there were previous attempts to regulate and guide the accounting profession. Before reviewing some of the provisions of Sarbanes–Oxley, let's look at a brief history of some (space prohibits reviewing all) attempts to regulate accounting standards that were deemed necessary to produce ethical behavior.

Beginning in the 1920s, accounting standards were driven by a period of industrial growth with a corresponding surge in stock prices. "Accounting standards were developed privately, often poorly designed and unregulated. As a result, they were subject to manipulation with accurate financial reporting easily compromised to drive stock prices, meet loan covenants, or attract new investors."[9]

The *Securities Acts of 1933 and 1934* were Congress's response to the Depression, which to some extent resulted from manipulation and fraud in the securities markets. Part of the acts' purpose was to promote ethical behavior through legislation and regulation. Congress established the Securities and Exchange Commission (SEC), regulated securities trading, mandated common accounting standards, and required CPA firm audits of publicly traded

[9] Howard Rockness and Joanne Rockness, Legislated ethics: from Enron to Sarbanes-Oxley, the impact on Corporate America. *Journal of Business Ethics*, Vol. 57 (2005), 31–54,.

companies. "The Acts signified a landmark change in corporate accountability and provide the foundation for growth of the CPA profession as external auditors."[10]

The *Federal Trade Commission* (FTC) in 1933 adopted the following rule to provide guidance on what it means to be an independent auditor. The FTC mandated both independence in fact and independence in appearance:

> The Commission will not recognize any such certified accountant or public accountant as independent if such accountant is not in fact independent. Unless the Commission otherwise directs, such an accountant will not be considered independent with respect to any person in whom he has any interest, directly or indirectly, or to whom he is connected as an officer, agent, employee, promoter, underwriter, trustee, partner, director or person performing a similar function.[11]

During this time period, an auditor could not be found liable to third parties (other clients who may use the client's financial information) who did not enter into a contract directly with the auditor.[12] Unless an auditor actively committed fraud, he or she would not be found liable to third parties who relied on a negligently prepared report. This decision held until 1968.

In 1947, the *Institute of American Accountants* (IAA), the industry trade group at the time, adopted a statement on independence, insisting that "independence, both historically and philosophically, is the foundation of the public accounting profession and upon its maintenance depends the profession's strength and its stature."[13] Around 1950, several major accounting forms expanded their service lines to offer new "management advisory services" or "administrative services," a move that raised some ethical concerns. In 1957, "Ethical Considerations in Rendering Management Services" was published in the *Journal of Accountancy,* exploring the issues arising from offering management services to audit clients. Also in 1957, the Securities and Exchange Commission issued its annual report and voiced concern about

---

[10] Howard Rockness and Joanne Rockness, Legislated ethics: from Enron to Sarbanes-Oxley, the impact on Corporate America. *Journal of Business Ethics,* Vol. 57 (2005), 31–54.

[11] Securities and Exchange Commission 17 CFR Parts 210 and 211, (Release No. 33-7507; 34-39676; IC-23029; FR-50) Commission Statement of Policy on the Establishment and Improvement of Standards Related to Auditor Independence.

[12] Ultramares Corp. vs Touche 255 N. Y. 170 Court of Appeals of New York, Decided January 6.

[13] J. L. Carey, *The Rise of the Accounting Profession,* New York, the AICPA, 1970, pp. 195–196. According to a study by professors at Brigham Young and Texas A&M, "hiring an audit firm to provide both internal and external audits, a practice that was banned by the Sarbanes–Oxley Act, actually reduced companies' accounting risk." Sarah Johnson, "The Cost of Auditor Independence," *CFO.com.,* February 12, 2009.

the breadth of services that auditors were providing. In 1958, the SEC's chief accountant, Andrew Barr, maintained that an auditor's performing managerial services for a client risked the possibility of the auditor's losing his objectivity.[14]

During the 1950s and 1960s, most accountants who reached the level of partner were assured of their tenure until they retired. If they stood up to clients regarding questionable practices, they expected their firms to back them. At that time, the Big Four accounting firms were not afraid to speak and write about major accounting principles. There was no marketing to new clients, because advertising was frowned upon, as were other forms of self-promotion. Partners were rewarded on the quality of the audit services that they provided.[15]

The *American Institute of Certified Public Accountants* (AICPA) in 1963 published Opinion #12 on Independence that stipulated, " ... normal professional or social relationships would not suggest a conflict of interest in the mind of a reasonable observer." This opinion, with some caveats, allowed combining auditing and management consulting.[16] The AICPA also determined, at that time, that the fees from management services would not have an impact on the audit because most management fees were not recurring.[17] The popular belief was that doing both consulting and auditing would be beneficial to the companies.[18]

> "The result (to place too much emphasis on the appearance of independence, rather than independence in fact) might be to deprive clients of valuable creative contributions to improved management which their auditor, through their familiarly with the client's business, acquired in the course of an audit, are in a better position than anyone else to make.

To split the accounting profession into two segments – one a group of ivory tower auditors who did nothing but attest to the fairness of financial statements, and the other a group of experts in management and tax problems – would not only reverse the actual trend of accounting practice which

---

[14] Gary J. Previts, Edward N. Coffman and Helen M. Roybark, *Keeping Watch! Recounting 25 Years of the Office of the Chief Accountant.* Abacus, 2003.

[15] Debbie Freier, "*Compromised Work in the Public Accounting Profession: The Issue of Independence*," GoodWork Project Report Series, Number 35, Harvard University, July 2004.

[16] Association of Certified Public Accountant Committee on Professional Ethics. 1963. Opinion No. 12 – Independence.

[17] Debbie Freier, "*Compromised Work in the Public Accounting Profession: The Issue of Independence*," GoodWork Project Report Series, Number 35, Harvard University, July 2004, p. 11.

[18] J. L. Carey, *The Rise of the Accounting Profession*, New York, the AICPA, 1970, p. 182.

has evolved over a century of experience, it would also add substantially to the cost of providing business with all the professional accounting service it needs.

To contend that a CPA acting as an auditor should have no relations with his client except those involved in his work as an auditor, for fear that the public might suspect a conflict of interest, would lead to an absurd situation."[19]

Whether combining consulting and auditing services is right or wrong, affects independence, or creates a conflict of interest is open to debate. But several consequences followed this practice of combining services. In the 1960s the real estate scandals began. The 1970s and 1980s evidenced international fraud and bribery, which led to the prohibition of nonaccounting related services, along with disclosure requirements for the amount and nature of nonaudit services.

In 1974, the American Institute of Certified Public Accountants established the Cohen Commission to investigate if "a gap may exist between what the public expects and needs and what auditors can and should reasonably expect to accomplish. If such a gap does exist, it needs to be explored to determine how the disparity can be resolved."[20]

The commission found fault with the accounting profession for failing to keep pace with the business environment and for not dedicating enough time or money to the field of auditing. Although the commission did not determine that consulting compromised the auditor's ability to remain independent, it did "recommend that the auditor fully inform the board of directors (or its audit committee) of all services and their relationship to the audit services provided, and that the board of directors (or its audit committee) duly consider all services provided by the auditor."[21]

The *U.S. Senate's Subcommittee on Reports, Accounting and Management* launched the Metcalf Committee in 1977 to investigate the accounting profession. It recommended that the profession improve its procedures for assuring independence in view of the public's needs and expectations. It also recommended as best policy to require that independent auditors of publicly owned companies perform only services directly related to accounting. It suggested that only certain management advisory services are appropriate to public audit clients, such as certain computer and systems analysis necessary to

[19] J. L. Carey, *The Rise of the Accounting Profession*, New York, the AICPA, 1970, pp. 195–196.

[20] Debbie Freier, "*Compromised Work in the Public Accounting Profession: The Issue of Independence*," GoodWork Project Report Series, Number 35, Harvard University, July 2004, p. 11.

[21] American Institute of Certified Public Accountants (Cohen Commission), *Commission on Auditors' Responsibility: Report, Conclusions, and Recommendations*, AICPA, New York, NY, 1978.

improve internal control procedures. The committee cautioned that other services should *not* be provided to audit clients, such as executive recruitment, marketing analysis, plant layout, product analysis, and actuarial services.

In 1977, the American Institute of Certified Public Accountants created a division for CPA firms, composed of a SEC Practice Section (SECPS) and a Private Companies Practice Section. The SECPS adopted criteria for the scope of services and prohibited an auditor from providing the following services to a public audit client: psychological testing, public opinion polls, mergers and acquisitions, assistance for a finder's fee, executive recruitment, and actuarial services to insurance companies. Members were required to report to the audit committee of each SEC client the amounts and nature of management advisory services performed on an annual basis. To oversee the activities of the SECPS, the AICPA established the *Public Oversight Board* (POB). The POB was charged with establishing and enforcing quality-control standards for public accounting firms and instituting a peer review process.

The SEC, in 1978, required companies to disclose any nonaudit services when the fees paid to the auditor were at least 3 percent of the audit fees paid. In the same year, the AICPA rescinded its ban on advertising and other forms of client solicitation. In 1979, the POB recommended that no rules should be imposed to prohibit certain services. It would be better, the POB said, to rely on the public disclosures of nonaudit services required by the SEC. In 1982, the SEC concluded that the required disclosure of fees for nonaudit service was not useful to investors in making decisions, and the 1978 disclosure requirement was repealed.

The 1980s were a time of intense competition among accounting firms, a major change from previous decades. The competitive situation was exacerbated by the trend of mergers, which limited the number of clients available. Some clients asked for bids, and others said that they would "shop around." The accounting firms responded to the new economic pressures in that competitive environment by merging with each other and expanding into highly lucrative nonaudit services. From 1983 through1985, revenues from audits at the Big Four grew by only 14 percent, while revenues for management consulting grew 33 percent and for tax practice, 28 percent.

The *National Commission on Fraudulent Financial Reporting* (the Treadway Commission) was formed in 1985 by the AICPA, the American Accounting Association (AAA), Financial Executives International (FEI), the Institute of Internal Auditors (IIA) and the Institute of Management Accountants (IMA). In 1986, the *AICPA Special Committee on Standards of Professional Conduct for Certified Public Accountants* found that "the competitive environment has placed pressures on the traditional commitment to professionals in the practice of public accounting." An increasingly competitive environment changed the job security of partners.[22]

The National Commission on Fraudulent Financial Reporting issued a study in 1987 that included 49 recommendations directed at the SEC, public companies, independent public accountants, and the education community. These recommendations were designed to promote reliable financial reporting and to help public companies, both large and small, tighten internal controls. This study was repeated in 2007 and as of this writing, has not been released.[23]

In response to the Treadway Commission, the *Auditing Standards Board* issued 10 new auditing standards in 1988. These Statements on Auditing Standards (SASs) include requirements affecting the auditor's responsibility to detect and report errors and irregularities, the consideration of internal control structure in a financial statement audit, and communication with a company's audit committee.

In that same year, three major accounting firms petitioned the SEC to modify the independence rules and allow expanded business relationships with their audit clients. By 1989, all of the Big Four had applied for a modification of the independence rules.

The *POB's Advisory Panel on Auditor Independence* (Kirk Panel) in 1994 issued a report. "Growing reliance on nonaudit services," the report stated, "has the potential to compromise the objectivity or independence of the auditor by diverting firm leadership away from the public responsibility associated with the independent audit function."[24] The stage for the collapse of Enron and Andersen was being set.

The *Sarbanes–Oxley Act* in 2002 established the Public Company Accounting Oversight Board and the Financial Accounting Standards Board.

VI The Sarbanes–Oxley Act (SOX)

The Sarbanes–Oxley Act was designed primarily to regulate corporate conduct in an attempt to promote ethical behavior and prevent fraudulent financial reporting. The legislation applies to a company's board of directors, audit committee, CEO, CFO, and all other management personnel who have

[22] American Institute of Certified Public Accountants. Special Committee on Standards of Professional Conduct for Certified Public Accountants. (1986). *Restructuring Professional Standards to Achieve Professional Excellence in a Changing Environment*, 1986.
[23] http://www.coso.org/Publications/NCFFR.pdf.
[24] http://www.springerlink.com/content/t2137117t883h718/.

influence over the accuracy and adequacy of external financial reports. The Sarbanes–Oxley Act has changed the basic structure of the public accounting profession in the United States.

The first section of the act created the Public Company Accounting Oversight Board (PCAOB), imposing external independent regulation on the profession and ending self-regulation under the AICPA. The PCAOB now sets the auditing standards and conducts inspections of CPA firms. It is also responsible for disciplinary actions against CPAs and for setting the ethical tone for the profession.

Section 301 of SOX addresses the responsibilities of the board of directors' audit committee. These responsibilities increased significantly. Under SOX, audit committees are directly responsible for appointment and compensation of the external auditor and must approve all nonaudit services provided by the external auditor. The audit committee members must be independent, which means that they may not receive fees from the company other than for board service and may not be affiliated in other ways.

Section 302 affects senior management. Both the CEO and the CFO must personally sign and certify that the company's financial report does not contain any known untrue material statements or omit a material fact. They must admit that they are responsible for establishing and maintaining internal controls. CEOs and CFOs are subject to a $5 million fine or a 20-year prison term, without an option for parole, for violation of the certification regulation, which falls under federal court jurisdiction.

Sections 303, 304, and 306 promote ethical conduct by the board of directors, corporate executives, and key employees. It is unlawful for an officer or director to take any action to influence or mislead the external auditor. CEOs and CFOs must forfeit bonuses and profits when earnings are restated due to fraud. Executives are prohibited from selling stock during blackout periods and are prevented from receiving company loans unavailable to outsiders.

The Sarbanes–Oxley Act takes a much stronger position on incarceration than previous attempts to legislate morality in business. It contains maximum prison terms for securities fraud, mail and wire fraud, and for destroying, altering or fabricating records in federal investigations. Finally, it requires the preservation of key financial audit documents and email for 5 years with a penalty for destroying any such documentation. All of these charges fall under federal jurisdiction.

Section 406 of SOX requires public corporations to have a code of ethics for senior executives or to state in their annual report that they do not have such a code and the reasons why they do not. The SEC provides the following guidance for the code: It should promote honest and ethical conduct, full and fair disclosure, compliance with the laws, internal reporting for violations, and accountability for adherence to the code.

Section 201 is a direct response to the conflict of interest arising from the consulting and external audit services provided to Enron by Andersen. It prohibits most of the other professional services that auditors historically performed for their audit clients, and the board of directors' approval is required for any additional service the external auditor provides that is not specifically prohibited by SOX.

In addition, PCAOB now has the authority to determine any other impermissible services. Section 203 mandates partner rotation; the lead auditor must rotate off an audit every 5 years with a 5-year time-out. Other audit partners must rotate after 7 years with a 2-year time-out.

Although it has always been the case, it has become even more apparent since the Enron/Andersen debacle that financial statements must be accurate and usable in a market system that relies on thorough information to make rational decisions. But pictures are not always accurate. They can be distorted to produce desired results, like "meeting one's numbers" or "smoothing out quarterly reports." We need to examine why and to what extent such distortions constitute unethical procedures. But first, we must provide an overview of what accounting is in order to better appreciate its nature and purpose, for it is only in the light of that purpose that we can effectively evaluate accounting behavior in ethical terms.

VII Recent Scandals that Provoked More Regulation

The WorldCom scandal immediately followed the Enron/Andersen scandal. WorldCom started its questionable practices when the company did not meet earnings expectations. Its fraudulent accounting led to a $9 billion restatement that was the largest in the history of the United States. "Accounting managers were given promotions, raises and made to feel responsible for a likely collapse of the stock price if they did not manipulate the books."[25]

Moreover, cooking the books didn't stop with the demise of Enron, Andersen, and WorldCom – or even with the passage of the Sarbanes–Oxley Act. Since then, there have been other scandals, the most notorious of which is HealthSouth, where recent estimates indicate that accounting fraud may have manufactured $4 billion of false earnings (2004). Reports say that the accountants focused on changing the contractual adjustments account – the

[25] S. Pelliam, "Questioning the Books: WorldCom Memos Suggest Plan to Bury Financial Misstatements", *The Wall Street Journal*, July 9, 2002, p. A=8.

difference between the gross billings and what the health care providers will pay – to increase revenues. This serves to increase net revenue; adjustments are made in the balance by falsifying fixed-asset accounts.

It is speculated that because many of HealthSouth employees were formerly employees of Ernst and Young, they knew the sort of adjustments that they could make without detection, and if the adjustments were noticed, the employees simply provided false documents to back the numbers up.

The SEC accused HealthSouth management of fabricating $2.74 billon in earnings. Five CFOs were convicted; 15 financial employees pleaded guilty. Former CEO Richard Scrushy is the first CEO to be charged under the Sarbanes–Oxley Act for signing a false certification of financial statements. Although he avoided conviction, he was indicted on 85 counts and subsequently lost a civil suit fining him $2.9 billion.

Whether and to what extent the Sarbanes–Oxley Act is successful are matters of conjecture. Nevertheless, because it is the foremost legislative attempt to promote ethical behavior in accounting, we have summarized in Appendix A what the act is and what it prohibits.

VIII Conclusions

In summary, the accounting profession was developed to give a true and accurate picture of the financial affairs of organizations. That picture is important to a variety of constituencies. Its accuracy is crucial. The creation of inaccurate pictures used to exploit those with a legitimate right to know the true picture is equivalent to the unethical behavior of lying. That constitutes a distortion of the accountant's true function. Such distortions then lead to regulations and mandated best practices.

In the final chapter of this book, we will examine numerous ways the profession is in crisis today. Largely, it is an ethical crisis. But before we can deal with some of the specific issues, we need to spell out what ethics involves. When applied to areas of accounting, it is not the simple matter we learned it to be when applied to everyday life. Accounting functions are complex procedures. We need a sophisticated set of ethics to deal with them. Consequently, at this point let us move on to a deeper examination of what constitutes ethics.

Chapter Two

Ethical Behavior in Accounting: What Is Ethics?

Ethical scandals in the accounting profession abound. In March 2009, David Friehling, Bernard Madoff's auditor, was arrested by federal prosecutors on charges of fraud, allegedly for signing off on fraudulent financial statements:

"Lev Dassin, acting U.S. attorney for the Southern District of New York, said … Mr. Friehling conducted sham audits that allowed Mr. Madoff to perpetuate the fraud. Mr. Dassin said that, by falsely certifying that he audited financial statements for Bernard L. Madoff Investment Securities LLC, Mr. Friehling 'helped foster the illusion that Mr. Madoff legitimately invested his clients' money.'"[1]

Let's go back to the beginning of the decade. In January 2000, the *New York Times* reported that the SEC found that partners and employees at PricewaterhouseCoopers routinely violated rules forbidding their ownership of stock in companies they were auditing. The investigation identified 8064 violations at the firm, which dismissed five partners.[2]

Scrutiny of auditing practices by SEC came "after a series of high-profile corporate accounting frauds that auditors missed at companies, including Cendant, Sunbeam, and Livent. Public shareholders lost hundreds of millions of dollars in these cases, and confidence in accountants was shaken."[3]

---

[1] Ami Efrati, "Accountant Arrested for Sham Audits," *The Wall Street Journal*, March 19, 2009.
[2] Gretchen Morgenson, "S.E.C. Seeks Increased Scrutiny and New Rules for Accountants," *New York Times*, May 11, 2000, Section C: p 1.
[3] Adrian Michaels, "Big Five Must Unite to Avoid Return to Their Audit Days," *Financial Times of London*, Thursday, May 11, 2000, Companies and Finance Section, p. 44.

Accounting Ethics, Second Edition. Ronald Duska, Brenda Shay Duska, and Julie Ragatz.
© 2011 John Wiley & Sons, Ltd. Published 2011 by John Wiley & Sons, Ltd.

And, of course, there is this well-known Enron/Andersen scandal. In October of 2001 Enron took a $1.1 billion charge related to write downs of investments, some of which was attributed to partnerships run by Andrew Fastow the chief financial officer. In December Enron filed for bankruptcy in the biggest bankruptcy case in history in a New York bankruptcy court. According to Nanette Byrnes, it was a "huge case:"

> "... A $50 billion bankruptcy, $32 billion lost in market cap, and employee retirement accounts drained of more than $1 billion. The lapses and conflicts on the part of Enron's auditor Arthur Andersen are equally glaring. Andersen had been Enron's outside auditor since the 1980s, but in the mid-1990s, the firm was given another assignment: to conduct Enron's internal audits as well.

For working both sides of the street, Andersen was rewarded richly. In 2000, the firm earned $25 million in audit fees from Enron, and another $27 million in consulting fees and other work."[4]

More recently, in 2005, KPMG was indicted for promoting abusive tax shelters. The Department of Justice and the Internal Revenue Service on August 29, 2005, reported as follows:

> "KPMG LLP (KPMG) has admitted to criminal wrongdoing and agreed to pay $456 million in fines, restitution, and penalties as part of an agreement to defer prosecution of the firm."[5]

Later, there were troubles with BDO Seidman:

> "In 2007, the CPA firm BDO Seidman LLP was found 'grossly negligent by a Florida jury for failing to find fraud in an audit that resulted in costing a Portuguese Bank $170 million. The verdict opens up the opportunity for the bank to pursue punitive damages that could exceed $500 million.'"[6]

Seven people, including the former chief executive and chairman of accounting firm BDO Seidman LLP, were charged criminally in an allegedly fraudulent tax-shelter scheme that generated billions of dollars in false tax losses for clients.[7] In July 2009 the PCAOB (Public Company Accounting Oversight

---

[4] Nanette Byrnes *et al.*, "Accounting in Crisis," *Business Week*, January 28. 2002, p. 44 ff.
[5] http://www.usdoj.gov/opa/pr/2005/August/.
[6,7] Chad Brady, "BDO Seidman Snags Guilty Plea" *AccountingWeb*, June 26, 2007. http://www.accountingweb.com/cgi-bin/item.cgi?id=103667.

Board) said that BDO Seidman had trouble testing revenue-recognition controls and that Grant Thornton LLP did not adequately identify GAAP errors.[8]

The PCAOB report highlighted several deficiencies tied to what it said were failures by BDO to perform audit procedures, or perform them sufficiently. According to the report, the shortcomings were usually based on a lack of documentation and persuasive evidence to back up audit opinions. For example, the board said, BDO did not test the operating effectiveness of technology systems that a client used to aggregate revenue totals for its financial statements. The systems were used by the client company for billing and transaction-processing purposes.[9]

BDO was not alone.

"On August 16, 2007, a year-long Audit Committee investigation of Dell accounting issues found that executives wrongfully manipulated accruals and account balances, often to meet Wall Street quarterly financial expectations in prior years. The probe was headed by an outside law firm, Willkie Farr & Gallagher of New York, and involved an outside accounting firm, KPMG. More than 5 million documents were examined during the probe."[10]

And in January 2009, the *New York Times* reported this fraudulent activity:

"In December 2008, Satyam, India's fourth largest computer software services outsourcer, revealed that its former chairman, CEO, and founder, B. Ramalinga Raju, wrote a four-page letter to the Bombay Stock Exchange, confessing that he orchestrated a massive accounting scam and kept it alive for at least 5 years. In the letter, Raju admitted that he created at least $1 billion in fraudulent cash entries on the company's books that went undetected for years. ... Many experts cast partial blame for the scandal on Satyam's auditor Price Waterhouse India, because the fraud went undetected for so many years."[11]

But these were not the only cases. Under "accounting scandals" in Wikipedia, there is a list, as of this writing, of 30 ethical irregularities since 2002 (a list by no means complete), involving the auditing companies of Arthur

---

[8,9] Marie Leone, "Audit Overseer Faults BDO, Grant Thornton," CFO.com, July 13, 2009.

[10] Edward F. Moltzen, "Dell Accounting Scandal 'Not A Happy Story,'" Channel Web, August 16, 2007. http://www.crn.com/it-hannel/201800702;jsessionid=TWRS3ZETWCRMPQE1GHO SKHWATMY32JVN.

[11] Heather Timmons and Bettina Wassener, "Satyam Chief Admits Huge Fraud," *New York Times*, January 7, 2009.

Andersen, Deloitte and Touche, Ernst and Young, Friehling and Horowitz, Grant Thornton, KPMG, and Pricewaterhouse Coopers.[12]

To what extent each of the accounting firms is culpable, we will leave to the courts and the Public Company Accounting Oversight Board (PCAOB) to determine. For our purposes, these cases indicate the necessity to scrutinize ethical behavior in accounting. Indeed, the Sarbanes–Oxley Act mandates the PCAOB to establish ethical standards.

As we have shown, there are numerous stories about questionable or "unethical" behavior by accountants. This is not to say that all accountants or accounting firms act unethically. By and large, we believe, most act honorably most of the time, or the entire structure would collapse. Stories such as the ones above are an indication that there is a need for greater ethical sensitivity and ethical behavior in the accounting profession. During the past quarter century, more attention has been directed to ethics and morals and on the need to apply ethical principles in business. But what is ethics? How do ethics apply to business in general, and to accounting in particular?

I What Is Ethics?

The remainder of this chapter will focus on the nature and dimensions of ethics and morality and on their application to accounting practices and the accounting profession.

The words "ethics" and "morals" have a number of meanings. Webster's Collegiate Dictionary gives four basic meanings of the word "ethics:"

- the discipline dealing with what is good and bad and with moral duty and obligation
- a set of moral principles or values
- a theory or system of moral values
- the principles of conduct governing an individual or group

Ethics, in all its forms, is concerned with right or wrong, good or bad. It is either a set of principles held by an individual or group or the discipline that studies those ethical principles. The task of that discipline is the analysis and evaluation of human actions and practices. For example, according to some people or groups, assisted suicide is ethically acceptable. The discipline of eth-

---

[12] Wikipedia, "Accounting Scandals," http://en.wikipedia.org/wiki/Accounting_scandals.

ics examines what "assisted suicide" means (analysis) and what reasons can be given in support of or against the practice (evaluation).

II Ethics: The Intellectual Enterprise

Every person has an ethical set of beliefs or ethical principles. For example, most people have some belief about whether practices such as euthanasia, abortion, capital punishment, and adultery are good or bad, right or wrong, acceptable or unacceptable. Most people think cheating and stealing are wrong, promises ought to be kept, and so forth. Each of these opinions constitutes a moral belief. If you were to write down what you believe about each of those actions or practices, that would constitute part of your ethic. One purpose of this chapter is to help you examine your own ethical beliefs.

To begin, we will look at the structure of an ethical belief. Every ethical belief contains two elements. It has what logicians call a subject and a predicate. A subject is what the belief is about. Usual subjects in ethics are actions or practices such as capital punishment, adultery, lying, and so forth. A predicate is what is said about the subject. "Wrong," of course, is an ethical predicate. So are such terms as "unfair," "unjust," "bad," "good," "should be done," "the right thing to do," and so on. Hence, for the person who believes that assisted suicide is wrong, "assisted suicide" is the subject of the belief and "wrong" is the ethical predicate. In the judgment (judgment here simply means the expression of our beliefs) "Cooking the books is wrong," "cooking the books" is an action or practice. The subject of an ethical belief is usually an action or practice, but sometimes is a system or institution.

III Actions

Human actions are the primary subject matter of our ethical judgments. By human action, we mean behavior or activity that is deliberate – that is, an action about which a person deliberates and freely chooses to perform. People deliberate about actions over which they have control and consequently are held responsible for those actions. We don't hold animals responsible for their actions, because there is no evidence that they do things "deliberately" in the same way that humans can and do.

Not all deliberate human actions, however, have ethical import. The action must have a certain gravitas. We can deliberately decide to wear a red rather than a blue tie, or to eat mashed potatoes with our fingers instead of a fork. But these are not actions with ethical impact. There are guidelines regarding what kind of tie goes with what and whether to eat potatoes with our fingers, but these are rules of fashion or etiquette, not ethical rules. The deliberate actions we designate as "ethical" or "unethical" are usually actions that benefit or harm other people or ourselves in some serious way.

IV Social Practices, Institutions, and Systems

Human actions are not the only subject matter for ethics. Besides actions, ethics examines and evaluates social practices. Whereas actions are individual activities, such as John's stealing in a specific situation, a social practice is a class of individual actions. When we say, "Stealing is wrong," we are evaluating a social practice and not a specific action. Thus, John's individual act of stealing is an instance of the general practice of stealing. Insider trading is a general practice. Tom's action of using insider information to buy a specific stock is an individual action, which is an instance of the general practice of using inside information.

Ethics also evaluates organizations, institutions, and even social, political, and economic systems. For example, we can evaluate the practices of an organization such as the American Institute of Certified Public Accountants (AICPA), a company such as a Big Four accounting firm such as Ernst and Young, the entire accounting profession, or even a system such as our free enterprise economic system, which stresses free market exchange and profit making. Individuals who say, "Capitalism is a corrupt system," are evaluating a system. The recent call for reform in the accounting profession implies that its practices are inadequate and need to be improved. It is, implicitly at least, an ethical judgment.

V Why Study Ethics?

Why should an accountant get involved in this study of ethics? Surely, every accountant already has a set of moral beliefs that he or she follows. Even so, there are several reasons for studying ethics:

- First, some moral beliefs an individual holds may not suffice because they are simple beliefs about complex issues. The study of ethics can help the individual sort out these complex issues by seeing what principles operate in those cases.
- Second, in some situations, because of conflicting ethical principles, it may be difficult to determine what to do. In these cases, ethical reasoning can

provide insights into how to adjudicate between conflicting principles and can show why certain courses of action are more desirable than others. The study of ethics can help develop ethical reasoning skills.

- Third, individuals may hold some inadequate beliefs or cling to inadequate values. Subjecting those beliefs or values to critical ethical analysis may show their inadequacy. Let's look at a few examples:

  (a) At one time, you probably thought certain things were wrong that you now think are okay, and you thought certain things were okay that now seem wrong. In short, you changed your mind about some of your ethical beliefs. Some time ago, for example, many managers believed that it was acceptable to fire someone for little or no justifiable reason. After ethical reflection and examination – which encourages us to become more knowledgeable and conscientious in moral matters – that practice now seems questionable. Although managers have an obligation to stockholders not to retain unneeded employees, don't the managers have some obligation to those who are fired?

  (b) In the past, the principle *caveat emptor* – "Let the buyer beware" – was an acceptable practice. Now, it is generally believed, in many cases, that the manufacturer has the obligation to inform the buyer of potentially harmful defects. Caveat emptor has become *caveat vendor* – "Let the seller beware."

  (c) Years ago, accountants thought it unacceptable to advertise. Today, it is a justifiable practice. It also used to be an accepted belief that an accounting firm fulfills the letter of the law simply by following generally accepted accounting principles (GAAP). Upon ethical reflection, however, does the firm have an ethical obligation to encourage more realistic financial pictures, even if it means going beyond GAAP?

- A fourth and very important reason to study ethics is to understand whether and why our opinions are worth holding. Socrates philosophized that the unexamined life is not worth living. Have you examined your life? As an accountant, what are your basic goals? Are they compatible with other values that you have? If you need to choose between keeping a job and violating your professional responsibilities, what would you do? When your responsibility to family clashes with your responsibility to your job, how do you resolve the conflict?

- A final reason for studying ethics is to identify the basic ethical principles that can be applied to action. These principles should enable you to determine what should be done and to understand why. When you are faced with a decision about what to do in a difficult situation, it is helpful to have a checklist of basic questions or considerations you can apply to help determine what the outcome should be. In engineering, we must learn the principles of construction so that we can apply them to certain activities. In accounting, we must learn the principles of accounting so that we can apply them to specific situations. So, too, in ethics, we must learn the principles of ethics, which govern human behavior, so that we can apply them to the difficult ethical situations we face. Thereby, we can ensure that we have examined the issue adequately, using all the ethical principles available.

The study of ethics can make us aware of the principles to use in determining what we should do in a situation involving ethical matters. Because ethical issues grow ever more complex in an ever more complex world, it behooves us to have a grasp of the underlying structure of ethical reasoning to help us navigate the ethical sea.

A caution is in order at this point: Just as some people excel at golf without knowing the principles of a good swing, some people can act ethically without knowing the principles of ethics, or without knowing why an action is ethically "right." But just as most of us can improve our golf game by learning the principles of a sound swing, it follows that we can improve the ethical decision-making dimension of our behavior by studying why certain actions and practices are correct. For example, well-meaning people are often led astray by their intuitions without understanding the concepts that justify those intuitions, or without appreciating the complexity of the situation. If you feel your only responsibility as a businessperson is to make a profit, that simple, yet inadequate, view will blind you to additional responsibilities you have to employees, employers, clients, and others in the community in which you do business. If you feel your responsibility as a management accountant is simply to do what is in the interest of the company, even though it gives a false picture of its financial affairs, you are ignoring other responsibilities.

VI   Being Ethical: How to Determine What to Do

Accountants have a number of ethical responsibilities – to themselves, their families, their profession, and the clients and company for which they work. But what is the accountant's basic responsibility as an accountant? To begin with, let's suggest a simple answer: Accountants should do their job! That's the ethical thing to do, and we will show why a little later. For now, suffice it to say that accountants implicitly promise to do their job when they enter the profession, and promises should be kept. Doing your job encompasses various specific responsibilities. These responsibilities are spelled out in the job description, the employee handbook, the managerial guidebook, the company's code of conduct, and/or finally, the profession's code of conduct or ethics. Thus, a professional code of ethics and/or a job description sets the standards. For example, the AICPA code of ethics clearly mandates certain types of behavior in its seven principles, as follows:

(1) In carrying out their responsibilities as professionals, members should exercise sensitive professional and moral judgments in all their activities.
(2) Members should accept the obligation to act in a way that will serve the public interest, honor the public trust, and demonstrate commitment to professionalism.
(3) To maintain and broaden public confidence, members should perform all professional responsibilities with the highest sense of integrity.
(4) A member should maintain objectivity and be free of conflicts of interest in discharging professional responsibilities.
(5) A member in public practice should be independent in fact and appearance when providing auditing and other attestation services.
(6) A member should observe the profession's technical and ethical standards, strive continually to improve competence and the quality of services, and discharge professional responsibility to the best of the member's ability.
(7) A member in public practice should observe the Principles of the Code of Professional Conduct in determining the scope and nature of services to be provided.

Later in the book, we will examine the broad-reaching principles of this code more thoroughly. At this point, however, let's briefly address the first and second principles.

According to the first principle, members should "exercise sensitive professional and moral judgments in all their activities." What is involved in sensitive judgment? What factors lead to making ethical judgments? If we can determine how moral judgments are constructed, we can discover ways to justify our moral beliefs – ways to ascertain the right answer (or most adequate answer possible) about what to do in particularly difficult situations. Ethics gives us a powerful tool to adjudicate ethical conflicts and resolve ethical issues.

The belief that "people should do their jobs" is probably in your set of moral beliefs, But why is that the right thing to do? Why should people do their jobs? Should they do them under any and every circumstance, even when it is not beneficial to them? The second principle stipulates that members should "accept the obligation to act in a way that will serve the public interest, honor the public trust, and demonstrate commitment to professionalism." Does that mean that accountants need to place their family's interests below those of the public? If the accountant has obligations both to a client and to a family member, does the accountant necessarily have to place the public's interest first? Further, what should the accountant do when the interests of the company – say, the need for more business – conflict with the needs of the client or the public?

Thus, even if we agree that people should do their jobs, there are occasions when doing so is problematic. There can be conflicts within the job; there can also be conflicts between the job, the profession, and the individual's personal life. What do we do in those cases? What standards can we use to adjudicate such conflicts? How can we tell what standards are acceptable, what actions are acceptable, what practices are acceptable? Moreover, how does the study of ethics help to answer these questions?

Recall that ethics involves the analysis and evaluation of moral beliefs or judgments. Let us expand on that definition. We noted that *analysis* of a moral belief or judgment might involve determining what one of the words in the belief or judgment means. For example, when the third AICPA principle above charges members to "perform all professional responsibilities with the highest sense of integrity," what does "integrity" mean exactly? The code suggests asking, "Am I doing what a person of integrity would do?" But how are we to know what integrity itself demands? Hence, analysis of a moral belief involves determining precisely what that belief is asserting – whether the action under scrutiny is an action that a person of integrity would perform.

After analysis, we can move to evaluation, a determination of whether the belief is correct. Many people think that moral beliefs are subjective. They think that merely holding a moral belief is sufficient to make it correct. They might say, "Well that's your opinion, so I guess it's true for you." This attitude, however, has no room for *evaluating* beliefs. It simply accepts anyone's belief as correct. But if simply holding a belief, however pernicious, makes it correct, then Hitler's belief that the Jews should be annihilated, the slave owner's belief that slavery is justified, and the infant sacrificer's belief that infanticide is acceptable would be correct. That is intolerable.

But how are we to evaluate beliefs? How can we tell if a moral belief is correct, what a person of integrity would do, or whether our judgment is sensitive enough? Moral judgments are not like factual judgments, which express beliefs about the way things are. Consequently, moral beliefs cannot be verified or justified the way factual beliefs can be. "The earth is a sphere" is a factual belief. We can justify that belief through observation and scientific theorizing. "It's raining" can be verified simply by looking outdoors. "Light rays bend when they travel around the sun" can verified through informed speculation using a hypothetical deductive method. But we cannot justify or verify moral beliefs that way. Moral beliefs involve values and values can't be seen or touched; they also involve emotions, desires, and subjective preferences. That's why many people conclude that each individual's belief is "true" for that individual. Everyone must judge, but sometimes those judgments are correct and sometimes incorrect. How are we to evaluate them? In many cases, we have a perfectly straightforward procedure for evaluating moral beliefs: Ask whether there are any *good reasons* why a certain action is morally acceptable or any *good reasons* why it is not.

Consider the following example. Imagine you are a teenager who has a very important date. You want to impress your date by showing up in a classy car. Your father has a Jaguar. You ask your father if you can borrow the Jaguar on Friday. He says, "Sure, no problem." Friday arrives, and when you request the car keys, your father says, "No, you can't have the car." How would you respond? Possibly with disbelief. You might say, "But you promised," or you might ask, "Why not?" If your father thinks (believes) he is not obligated to give you the car, either the belief itself is not justified (correct), or he needs to justify it.

Suppose he answers your "Why not?" with "I don't feel like it." You wouldn't accept that as a good reason. That's no reason. You would probably remind him that he had promised you the car. Promises, after all, are made precisely because people might not feel like doing what they've said. If people always felt like doing what they said they'd do, we wouldn't need promises. Your father's justification, therefore – that he won't give you the car because he doesn't feel like it – carries no weight. He, like everyone else, is expected to overcome his feelings and honor his commitments. Imagine if we all did whatever we felt like. Human institutions would collapse – a spouse could wake up one morning and declare, "I don't feel like being married today." At any rate, your father, if he believes he has no obligation to give you the car simply because he doesn't feel like it has gotten it wrong. His belief is incorrect.

But there might be a way he is correct. Suppose you ask, "Why not?" and he says, "Because the brakes failed on my way home, and there was no time to get them fixed." This is a perfectly good reason for not giving you the car – for him not keeping his promise. Furthermore, his belief that he is not obliged under those circumstances to keep his promise, that he is obliged *not* to keep it, and that you are obliged to let him out of it are justified.

This example illustrates how moral beliefs are evaluated as correct or incorrect. The beliefs can be justified if there are good reasons for accepting them. Good reasons justify moral beliefs in the way that observations justify factual beliefs. Furthermore, these good reasons form the basis of ethical principles and are at the core of ethical theory.

What characterizes a good reason is based on precepts of common morality that we learned growing up: Do good. Don't harm. Don't lie. Don't cheat.

Don't steal. Be fair. Respect others. Treat others as you would be treated yourself. Follow your conscience. Keep your promises or your word. Thus, if someone falsifies an expense account, we agree that what the person did was wrong because it constitutes lying or stealing. Likewise, we agree that what the father in the example above did, in not loaning the car to his child because the father didn't feel like it, was wrong because he didn't keep his promise.

There are two kinds of reasons to justify our moral beliefs: reasons that validate doing something and those that validate not doing something. It is much harder to take a positive course of action than to prohibit a course of action, because taking a positive action opens up an indefinite number of options. It is much clearer to prohibit an action, for if we know that an action will harm another, we need only to avoid it. Often, therefore, we are clear about what we should not do (negative injunctions) but not clear about what we should do (affirmative duties).

What are some of the good reasons for doing something? A very good reason for doing anything is that the action is good for you, that it is in your interest or benefits you. Another good reason is that the action is good for or benefits society. Other good reasons are that the action is just or fair, or because it is something you promised to do – as long as what you promised to do will not bring harm to someone. There are also reasons for not doing something, and they are the more common rules of morality. We should not do something because doing so would harm people or use people – we should not cheat, lie, or steal. We should not do something that harms others or ourselves – we should not be unjust or unfair; we should not break promises.

Let's see how those reasons work when we apply them to the belief we discussed earlier: "People should do their jobs." Why should people do their jobs? In the first place, doing the job usually benefits the person, by giving him or her a salary and meaningful work. Thus, doing the job is good for that individual. In the second place, because the division of labor provides the most efficient way for society to operate, a job is a necessary cog in the wheel of progress, and doing it will benefit society. Finally, in taking a job, the individual makes at least an implicit promise to do it; promises should be kept.

VII Questions to Ask to Justify An Action: The Basis of Ethical Theory

Thus we see that the way to justify an action is to examine the reasons for and against it. One way to examine those reasons is to ask several basic questions. We will now consider these questions.

Is the action good for me?

Obviously, if a certain action benefits an individual or is good for that person, that is a good reason for doing it. As we saw, a good reason for working is that it provides us with the wherewithal to live and, ideally, to engage in a fulfilling activity. There is a great deal of emphasis today on the importance of meaningful work. But what is meaningful work if it is not work that is beneficial to the person? We have a need to be creative and productive, and meaningful work will help us fulfill that need. Hence, it is good for us.

On the other hand, if an action harms the individual, that is a good reason for not doing it. People frequently equate ethical behavior with actions that are detrimental to them and hesitate to defend actions that are beneficial. That is a mistake. A healthy self-interest is a good thing. If you don't care about your own benefit, who will?

However, several caveats are necessary here. What is beneficial to someone is not necessarily what that person wants or desires. Our wants and desires are a mixed bag. For example, I want the piece of cake, but it is not good for me because I need to lose weight. We must clarify what we mean by good. For our purposes, let's say that something that fulfills basic human needs is good, although there may also be other things that are good.

As human beings, we have several levels of need corresponding to several dimensions of human nature. There are material needs that fulfill the bodily dimension – needs for food, shelter, and clothing. Beyond that, because human beings are social, there are needs relating to other people, as in friendship. These are the needs to fulfill the social dimension. Finally, because human beings are potential producers, there is a need for purposeful projects, goals, and actions – in short, meaningful activity. These are the needs that fulfill the active dimension.

To fulfill these material, social and creative needs is an important *reason* for performing an action, and in some cases, we can justify our belief that an action is good simply by showing it is good for us in those ways. But there are more questions.

Is the action good or harmful for society?

The second question to ask of any action is whether or not it is going to be good for society. When we think ethically, we don't usually stop at considering the benefit of the action for ourselves, but we go further and consider its benefits for everyone affected. After all, not every action performed in the world affects us directly. You may recall that in 1982, capsules in some Tylenol bottles were poisoned, several deaths resulted, and Johnson and Johnson pulled the defective Tylenol from the shelves. If neither I nor anyone else I knew used Tylenol, then whether or not Johnson and Johnson recalled the product really didn't affect me. Therefore, that action was neither good nor bad for me. From a detached, objective point of view, however, I can see that it was a good thing to do, because removing the defective product from the shelves prevented harm to those who might have used it. Simply, if a good reason for doing an action is that it benefits me, then that's true for everyone, so the more people benefited the better. Of course, when the action benefits society but harms me, there is a problem, but we will return to that shortly.

Is the action fair or just?

A third question to ask is whether or not the action is fair. When you were a child, your mother probably served you a piece of cake numerous times. But suppose you had a brother and sister and your mother gave all of you pieces of cake, but the one she gave you was bigger than the pieces she gave your siblings. Wouldn't you think (even though you might be afraid to admit it) that she was being unfair?

The principle of justice, which all of us recognize, is that the same (equals) should be treated the same (equally). There is often disagreement about who and what are equal, but unless there is some relevant difference, all persons should be treated equally. Therefore if there is no relevant difference between you and your siblings, you should all receive roughly the same size piece of cake. If it is your sister's birthday, however, you are not equal in all relevant respects; her birthday creates a good reason for her to get a larger piece.

This notion of fairness gives rise to another reason for or against a course of action: entitlement. To be entitled to something means that the person has a right to it and that the person's rights should be respected. We turn now to the next question.

Does the action violate anyone's rights?

To the extent that all humans are equal, they are *entitled* to be treated in a certain way. The principle of equal justice gives us a right to be treated equally. A word about rights (entitlements): There are two kinds of rights – negative and positive. Negative rights are rights to things that no one has to provide for us, that we already have, and that are to be respected and not taken away, such as a right to life, a right to liberty, and, some would argue, a right to property.

Take the right to liberty: If we are equal to others, by what right can they restrict our liberty? Why is their liberty more important than ours? The right to liberty is essential in a free market system because free exchange is key to efficient market transactions. Deceptive advertising and coercive marketing practices are condemned because removing information that is necessary for informed consent violates the consumer's liberty. Further, government regulations are often objectionable because they interfere with the business entrepreneur's liberty to do business.

Whereas a negative right is intrinsic, a positive right is an entitlement in which something must be provided – a right to recipience (to receive something). A child has a positive right to be educated, for example. In our society, customers have a right to quality merchandise and should not be subject to *caveat emptor*. Likewise, stock purchasers have a right to accurate information about the financial picture of a company. Thus, we see that for every positive right, there is a corresponding obligation. If, however, there is not someone with the capability and responsibility to provide something, it is futile to claim a right of recipience. In a society without health care services, for example, it makes no sense to claim a right to adequate health care. Who is obligated to provide it? (Note: Even if there is adequate health care, it is still necessary to specify whose responsibility it is to provide it.) Similarly, in a society with insufficient jobs, it makes no sense to claim a right to employment. Who is obligated to provide it?

At any rate, if an action treats people fairly and does not violate their rights, there is no reason not to perform it. Conversely, if an action treats someone unfairly and/or violates the person's rights, there is reason not to do it.

Have I made a commitment, implied or explicit?

Another question to ask in justifying an action deals with relationships: Do I have a commitment? The question asks whether or not any promises to act in a certain way were made. If so, those promises ought to be kept. Thus, if the answer to the question "Did I promise to do this?" is "Yes," there is a good reason to perform the action. Explicit promises and contracts are commitments as well as implicit promises.

People are promise-makers. It is one aspect that distinguishes us from the rest of the animal kingdom, and our social structure could not function otherwise. Any lasting relationship rests on promises and the expectation of guaranteed behavior in spite of future contingencies. Customers expect to reap the benefits an insurance ad promises; they do not expect to be cheated because they didn't read the small print. Human beings need to make and depend on long-term commitments. As a professor, I commit myself to teaching a certain number of classes at a certain time for a certain duration. My commitment extends into the future and binds me to a course of action.

Thus, if you make a commitment, you have a good reason for doing something. But there is a caveat: Should you honor your commitment if doing so causes harm? Suppose you borrow a gun from your neighbor and promise to return it when he asks. Should you return it, as promised, if he asks for it in order to shoot someone? Clearly, in this case, the harm that would result from honoring your commitment outweighs your responsibility to keep that promise.

VIII Using the Reasons

Let's examine how to use these reasons to justify an action. If I am planning to produce some commodity that brings a profit to the company, earns a commission for me, benefits society, does not treat anyone unfairly, or does not violate a promise or commitment, there are nothing but good reasons to do it. Suppose, however, that I am contemplating falsely declaring profits in a financial statement developed for a merger. The merger does not benefit my company, its executives, or the general society; my action is deceptive and hence unfair, and it violates the relationship of trust my corporation has with the community. In this scenario, there are nothing but good reasons against performing the action. (This assumes that you believe your fraud will not be detected and that you will benefit from it. If you know you'll get caught, that gives you still another good reason not to do it.)

Thus, we have a decision-making procedure. Ask yourself the questions of common morality. If there are good reasons to perform the action – for example, it benefits you, it is beneficial to society, it is just, and it fulfills a commitment – then do it. If the opposite is true – the action does not benefit you, it is not beneficial to society, it is unjust, and it breaks a commitment – then don't do it. Let's look at examples of two different actions: first, getting an education and second, abusing heroin.

Presumably, getting an education is beneficial to you because it fulfills you in a number of ways. Moreover, it is presumed in this society that the more people who are educated, the better the society will be. Thus, if you get an education, not only will you benefit, but society will also benefit. If, in attaining the education, you need not violate any commitments and no one is unfairly deprived because of your education – that is, you are not using up someone else's spot, or you are not attending college while your twin brother is employed in a menial job to help finance your education – the action does not violate fairness and commitments. It is a *prima facie* example of an action that should be done. In fact, you would be hard pressed to justify not getting an education under those circumstances. What valid reasons could you give?

Right now, you are reading this chapter, an action that can be described as getting an education. Ask yourself why you are doing it. Most likely, you will answer that it benefits you by enabling you to learn, to pass a course, or to help you in some other way. The action of learning this material can also make you a more productive and, ideally, more ethical employee; hence, your company, family, and society will all benefit. Let's assume you are taking this action at no one's expense – that is, studying this text is not interfering with your personal responsibilities and is not putting anyone else at a disadvantage. If all the above are true, then you have very good reasons to pursue this action. Taking this course in ethics is a justified action.

Suppose, however, that you just hate taking this course even though you recognize the value of getting an education. In this case, you are torn between doing something you don't like that may be good for you, and giving in to your likes and dislikes, which may be bad for you. But can conceding to your likes and dislikes ever be good for you? As we pointed out earlier, we should not confuse what benefits us with what we desire, want, or like. Nevertheless, sometimes getting what we want can be beneficial (a higher-paying job, for example) and doing what we hate may be harmful (taking the subway in a crime-ridden area). At times, we may also need to defer pleasure (eating that ice cream sundae) or suffer pain (getting a flu shot) for some long-range benefit. There are also times when we need to pursue pleasure in life.

Now let's consider our other example – abusing cocaine. Is abusing cocaine good for you? Unquestionably not. Is it good for society? Absolutely not. It lowers productivity, increases medical costs, raises crime rates, and undermines society. Is it fair or just? Certainly not. Although the action itself of taking cocaine may not involve unfairness or injustice, it can lead to unfair or unjust actions, such as not fulfilling your commitments or ignoring your responsibilities. In this example, then, we have a proposed action that has no good reasons to support it. It is a *prima facie* case of something we should not do.

IX Ethical Dilemmas

Responses to the questions above give reasons that justify or do not justify an action. You don't have to take an ethics course to ask those questions. The answers provide the principles of "ethical theory." Ethical theories establish the foundation for all ethical rules or judgments.

It is important to note that no ethical theory would be necessary if the actions to take in all cases were clear-cut. The examples above show that there are many situations in which the action to take is perfectly clear. Suppose, however, the action is not clear. Assume that by taking this ethics course, you could not keep a promise to your children to go on vacation this spring. In that case, taking the course might benefit you but be unfair to your children. Thus, circumstances can alter the appraisal of an action. In situations like this, when there are reasons for doing something and reasons for not doing it, we are faced with an *ethical dilemma*. An ethical dilemma is a problem that arises when a reason to act in a certain way is offset by a reason not to act that way. To resolve these dilemmas, ethicists rely on what they consider the primary ethical principle underlying the action. Thus, when faced with a conflict, ethicists who give precedence to rights or fairness over harm fall into one camp, and those who give precedence to benefits over rights or fairness fall into an opposing camp. For example, drug testing may prevent harm – a good reason for doing it – but it may violate a right to privacy – a good reason for not doing it. Blowing the whistle on a firm's fraudulent accounting procedures may prevent harm as well as fulfill the accountant's responsibility to the general public, but it might violate the accountant's sense of loyalty to the company. For those who give precedence to harm considerations, there is a reason to blow the whistle. For those who give precedence to rights considerations, there is a reason not to do so.

Thus, ethical dilemmas occur when there is a conflict of reasons, and ethical theories arose to resolve dilemmas. Each rival ethical theory maintains that when there is a conflict of reasons, there is an overriding reason that takes precedence over all other reasons. That reason is articulated in the principle that expresses the theory. Those who appeal to fairness and rights over consequences are called deontologists. Those who appeal to consequences over fairness and rights are called consequentialists. Let us look at a classic dilemma to see how ethical theories are involved in its solution.

X Some Classic Moral Dilemmas

The story of Jean Valjean in Victor Hugo's *Les Miserables* is a classic moral dilemma. Valjean, an ex-prisoner living under an assumed name, has been in violation of parole for years and is being hunted relentlessly by a police officer named Javert. Javert, passionately committed to upholding the law, is obsessed with tracking Valjean down and has reason to suspect that Monsieur Madeleine – the mayor of a small French town and owner/manager of the town factory – is the prisoner he seeks. To entrap Valjean (Madeleine), Javert lets it be known that an innocent vagrant is about to be identified as Valjean. Valjean realizes that if he does not reveal his true identity, an innocent man will go to prison in his stead. What should Valjean do? It certainly won't benefit him to go to prison; nor will it benefit the town that depends on his managerial and governing skills. On the other hand, it is not fair that an innocent vagrant should suffer in place of Valjean.

This is an example of a classic dilemma, the stuff that makes great drama. It presents a situation in which whatever action is taken, something is wrong and something is right – a "damned if you do and damned if you don't" scenario. In Valjean's case, doing what benefits society is unfair, and doing what is fair harms society.

Another example of a dilemma is President Harry Truman's decision whether or not to drop the atomic bomb on Hiroshima and Nagasaki. Defenders of the action believe that losing 80,000 lives by dropping the bombs is justified because it saved approximately 3 million lives that would have been lost if Japan had been invaded. Those who condemn the action believe that no matter what the consequences, the action was immoral and unjust because it involved taking innocent lives.

There are dilemmas in accounting, too, although not as dramatic. Suppose as company controller, you need a large influx of cash to develop and market a new product that will keep the company afloat. You may be able get a bank loan, but not if you report the current inventory on the now-outmoded product at its true value. If you fudge the numbers and misrepresent the company's financial health, you can get the loan and keep the company going. Here, again, is a situation in which being honest and preserving your integrity (not fudging the numbers) outweighs the positive consequences of benefiting a large number of people (getting the bank loan).

As noted earlier, ethical dilemmas give rise to ethical theory, which is the focus of our next chapter.

Chapter Three

Ethical Behavior in Accounting: Ethical Theory

Dilemmas help to illuminate the nature of ethical theories. Contemporary ethical theories provide ultimate principles that can be used to solve a dilemma. If, in the case of *Les Miserables* Jean Valjean's dilemma (discussed in the previous chapter), we give priority to what is good for all the people affected over considerations of fairness, we adopt the stance of theorists called *utilitarians*. For utilitarians, the ultimate justifying reason for an action is that the action brings about more good for more people than it does harm. If, on the other hand, we give considerations of fairness priority over the consequences of the action, we adopt the attitude of theorists called *deontologists*, who believe that actions themselves are ethical in spite of their consequences. For deontologists, the end does not justify the means. Finally, if we consider only what is good for ourselves and give self-interested concerns priority over what is good for others and what is fair, we adopt the position of theorists called *egoists*. It may be a bit strange to talk of an "ethical" theory that gives priority to self-interest , but there are a few defenders of egoism, so we will look at it briefly later. To conclude then, an ethical theory espouses a principle that provides the overriding justifying reason to pursue any course of action.

Both egoism and utilitarianism determine whether an action is ethically acceptable according to the action's consequences. Egoism gives priority to the reason, "It benefits me." When there is a conflict between something good for me and society, or a conflict between something good for me and its fairness, egoism recommends the self-serving action. Thus, egoist theory maintains that an individual should always act in his or her own best interest. As we mentioned, egoism has its advocates, even though it may seem paradoxical for an ethical theory to give primacy to self-interest.

Accounting Ethics, Second Edition. Ronald Duska, Brenda Shay Duska, and Julie Ragatz.
© 2011 John Wiley & Sons, Ltd. Published 2011 by John Wiley & Sons, Ltd.

Utilitarianism gives priority to concern for everybody's good, including the individual's, which is factored into the total overall good. If self-interest conflicts with the overall good, self-interest is set aside. Thus, utilitarianism recommends actions that bring about the greatest good for the greatest number of people.

Finally, the theory that gives precedence to the issues of fairness, rights, and commitment, and advocates doing the right thing – no matter what the consequences to self and others – is called deontological theory. Under this theory, the end does not justify the means.

Let us summarize. Sometimes in deciding what to do, no conflict arises between reasons. In these situations, what is good for me is also good for society and is fair and just. Then there is every reason to perform the action, which fulfills all three theories' principles. In a case where there is conflict, however, disagreement arises about which principle to follow. Which reason takes priority? If we decide always for ourselves, we are egoists. If we consider the benefits to society, we are utilitarians. If we are moved by questions of fairness or justice, we are deontologists. The integrity of each of these theories rests on its appeal to a very important reason to choose a course of action.

We all use all three sets of reasons. Because these reasons sometimes conflict, though, and cause uncertainty about what to do, skeptics conclude that ethical knowledge is not possible and that ethical beliefs cannot be justified. We contend, however, that individuals are unsure about what to do only in rare dilemmas. In other situations, a systematic investigation can lead to a resolution of the problem. We *can* determine what to do.

Let us examine each of these contemporary ethical theories more fully.

I Egoism

Most people think the principle of egoism – that an individual ought always to act in the his or her own self-interest – is inherently unethical. It appears to advocate selfishness, and in our society, if not in all societies, selfishness is considered wrong. How can a principle that promotes selfishness be an ethical theory? Why would anyone pursue such a faulty theory? What insights support it? Its supporters usually defend egoism by objecting to moralists who emphasize altruism over the pursuit of self-interest. Egoists assert, as we have noted earlier, that self-interest is a good thing. Egoism can go too far, however, because *always* pursuing self-interest leads to selfishness, and selfishness is immoral.

To understand this more clearly, it is necessary to explain the difference between selfishness and *self-interest*. Acting in self-interest is doing what is in one's own best interest – what benefits one. Self-interested pursuits are not bad. Psychologists have pointed out the necessity of self-love and self-esteem, and the desirability of an individual's vigorous pursuit of his or her projects and dreams. It is healthy, therefore, to pursue your own interests. After all, if you don't, who will? That is why an action that benefits you is a good action, and a good reason for doing something is that it will be good for you.

The problem arises when the pursuit of one's own interests is at the expense of others. Selfishness is pursuing one's own interest *at the expense of another.* If you can make a sale only by persuading a customer who can't afford the product to buy it, that is selfish behavior. To justify your action by saying that it will help you is to justify it egoistically. Thus, a principle that says, "*Always* do what is in your own interest," is a principle that *necessarily,* at some time or other, promotes selfishness – that is, achieves one's own interests only at the expense of another. Because selfish behavior is unethical behavior and egoism mandates selfishness, we reject egoism as a viable ethical theory. Clearly, it is not acceptable in the accounting profession, where the code of ethics mandates the accountant's "obligation to act in a way that will serve the public interest."

There are additional formal objections to egoism, which we will mention briefly. First, egoism is incompatible with many human activities, such as giving advice. Ask yourself how someone who is always acting in his or her own interest can give you trustworthy advice. The incompatibility of egoism with friendship is also easy to show. Would you consider a friend "true" if you knew that he was acting as a "friend" just for what he could get out of the friendship? We expect friends to put themselves out for us, and we expect to put ourselves out for our friends. The consistent egoist, then, can be seen to recommend against friendship.

Egoism is also incompatible with many business activities, such as being an agent or fiduciary for another. There are times when, as an accountant, you will not have the expertise necessary to provide a client with the best service. In such a situation, you may have to recommend another professional and lose the business. You do not do this because you are concerned about your long-range self-interest. You do it because you have a responsibility as a professional to act in the client's best interest.

A further difficulty with egoism is that it cannot adjudicate disputes, which is one of the tasks of ethics. If we are each to look out for ourselves, how can egoism resolve a conflict in which two of us need the same thing – for example, we each need the last seat available on the next flight to Chicago? To say that both people should look out for their own interests does not resolve the conflict; it gives no practical recommendation.

Moreover, egoism leads to a strange anomaly: It cannot be promulgated – that is, it cannot be published, taught, or even spoken out loud. If, as an egoist, you genuinely believe you should always act in your own interest, what is the effect of conveying that belief to others? It will only alert them to situations in which your interests conflict with theirs, and that is certainly not in your self-interest. The egoist doctrine recommends not teaching the egoist theory, because doing so is not in one's own interest. On the contrary, teaching the egoist theory is acting *un*ethically, according to that theory.

A standard philosophical objection to egoism is that it is impossible to formulate in a way that is not either illogical or absurd. For example, if we say, "Everyone should act in his or her own self-interest," it recommends an unworkable situation when, as above, two people both need the same thing. If we reformulate the principle to read, "Everyone should act in my own interest," to whom does "my" refer? If "my" refers to whoever makes the statement, its meaning duplicates the first formulation, which is illogical. If, however, "my" refers to a specific person, it then becomes patently absurd. If Sue says, for example, "Everyone should act in my [Sue's] interest," isn't that ridiculous? Why should everyone in the world, billions of people who do not know Sue, act in her interest? Why should even those who know Sue act in her interest? Perhaps the theory could be restated as "I should always act in my interest." But if "I" refers to the individual making the pronouncement, it, again, is exactly the same as the first formulation and thus illogical. If "I" doesn't mean everyone, the statement ceases to be a principle at all, because principles are supposed to be generally applicable.

There is a final objection to egoism. Egoism is based on a distorted egocentric view of the universe. Certainly, I am the most important person in my life. I am inside my own skin, I am always with myself, and I see the world from my eyes and my perspective. Thus, from my point of view, I am the center of the universe. But how limited that view is! The moral point of view demands that I recognize the billions of other people in the world, more or less like me, who all have a subjective viewpoint. Why, then, am I so important? The answer, of course, is that I am not. Thus, the limits of egoism make it an inadequate principle.

If egoism is inadequate, then what is its appeal? The appeal seems to derive from the fact that acting out of self interest is such a strong motivating factor. Philosopher Thomas Hobbes[1] claimed that if we look deeply into human motivation, we can see that all actions are directed by self-interest. Philosopher and economist Adam Smith[2] also believed that self-interest was a primary

[1] Thomas Hobbes, *Leviathan*, 1651, Chapters 13 and 14.
[2] Adam Smith, *The Wealth of Nations* (Ed. Edwin Canan, New York: Random House, 1937), IV, ii, 9.

motivator of human behavior. Consider Holden Caulfield's observation in J.D. Salinger's *The Catcher in the Rye*:

> "Even if you did go around saving guys' lives and all, how would you know if you did it because you really wanted to save guys' lives, or whether you did it because what you really wanted to do was be a terrific lawyer, with everybody slapping you on the back and congratulating you in a court when the god dam trial was over, the reporters and everybody? How would you know you weren't being a phony? The trouble is, you wouldn't."[3]

Salinger's Holden Caulfield says he does not know if we are acting in our own interest all the time, but there are some philosophers who think that human beings naturally act in their own interest all the time. If everyone always does look out for their own interests then recommendations suggesting any course of action must take that into account. Remember the old maxim, "You'll catch more flies with honey than vinegar"? If someone is naturally disposed one way you better make recommendations that conform to that disposition rather than go against it.

Such a belief, that everyone *always* acts in their own interest is called *psychological* egoism because it is a theory about how people behave, and psychology is the study of human behavior. Psychological egoism is distinguished from ethical egoism in that psychological egoism describes how we *actually* behave, whereas ethical egoism prescribes how we *ought* to behave. If psychological egoism is true, then any moral principle that prescribes that a person act contrary to his or her own interest is sheer nonsense, because it recommends that people do what is psychologically impossible.

Is psychological egoism credible? It would seem not, for there are countless examples of people not acting in their own interest – Mother Teresa, for example, who ministered to the poor, sick, and dying, or the soldier who throws himself on a live grenade to save his comrades. Nevertheless, there is a strong contingent of thinkers who utilize psychological egoism as a model to explain human behavior and from which to make predictions. When economists adopt this theory, the economic and business models they develop assume that everyone is self-interested. This has to affect their view of what is acceptable or not acceptable. There is a moral maxim "ought implies can". *If* you are necessarily always self-interested you will not be able to act otherwise. If all are self-interested it is foolhardy to tell people to go against their nature, just as it is foolhardy to expect stones to fly.

[3] J.D. Salinger, *The Catcher in the Rye* (New York: Signet Books, 1951), p. 155.

According to Adam Smith, "It is not from the benevolence of the butcher, the brewer, or the baker, that we expect our dinner, but from their regard to their own self-interest. We address ourselves, not to their humanity but to their self-love, and never talk to them of our own necessities but of their advantages."[4] Hence, it makes economic sense to appeal to people's self-interest.

So to the extent that economists and social scientists assume everyone is self-interested, they develop economic and business models on that assumption. The self-interested maximizer is even given a name, *Homo economicus,* economic man. It is in this way, that economics, which looks value neutral, since it assumes everyone always acts in their own interest, attempts to set up systems that will be most productive, systems which, if they are to work, must appeal to the way human beings are. For the economist, that is selfish. No wonder, then, if selfishness is the opposite of ethical, and business is viewed as an activity in our economic system designed around facilitating selfishness, people often claim that business ethics is an oxymoron, a contradiction in terms.

What can be said of this psychological egoism? Without getting too philosophically technical, we need only remind ourselves of the sacrifices that humans make for one another. Even if the psychologists call self-sacrificing behavior underlyingly selfish, it's the kind of behavior we want. Thus, even the most hardened economist justifies the appeal to self-interest by arguing that it will benefit society.

But not all economists are psychological egoists. Many believe that while self-interest is a strong motivating factor, it is not the only one, although it can be used as an incentive to produce good for society.

One example is Adam Smith, who maintains that the conjunction of the forces of self-interest, competition, and supply and demand – the doctrine of the "invisible hand" – guide society, by assuring that self-interest will lead to societal benefits.[5] Note, however, that Smith is not an extreme psychological egoist, since he does not believe self-interest is the only motivator:

> "Howsoever selfish he may be supposed, there are evidently some principles in his nature, which interest him in the fortune of others and render their happiness necessary to him, though he derives nothing from it except the pleasure of seeing it."[6]

[4] Adam Smith, *The Wealth of Nations* (Ed. Edwin Canan, New York: Random House, 1937), IV, ii, 9.
[5] Adam Smith, *The Theory of Moral Sentiments*, 1759.
[6] Adam Smith, *The Theory of Moral Sentiments*, 1759, p.I.i.1.1.

But if egoism is inadequate as a theory, what about utilitarianism and deontological theory?

II Utilitarianism

The principal maxim of utilitarianism is best expressed by John Stuart Mill: "Actions are right in proportion as they tend to promote happiness, wrong as they tend to produce the reverse of happiness." Mill continues that "the happiness" to which he refers is "not the agent's own greatest happiness, but the greatest amount of happiness all together." The appeal to the happiness of all is Mill's answer to the egoists.[7]

Utilitarianism has recently been expressed in a slightly different way: "Do that action which will bring about the greatest good for the greatest number of people." Utilitarianism is significantly different from egoism because the consequences used to judge an action's worth are not simply the consequences for the agent but also include the consequences for everyone concerned with or affected by the action, including the agent.

We can illustrate the differences as follows:

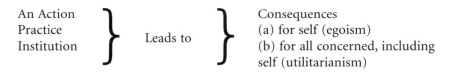

An Action
Practice
Institution
} Leads to } Consequences
(a) for self (egoism)
(b) for all concerned, including self (utilitarianism)

Good consequences make it a good action; bad make it a bad action.

Utilitarianism is in greater accord with our moral sensibilities than egoism is, and it reflects what we do when we find reasons to justify an action or practice. Doing something to make yourself happy is acceptable unless doing so makes someone else miserable. If you do something that maximizes your own happiness, makes others happy, and leaves precious few people miserable, that action is justifiable.

Let's look at an example. Suppose an accountant sets up a check-kiting scheme where he deposits company money in his own account for a few days, thereby gaining interest on the money, before he puts the money in the company account. That action may be in his interest, but it is certainly not in the interests of the greatest number of people. It is unethical because (here is the reason) it clearly harms more people than it helps. Utilitarians praise individuals and companies that provide services or goods for society

[7]John Stuart Mill, *Utilitarianism*, 1863, Chapter 2.

and cause little harm. They condemn individuals and companies that cause more harm than benefit.

A utilitarian uses the following procedure to justify or condemn an action: Take any action. Compute the benefits and harms of the consequences for everyone affected. If the action brings more total happiness than unhappiness for more people, it is justified. If it causes more total unhappiness for more people, it is wrong. Thus, utilitarianism is the ethical theory that uses a cost-benefit approach.

There are, however, some difficulties in using the utilitarian approach. It seems obvious that it is wrong for a company to misrepresent its worth to a bank that is considering giving it a loan. Deceiving the bank is wrong. The bank has a right to know the company's true condition. But suppose the company executive justifies such behavior by saying, "Well, the bank is just too strict, so if I lie to the bank, I'll get the loan, save the business, and in the end everyone will be better off." To justify lying, however, by appealing to possible good consequences – even if it is certain that those consequences will follow – points to one of the weaknesses of utilitarianism. Let's examine some of the other problems that can arise with utilitarian principles.

A major problem with utilitarian theory is the *distribution problem*. The phrase "the greatest good for the greatest number of people" is ambiguous. Are we obliged to bring about the maximum good, or are we obliged to affect the maximum number of people? Suppose you have five units of pleasure – let's say five pickles – to distribute to five people. How, according to the formula, should you distribute the pickles? The easiest answer is to give each person one pickle. Then, supposedly, each person will receive one unit of pleasure, and you will have distributed the units to the greatest number of people – five. But imagine that two people passionately love pickles and two people don't care one way or another about pickles. Wouldn't it make sense then to give two pickles apiece to the two people who passionately love them? And to give none to the two who don't care?

This can be represented as follows (A):

A	=	2 pickles	=	2 units of happiness
B	=	2 pickles	=	2 units of happiness
C	=	1 pickle	=	1 unit of happiness
D	=	0 pickles	=	0 units of happiness
E	=	0 pickles	=	0 units of happiness
Totals		3 recipients		5 units of happiness

If you distribute the pickles equally (keep in mind that two people don't like pickles so that receiving one gives zero units of happiness), it looks like this (B):

A	=	1 pickle	=	1 unit of happiness
B	=	1 pickle	=	1 unit of happiness
C	=	1 pickle	=	1 unit of happiness
D	=	1 pickle	=	0 units of happiness
E	=	1 pickle	=	0 units of happiness
Totals		5 recipients		3 units of happiness

Thus, (B) distributes to the greatest number of people but does not create the greatest amount of happiness, whereas (A) creates the greatest amount of happiness but does not distribute to the greatest number of people. This illustrates the problem of distributive justice: a problem of fairness, a problem of how the goods and the burdens of the world are to be distributed. It is a problem that the utilitarian decision procedures do not manage well, one that seems better handled by deontologists. This problem arises in the utilitarian justification of capitalism – that the economic system of capitalism produces the highest standard of living in the history of mankind. That may be true, but the rejoinder is that in maximizing all those goods, some people get a lot and others get little or nothing. Thus, the critics of capitalism say that although capitalism might create the greatest amount of material goods in history, it doesn't distribute those goods to the greatest number of people. Utilitarianism leaves us with the question, "How are we to fairly distribute those goods?"

Another problem for utilitarianism is the *deciding what counts as "the good."* We alluded to this problem earlier in the discussion of the dimensions of human fulfillment, and contrasted the good – what we need – with what we desire. Utilitarian John Stuart Mill and his mentor, Jeremy Bentham, equated "the good" with happiness, and happiness with pleasure. But there are numerous difficulties with this theory. Let's examine some of them.

Generally, goods can be divided into two types: intrinsic goods or extrinsic (instrumental) goods. An intrinsic good is something desired or desirable for its own sake. An extrinsic (instrumental) good leads to or is instrumental in obtaining another good. Happiness is clearly an intrinsic good. Money is an extrinsic good. When someone asks why you want money, you can answer, "Because it will make me happy." Thus, the extrinsic good of money leads to the intrinsic good of happiness. But if someone asks why you want to be happy, there is no further answer.

Mill recognizes happiness as the intrinsic good. Other utilitarians acknowledge other things such as freedom or knowledge as intrinsic goods. Some claim there is a plurality of intrinsic goods. Thus, we have a disagreement about what counts as intrinsic goods. *Pluralists* believe that there are a number of intrinsic goods; *eudaemonists* believe that happiness (well-being) is the only intrinsic good; *hedonists* believe that happiness is the same as pleasure. Mill, then, was a hedonistic utilitarian. Others, and especially economists, do not identify objective goods but appeal to individual preferences, or "satisficers" – what people prefer or what they think will satisfy them.

Such an identification is problematic, however, because what you prefer is not always good for you, and/or what satisfies you in also not always good for you. Hence, we can ask the utilitarian, "Are you promoting actions that actually *are* good for people or actions that only *seem* good for them? If, as in business and economics, the concept of an objective good is discarded in favor of individual preferences, good can be judged only by demand. But that assumes that what people prefer (want) is what they need (good). That assumption is unwarranted. As we noted earlier, although defenders of capitalism assert that it brought about the highest standard of living in the history of the world, critics declare that a high standard of living is not necessarily a good thing. We might agree, therefore, on where an action leads but disagree on whether that goal is good. Utilitarians, then, along with other ethical theorists, need to determine what things are good, a determination that often provokes ethical disputes, because one person's good is another person's poison.

A further problem with utilitarianism is that *of predicting the future* – deciding whether an action is right by looking at its consequences. Predictions, however, can be tenuous, even risky. Thus, the inability to predict accurately creates several problems. Should utilitarians do what they *think* will bring about good, or should they do what will *actually* bring about good? And how are they to know? Often, what we think will be good turns out to be bad or has unforeseen consequences. Economists speak of "externalities" – undesirable, unpredicted side effects of some activity.

But the difficulty with utilitarianism that many critics think is the most serious is the *problem of illicit means*. Many of us were raised with the maxim that the ends do not justify the means. From a utilitarian perspective, however, it is precisely the ends that do justify the means, even if the means are immoral.

The earlier example of misrepresenting assets to the bank illustrates this problem. Even if we justify the misrepresentation by saying that no harm will be done – the company will survive, and the bank will not get hurt – it is still lying. History is replete with examples of actions we consider immoral being performed for the sake of effecting some desirable end. Suppose you could save 100 people by killing three innocent children. Should you do it? The happiness of the 100 people saved would seem to outweigh the pain of losing three children. But our moral sentiments – that taking of the lives of innocent children is immoral – are outraged at the suggestion. Or suppose that you could achieve law and order by convicting an innocent man. Suppose further that the wrongly accused man has already been convicted of several despicable acts; does that change anything? What if an accountant could benefit her company by misstating receivables? Lockheed could retain employees by bribing Japanese government officials? A manufacturer could keep his plant open and 150 people on the payroll by lying to a government inspector? Suppose I can keep a healthy economy in the southern states by preserving slavery? Suppose I can dampen inflation by keeping unemployment artificially high? All of these actions (means) are ordinarily viewed as immoral in spite of the good consequences (ends) they may bring about. Utilitarians who justify an action by citing its good consequences are accused of missing an important part of ethics – that some actions are wrong in principle, no matter what the consequences.

The philosopher W.D. Ross raises one more very important objection to utilitarianism, which he calls its "essential defect":

> "The essential defect of utilitarianism is that it ignores, or at least does not do full justice to, the highly personal character of duty. If the only duty is to produce the maximum of good, the question who is to have the good – whether it is myself, or my benefactor, or a person to whom I have made a promise to confer that good on him, or a mere fellow man to whom I stand in no such special relation – should make no difference to my having a duty to produce that good. But we are all in fact sure that it makes a vast difference."[8]

Ross reminds us that we give ethical priority to the duties that arise from special relationships. If lying to the bank is repugnant to you as an accountant, for example, it is because you have a special duty to present companies' financial pictures accurately. That is what accountants do.

III Kant and Deontology

Ross belongs to a group of ethical theorists who maintain that there are ethical concerns with actions themselves that prohibit the actions, in spite of the consequences. These theorists are called deontologists. Deontologist derives from the Greek word "deontos," meaning "what must be done." It is sometimes translated as "obligation" or "duty." The foremost deontologist was the 18th century philosopher Immanuel Kant.[9]

Kant preceded utilitarianists Bentham and Mill, so he did not directly confront their theories. Still, if we apply his principles to utilitarianism, they will

[8] W.D. Ross, *The Right and the Good* (Oxford University Press, 1930), p. 60.
[9] The fundamental ethical theory of Immanuel Kant is found primarily in *The Groundwork of the Metaphysics of Morals*, 1785. See especially Chapter 1.

show it as a misguided theory because it fails to consider one of the characteristics of a moral action – a moral motive. Kant calls the motive *duty*. We can describe it as a sense of moral obligation and contrast it to inclination or desire. According to Kant, if you are acting merely from inclination or desire, you are not acting morally at all. Rather, you are behaving the way nonhuman animals behave. For Kant, it is humans' ability to act on a *moral* level – to transcend animal instincts and inclinations – that makes us special, makes us moral, and gives us dignity and rights.

How does Kant establish this? Let's compare a human being's way of acting with a spider and with a beaver. A spider spins webs. Why? Because of an instinct or inclination. Nature makes spiders that way, and if they don't spin webs, they won't live. Beavers chew trees and build dams. Why? Because nature makes them that way. Think how ridiculous it would be to imagine a spider refusing to spin a web or a beaver refusing to chew a tree. They have no choice. They are not *free*. They are inclined by nature to do those things and consequently will do them.

According to Kant, human beings, too, have inclinations. We are inclined to pursue things we want. We have psychological propensities and inclinations to pursue goals. But we have two capabilities other animals don't have: (1) the ability to choose between alternate means or ways to achieve the goals to which we are inclined; and (2) the freedom to set aside those goals or inclinations and act out of a higher motive. The first capability makes us somewhat, but not significantly, different from other animals. Beavers have an inclination for food and shelter, yet are equipped by nature with only their instinct to chew bark and build dams to fulfill that inclination. Although we have the same inclination for food and shelter, we do not have the beaver's limitations. We can choose from a vast array of diverse means – we can hunt, fish, plant crops, build lean-tos, dig caves, build houses, and so on. We have choices about how to fulfill our inclinations.

The second difference between humans and the rest of the animals, the one Kant thinks is particularly significant, is that humans can act against their inclinations for the sake of duty.

IV   Deontological Ethics

The question "What should I do?" can take two forms. If we are interested in fulfilling our inclinations, the question is qualified: "What should I do if I want to fulfill my inclinations?" At times, however, the question is not what to do to fulfill our inclinations but what to do to fulfill our obligations or duty. Here, the question is unqualified: "What should I do?" There are no ifs, ands, or buts. The answers come out as rules. Kant calls these rules "imperatives." To Kant, all practical judgments – that is, judgments about what we ought to do – are imperatives. The unqualified "oughts," Kant calls "categorical" imperatives. But, as we saw, there are also qualified oughts – oughts determined by some prior inclination – which he calls "hypothetical" imperatives.

When we make decisions based on qualified oughts, what determines the goodness or badness is whether or not the decisions accomplish the goal. For example, if you're in a third-floor classroom and you want to get to the cafeteria in the next building, what should you do? You could jump out the window, but you'd probably break a leg, if not more. Such a course of action would be "imprudent," according to Kant. The "prudent" thing to do would be to take an elevator or walk down the steps.

If we say that we should be ethical in business because it accomplishes what we want, then we are saying it is prudent to be ethical. But that gives us only a hypothetical imperative, which to Kant is not an ethical imperative. Thus, for Kant, if we are being ethical because it's good business, we don't have the proper ethical concern. Note that Mill and utilitarians deal with only hypothetical imperatives – if you want the greatest good for the greatest number of people, do "X." But Mill cannot answer two questions: Why should anyone *want* the good of others over his or her own good? And what difference does it make what motives anyone has for an action? But, clearly, it does make a difference. If we give to charity for a tax write-off, that isn't as fine a motive as giving because alms-giving is a duty. Unless we are acting out of our duty, then, we are not acting out of moral concern.

According to Kant, therefore, if we're doing something simply to fulfill a desire, we are not acting out of a moral motive. It follows, then, that if we are doing the right things in business simply because it will improve business, we may not be doing anything wrong, but we are certainly not acting from an ethical motive. To act morally, we do something simply because it is the moral thing to do. It is our duty, a categorical imperative to do "X." This insight is usually expressed by those who say, "It's the right thing to do." But doing "X" because it is our duty is not very informative. What is our duty? Kant presents several formulas for the categorical imperative[10] to help us decide. We will look at two of them:

- Act so that you can will the maxim of your action to become a universal law.
- Act so as never to treat another rational being merely as a means.

[10] Immanuel Kant, *The Groundwork of the Metaphysics of Morals*, 1785, Chapter 2.

V The First Formula of the Categorical Imperative

The first formula for the categorical imperative, "Act so that you can will the maxim of your action to become a universal law," needs some explaining. A maxim is your reason for acting. Suppose you borrow money from a friend. When it is time to repay it, you don't have the cash. You decide not to repay your friend at all because you know he won't really press you for it and you don't want to borrow money from a bank. Your reason, then, for not paying him is that it's inconvenient. Thus, the maxim of your action becomes, "Don't repay debts (keep promises) if it is inconvenient to do so."

Now let's will that maxim to become a *universal law* – that is, universalize our rule. Promises are made to guarantee that we honor our commitments even when things are tough, when we are *not inclined* to keep them. What would happen, then, if everybody broke promises because it was inconvenient to keep them? Well, people would end up not trusting each other and society would be chaotic. But that is judging a universal practice by the consequences, and it assumes that chaos is not beneficial. Isn't that just a more complex utilitarianism, where we judge the universal practice rather than the particular action? Yes, it is. Kant therefore needs to go further, and he does. He recognizes that the consequence of not paying debts or keeping promises is that people will not want to loan money or accept promises. Whether that consequence is favorable or unfavorable, however, is not the determining factor.

The categorical imperative stresses that we must "will" the maxim to become a universal law. For Kant, the will is practical reason, and we cannot will that promises not be kept. This is not because it results in unfavorable consequences, but because it creates a "will-contradiction." A will-contradiction is when you want to eat your cake and still have it. If you universalize promise breaking, no one would trust anyone else, and no one could make a promise to another because a precondition of promise making is trust. To will promise breaking, therefore, you must will promise making. That is the contradiction, and that's what goes wrong. The same sort of contradiction holds for stealing, lying, cheating, adultery, and any number of other activities we believe are immoral. The only way the action will work is if others do not behave as you do. But that's a double standard.

The implications for business and accounting are obvious. There must be an atmosphere of trust to allow business to function. If you will to break promises, however, you will other people *not* to break them; otherwise, promise making will not exist. But to will others not to follow your rule is to make an exception of yourself. When we universalize, therefore, we move beyond our egocentric view. We see that we are the same as others and that this is the basis for the rule of justice: Equals should be treated equally.

VI The Second Formula of the Categorical Imperative

Kant does not stop with the first formula of the categorical imperative. He moves on to another. Unlike other animals, human beings transcend nature's inclinations and limitations; humans are free; humans are autonomous. Kant thus calls humans "ends in themselves." We can determine and self-regulate our moral life; we can establish values and ends. Consequently, human beings are special, which leads to Kant's second formula: "Act so as never to treat another rational being merely as a means."

Under this view, everyone is morally equal and ought to be treated with respect and dignity. Everyone's rights ought to be respected; no one ought to be used *merely* as a means or instrument to bring about consequences that benefit the user. This is the deontological answer to the utilitarian's problem of illicit means. It is not justifiable to use or exploit someone to make society better. Hence, Jean Valjean should not use the vagrant to escape imprisonment. Employers should not exploit employees to further the employers' own gains. Companies should not mislead customers with false advertising to make sales and boost profits. Corporations should not deceive banks by cooking the books to get a loan.

This formula of the imperative shows what is wrong with slavery and sexism. They dehumanize fellow human beings into instruments to be used by the exploiter. They ignore the fundamental principle that everyone is morally equal and should be treated with respect and dignity. Customers' and other stakeholders' rights rest on this principle. Businesses have no right to use stakeholders in the name of profit. They must respect the rights and autonomy of customers, employees, and others to whom they relate. Thus, ethical reasons that rest on concerns for justice, fairness, dignity, and rights are often deontological in inspiration.

As you might expect, though, as with every ethical theory, there are some shortcomings of deontological thinking. The first is the criticism of the utilitarians, who want to know why a person should do his or her duty if it isn't going to lead to happiness. Why be moral simply to be moral? Utilitarians might wonder: If the end doesn't justify the means, what does? They surmise that Kant's deontological position embraces the belief that we ought to be moral because virtue will be rewarded. But if that is so, it reduces deontology to egoisim or at least utilitarianism.

Further, there is a problem of what to do when there is a conflict of duties. W.D. Ross, the contemporary deontologist we mentioned earlier, believes that we have certain duties that are *prima facie* – we should fulfill them unless they conflict. They include duties to keep promises, to do good, and to not do harm, for example. Ross suggests that when *prima facie* duties conflict, we need to determine an actual duty. But what criterion do we employ? Take an example. Suppose you promised your friend that the next time she was in town you would have a long-delayed heart-to-heart talk. Suppose you also promised your son that you would take him to the ball game on Wednesday. Your friend calls Tuesday night and says she will be in town for a brief time tomorrow, and the time conflicts with the time of the ball game. How do you decide which duty to fulfill? Most likely, you decide by weighing the consequences, and if you keep the promise that causes the least harm, you are using a utilitarian reason to resolve the issue.

Suppose the demands of justice for one person conflict with the demands of liberty for another. In a conflict of rights, utilitarians insist that the only consideration is the consequences of the action. Thus, sooner or later, utilitarians conclude, deontologists have to give priority to considerations of consequences.

One last objection is sometimes raised against Kant's second formula. What exactly does "merely" mean in "… no one ought to be used *merely* as a means or instrument to bring about consequences that benefit the user as a means"? We often use people. For instance, students use teachers; teachers use students. We use someone who buys something from us, if only to help us make some money. But is someone being used *merely* if the person gives permission to be used? Can an employee be exploited if the employee signs a contract specifying that he or she will perform certain services? The fault is that Kant's concept of "use" is unspecified. One person's use is another's exploitation.

VII Virtue Ethics

Having examined utilitarian and deontological perspective, we must now turn our attention to one more approach to ethics. This approach has recently been called the ethics of virtue or character. It addresses the question of what a person should be or become, rather than the question of what a person should do. What type of virtues should a person seek to develop? What makes a good person? What makes a good businessperson? Are these virtues the same or compatible? Is honesty a virtue that businesspeople should develop?

The word virtue comes from the Latin *virtus*, meaning power or capacity, and *virtus* was used to translate the Greek word *arête,* which means excellent.

For ancient Greek philosophers, especially Aristotle, the good life (the life of well-being) was a life in which an individual did things in accord with his or her excellent capacities – "activity in accord with virtue."[11] Excellent capacities led to well-being.

Aristotle and his mentor Plato introduced a model for us to follow. A thing should fulfill its potential – should be, so to speak, all that it can be. That potential is to achieve a determinate end or goal or purpose. Just as a knife has a purpose to cut and is a good knife if it cuts well, so a person has purposes, goals, and ends, which are good if the person accomplishes or fulfills them.

Accountants should be truthful in all their professional dealings. They should benefit others. They should avoid harming or exploiting others. They should live up to their responsibilities because they have committed to them. Accountants should behave with integrity. If they accomplish these goals – activities in accord with virtue – they will likely be excellent accountants.

But what happens if personal goals conflict with professional goals? For example, loyalty is viewed as a virtue, but is loyalty compatible with hard-nosed auditing practices? This chapter has presented some theoretical considerations we can apply to reconcile such conflicts. These considerations give us the ethical approaches that we can use to evaluate various accounting practices.

We can look at ethical theory in two different ways – as providing principles to use in resolving ethical issues, or as presenting the underlying principles that inform our ethical decision-making processes. Generally, most people do not often deliberate on these underlying principles. Rather, they follow their feelings or intuitions, or they practice the everyday rules they've heard all their lives. Ethical principles enable us to analyze and evaluate these feelings and intuitions. But the everyday rules we apply in our decision-making process are also important – in accounting, for example, professional standards of conduct and the AIPCA code of ethics. The next chapter examines these issues.

---

[11] Aristotle, *Nichomachean Ethics*, Book 1, Chapter 10.

Chapter Four

Accounting As a Profession: Characteristics of a Profession

In the mid-20th century in the United States, when the discipline of accounting was seeking the status of a profession, the Commission on Standards of Education and Experience for Certified Public Accountants issued a report that listed the following seven characteristics of a profession:

(1) a specialized body of knowledge
(2) a recognized formal education process for acquiring the requisite specialized knowledge
(3) a standard of professional qualifications governing admission to the profession
(4) a standard of conduct governing the relationship of the practitioner with clients, colleagues, and the public
(5) recognition of status
(6) an acceptance of social responsibility inherent in an occupation endowed with the public interest
(7) an organization devoted to the advancement of the social obligations of the group[1]

It is obvious that accounting meets the first two characteristics. Accounting is a complicated discipline that requires formal study to become an expert. To become a certified public accountant usually requires a bachelor's degree in accounting, as well as passing the rigorous Certified Public Accountants (CPA)

---

[1] From "Background Paper on CFP Board's Initiatives Announced June 14, 1999," http://natasha. cfp-board.org/internet/WP_text.html.

Accounting Ethics, Second Edition. Ronald Duska, Brenda Shay Duska, and Julie Ragatz.
© 2011 John Wiley & Sons, Ltd. Published 2011 by John Wiley & Sons, Ltd.

exam. Retaining CPA status requires staying abreast of the latest developments with continuing education.

In meeting the third standard, the accounting profession is like many other groups that have banded together to serve the general public from a position of expertise. Doctors, attorneys, teachers, engineers, and others form professional groups dedicated to serving their clientele. These groups generally determine the qualifications necessary to obtain membership. Continued membership requires abiding by the group's standards of behavior, including the requirement to act in the client's best interest. Only individuals who meet the qualifications will be admitted into the profession, and individuals can be expelled from the profession if they do not live up to its standards.

The fourth characteristic states that a profession needs "a standard of conduct governing the relationship of the practitioner with clients, colleagues, and the public." But what should be included in that standard of conduct? Standard six specifies the need for "an acceptance of social responsibility inherent in an occupation endowed with the public interest." But what social responsibility does the accounting profession owe to the public?

We can find answers to these questions in the analysis of ethical standards of professionalism developed by Doctor Solomon Huebner, the founder of The American College. Huebner established the college to provide advanced education for insurance salespeople. His goal was to elevate insurance salespeople into professional agents. Several years before he founded the college, Huebner delivered an address at the annual meetings of Baltimore Life and New York Life Underwriters, in which he laid out his vision of what it means to be a professional, as fine a statement of what it takes to be a professional as exists.

Huebner cited four characteristics of the professional:

(1)   The professional is involved in a vocation useful and noble enough to inspire love and enthusiasm on the part of the practitioner.
(2)   The professional's vocation in its practice requires an expert's knowledge.
(3)   In applying that knowledge the practitioner should abandon the strictly selfish commercial view and ever keep in mind the advantage of the client.
(4)   The practitioner should possess a spirit of loyalty to fellow practitioners, of helpfulness to the common cause they all profess, and should not allow any unprofessional acts to bring shame upon the entire profession.

Let us apply Huebner's first characteristic to accounting. Clearly, accounting is a useful vocation; modern organizations could not function without accounting skills. What about nobility? According to the American Institute of Certified Public Accountants (AICPA) code of ethics, "The accounting profession's public consists of clients, credit grantors, governments, employers, investors, the business and financial community, and others who rely on the objectivity and integrity of certified public accountants to maintain the orderly functioning of commerce."[2] Contributing to the orderly functioning of commerce certainly makes the accounting profession noble.

But the most interesting of Huebner's characteristics of the professional is the third, for it prescribes the standard of conduct that should govern an accountant and the social responsibility inherent in the occupation of accounting. It requires the professional "to abandon the strictly selfish commercial view and ever keep in mind the advantage of the client." As noted earlier, the Commission on Standards of Education and Experience for CPAs states that membership in a profession demands a *standard of conduct* that governs the member's relationship with clients, colleagues, and the public and an *acceptance of social responsibility* that is central in an occupation committed to the public interest. Advancing the concept of professionalism brings ethical behavior to the world of business. In short, making a commitment to a profession involves taking on ethical responsibilities that require rejecting a strictly selfish commercial view.

What is a strictly selfish commercial view? It is the view of those for whom business's *only* concern is making money or increasing profit. It is the view that extreme advocates of the free-market system voice in echoing economist Milton Friedman and others who insist that "the primary and *only* responsibility of business is to increase profit."[3]

Such a view distorts the position of Adam Smith, the 18th century economist-philosopher and father of the capitalistic free-market economy. As we discussed in Chapter 3, Smith argued in *The Wealth of Nations* that a great deal of good derives from a system that allows people to pursue their own interests. His doctrines became the theoretical foundation and justification of the capitalist free-market economic system. Smith, however, did not adopt a strictly commercial point of view, in that he asserted that the pursuit of self-interest be constrained by ethical considerations of justice and fairness. "Every man is left perfectly free to pursue his own interest, his own way," said Smith, "and to bring both his industry and capital into competition

[2]AICPA Code of Ethics, 53.2.01.
[3]The Social Responsibility of Business is to Increase Profits, by Milton Friedman. New York Times. September 13, 1970.

Smith + Friedman had similar views on ethical standpoint

with those of any other man, or order of men, as long as he does not violate the laws of justice."[4] Thus, there are times when justice and ethics demand that the professional sacrifice his or her own interests for the sake of others.

The strictly selfish commercial view, on the other hand, encourages the pursuit of self-interest with no limits – a pursuit that inevitably leads to selfishness. As we saw in the discussion of egoism in the previous chapter, there is a distinction between behavior that is completely acceptable (self-interested behavior) and behavior that is ethically inappropriate (selfish behavior). The *New Testament* teaches that we should love our neighbor as ourselves, thereby reminding us that if we don't have a healthy self-love and self-interest, we do both our neighbors and ourselves a disservice. Nevertheless, if we pursue our self-interest *at the expense of another*, we act unethically. In an ethical world, occasions arise in which we must sacrifice our own interests for others or for the common good.

We can argue that it is precisely because of the professional's specialized knowledge that this view should be abandoned. Whenever specialized knowledge is required to provide services to other people, it creates an asymmetry of knowledge and thereby an asymmetry of power. This results in a dependency relationship, whereby one person needs to rely on the word and advice of another. The potential exists to abuse the position of power and take advantage of a dependent person. For example, a doctor seeking extra compensation could recommend a procedure that a patient does not need. The patient would depend on the doctor's recommendation because the patient does not have the doctor's specialized medical knowledge. The ethics of our society mandate that those with superior knowledge have an obligation not to abuse that knowledge or to use it on the unknowing to gain unfair advantage. Hence, the professional must adhere to ethical precepts. But what specific obligations must the professional follow?

As a professional, the accountant has the following three obligations:

(1) to be competent and know about the art and science of accounting
(2) to put the interests of the client before the accountant's own, avoiding the temptation to take advantage of the client
(3) to serve the public interest

The AICPA code of ethics clearly articulates these responsibilities. It explains the first obligation as follows:

[4] Adam Smith, *The Wealth of Nations*, IV, IX 5 s.

Competence is derived from a synthesis of education and experience. It begins with a mastery of the common body of knowledge required for designation as a certified public accountant. The maintenance of competence requires a commitment to learning and professional improvement that must continue throughout a member's professional life. *It is a member's individual responsibility.* In all engagements and in all responsibilities, each member should undertake to achieve a level of competence that will assure that the quality of the member's services meets the high level of professionalism required by these Principles.[5]

The second obligation accrues to all professionals – the obligation to look out for the client's best interest. When an accountant is hired to perform a service for the client, there is, at the very least, an implied understanding that the accountant will look out for the client's interests. "A distinguishing mark of a profession," according to the code, "is acceptance of its responsibility to the public ... which consists of clients."[6]

The same passage of the code also recognizes the accountant's obligation to the public:

A distinguishing mark of a profession is acceptance of its responsibility to the public. The accounting profession's public consists of clients, credit grantors, governments, employers, investors, the business and financial community, and others who rely on the objectivity and integrity of certified public accountants to maintain the orderly functioning of commerce. This reliance imposes a public interest responsibility on certified public accountants. The public interest is defined as the collective well-being of the community of people and institutions the profession serves.[7]

Thus, accountants must accept the social responsibility inherent in their profession to serve the public interest. Note that this responsibility arises, as stated above, "to maintain the orderly functioning of commerce." Also note that the public interest – "the collective well-being of the community of people and institutions the profession serves" – is remarkably similar to the concept of "stakeholder," prevalent in business ethics literature. In light of Arthur Andersen's involvement in the Enron debacle, it is essential to recognize, no matter what the facts, that Arthur Andersen had an obligation to look out for the public interest, to protect the integrity of the free-market system. We can apply this same responsibility to the public interest to the tax accountants in the KPMG tax evasion scandal. Certainly, the accountant should act in the client's

---

[5] AICPA Code of Ethics, 56.V.02.
[6,7] AICPA Code of Ethics, 53.2.01.

interest, but not if it is unfair to or brings harm to the public. It is important to remember the scathing criticism in the KPMG indictment:

> It is hard to imagine anything that can serve to undermine our voluntary system of taxation more than the crimes charged today, where so many professionals banded together with wealthy individuals to perpetrate this massive fraud on the tax system.[8]

The laws that require publicly held companies to be audited impart a special responsibility to the accounting profession. Accountants are the public's designated gatekeepers; because they hold that privileged position, therefore, they are answerable to the general public.

This brings us to Huebner's last characteristic of a professional: "The practitioner should possess a spirit of loyalty to fellow practitioners, of helpfulness to the common cause they all profess, and should not allow any unprofessional acts to bring shame upon the entire profession." This corresponds to the AICPA's seventh characteristic of a profession: "an organization devoted to the advancement of the social obligations of the group." Thus, the AICPA and its members have a critical responsibility to society. If performing both auditing and consulting services for the same company interferes with an accountant's objectivity, for example, the AICPA must develop ways that will allow the accountant to meet her obligations to the general public.

Because of their joint responsibility to various groups – clients, colleagues, and the public – it is inevitable that accountants will sometimes face conflicting pressures. How can the accountant handle these pressures? The AICPA code of ethics says, "In resolving those conflicts, members should act with integrity, guided by the precept that when members fulfill their responsibility to the public, clients' and employers' interests are best served."[9]

This passage presents an intriguing motivation for behaving ethically. Because doing what is right for the public best serves clients and employers, the passage suggests, there cannot be a substantial conflict between the public, clients', and employers' interests. Thus, if an employer pressures a management accountant to cook the books, the accountant should refuse – not only is altering financial information not in the public's best interest, but it is also not in the employer's best interest. The AICPA code assumes that honesty is always the best policy, and that ethical business is always good business. In

---

[8] KPMG Superseding Indictment. US Department of Justice. US Attorney – Southern District of NY. October 17, 2005.
[9] AICPA Code of Ethics, 53.2.02.

effect, this means that an action that appears to be in a client's or employer's interests cannot be if the action is not in the public's interest. Appearances can be false and misleading. Consider this: Would Enron have been better off if its accountants had exposed some of its more opaque transactions?

Because accountants are charged with maintaining the orderly functioning of commerce without succumbing to a strictly commercial point of view, the public has a right to expect accountants to act with ethical probity, as mandated by the AICPA code:

> Those who rely on certified public accountants expect them to discharge their responsibilities with integrity, objectivity, due professional care, and a genuine interest in serving the public. They are expected to provide quality services, enter into fee arrangements, and offer a range of services – all in a manner that demonstrates a level of professionalism consistent with these Principles of the Code of Professional Conduct.[10]

Joining a professional group such as the AICPA is tantamount to promising to abide by the group's ethical standards. As such, that promise must be kept. Breaking promises is unacceptable (recall the discussion of Immanuel Kant's ethical theories in Chapter 3), because it is usually in pursuit of an individual's own inclinations without regard for others. The code specifically points out that joining the AICPA places an ethical burden on the member:

> All who accept membership in the American Institute of Certified Public Accountants commit themselves to honor the public trust. In return for the faith that the public reposes in them, members should seek continually to demonstrate their dedication to professional excellence.[11]

An interesting question remains: If being a professional requires membership in an organization, but all accountants are not CPAs and therefore do not belong to the AICPA, are all accountants professionals? If not an AICPA member, is the accountant bound by the same ethical obligations?

It seems evident that all certified public accountants fulfill the criteria of being professionals. They are admitted into the CPA fraternity by meeting professional qualification standards and passing the rigorous CPA exams to demonstrate that they have the requisite expertise.

But what about accountants who have not acquired the CPA designation? They may have the necessary expert knowledge without passing the CPA exam

---

[10] AICPA Code of Ethics, 53.2.03.
[11] AICPA Code of Ethics, 53.2.04.

or becoming AICPA members. They deal with clients and thereby have the same obligation to those clients as CPAs do. Thus, they should be subject to some of the other professional standards, such as abiding by the provisions in a code of ethics, whether it is the AICPA code or another professional code. The standards of behavior do not rest on the code itself. Rather, codes specify universally valid standards of conduct that accountants should follow. The next chapter examines these codes of ethics and explores the principles on which they are based.

Chapter Five

Accounting Codes of Conduct[1]

Accountants have a responsibility to present the most truthful and accurate financial pictures of an organization. As auditors, they have a responsibility to evaluate other accountants' pictures and attest to their truthfulness and accuracy. In doing so, accountants accomplish the purposes of their profession – to meet the needs of the clients or companies for which they work, or to serve the best interests of the stockholders/stakeholders who are entitled to truthful representations of an organization's financial status.

Individuals have an ethical obligation to perform their jobs. (As we discussed in Chapter 2, the act of accepting a job entails a promise to do that job, and promises should be kept.) Job responsibilities are usually spelled out in a job description, employee handbook, managerial guide book, company code of conduct, and/or, finally, the profession's code of conduct or ethics.

The accounting profession has developed multiple codes of ethics that set the standards for accountants' behavior, standards that require more than simply adhering to the letter of the law. We suggest that these sophisticated codes are the equivalent of a binding organizational moral law. Consequently, the codes determine what is ethically required of an accountant. *Business Ethics*[2] enumerates six ways that codes of conduct can be valuable:

(1) A code can motivate through using peer pressure, by holding up a generally recognized set of behavioral expectations that must be considered in decision making.

---

[1] The full AICPA code can be downloaded at http://www.aicpa.org/about/code/index.html.
[2] Norman Bowie and Ronald Duska, *Business Ethics*, Prentice-Hall, 1985.

Accounting Ethics, Second Edition. Ronald Duska, Brenda Shay Duska, and Julie Ragatz.
© 2011 John Wiley & Sons, Ltd. Published 2011 by John Wiley & Sons, Ltd.

(2)   A code can provide more stable permanent guides to right or wrong than do human personalities or continual *ad hoc* decisions.

(3)   Codes can provide guidance, especially in ambiguous situations.

(4)   Codes not only can guide the behavior of employees, they can also control the autocratic power of employers.

(5)   Codes can help specify the social responsibilities of business itself.

(6)   Codes are clearly in the interest of business itself, for if businesses do not police themselves ethically, others will do it for them.

In the United States, there are two major codes for the accounting profession – the AICPA (American Institute of Certified Public Accountants) Code of Professional Conduct, adopted in its current form in 1973, significantly revised in 1988, and updated for all official releases through October 2009,[3] and Institute of Management Accountants (IMA) Standards of Ethical Conduct for Practitioners of Management Accounting and Financial Management, adopted in April 1997.[4]

There are also codes for accountants in other countries, the most notable of which is the International Federation of Accountants (IFAC) Code of Ethics for Professional Accountants, updated in 2009 by the International Ethics Standards Board for Accountants (IESBA), which develops ethical standards and guidance for professional accountants. The IESBA encourages member bodies to adopt high standards of ethics for their members and promotes good ethical practices globally. The Public Interest Oversight Board (PIOB) oversees the work of the IESBA, which also fosters international debate on ethical issues that accountants face. Four of the principles of the IESBA code – integrity, competence, confidentiality, and objectivity – are identical to those in the AICPA code. (The IMA code also addresses the principles of integrity, competence, confidentiality, and objectivity – see Appendix B) The fifth IESBA principle – professionalism – is covered in other areas of the AICPA code.[5]

This chapter examines what constitutes appropriate behavior for accountants. Because we do not have the time or space to examine all accounting codes of conduct, we will concentrate on the AICPA code.

---

[3] http://www.aicpa.org/about/code/index.html.

[4] The IMA code is available at http://www.accountingformanagement.com/code_of_conduct_for_management_a/htm.

[5] Information about the International Federation of Accountants code can be found at http://www.ifac.org/Ethics/ The code can be downloaded at http://www.ifac.org/Members/Pubs-Downloading.tmpl?PubID=1247239638617226&File=Ethics/code-of-ethics-for-professi-2.pdf&Category=Ethics.

I AICPA Professional Code of Conduct

The AICPA Code of Conduct is composed of two sections; the first section is devoted to principles, the second to rules. The principles are general norms of behavior, and they provide the framework for the more specific rules. The Council of the AICPA designates bodies to interpret the rules and provide technical standards for them. These interpretations result in Ethical Rulings, which govern specific activities but can also be applied to other similar behavior.

The AICPA code begins by explaining its purpose and scope. It was adopted "to provide guidance and rules to all members – those in public practice, in industry, in government, and in education – in the performance of their professional responsibilities."[6] Its purpose, then, is to guide, and its scope encompasses all certified public accountants who belong to the AICPA. It is binding on them and only them. Because, however, the code promulgates the "basic tenets of ethical and professional conduct for accountants,"[7] it can serve as a handbook on ethics for *all* accountants.

The code specifies three constituencies to whom accountants have ethical responsibilities: the public, clients, and colleagues. In the accounting profession, particularly for "public" accountants, the responsibility to the public is paramount. This primary responsibility is different in accounting than in various other professions, such as law and medicine, in which the primary responsibility is to the client or patient. The accountant's responsibility to the public is so important that it overrides his or her obligations to companies or clients. In the case of an external audit, for example, even though the firm being audited hires and pays the accountant, the accountant's first responsibility is to those in the public constituency entitled to view the company's financial statements. This creates an anomalous situation in which the accountant technically is not working for the person or company that pays him or her.

Because accountants have responsibilities to the public, clients, and colleagues, we need to examine all the relationships and the incumbent obligations. Studying the provisions of the AICPA code helps to clarify the various relationships.

Let's turn now to an examination of the principles in the AIPCA code. Chapter 6 will focus on the rules.

---

[6] AICPA Professional Code of Conduct, Introduction.
[7] AICPA Professional Code of Conduct, Preamble, Section 51.02.

II Code Principles

"The Principles of the Code … express the profession's recognition of its responsibilities to the public, to clients, and to colleagues. They guide members in the performance of their professional responsibilities and express the basic tenets of ethical and professional conduct. The Principles call for an unswerving commitment to honorable behavior, even at the sacrifice of personal advantage."[8] There are six principles, as follows:

- Principle I – In carrying out their responsibilities as professionals, members should exercise sensitive professional and moral judgments in all their activities.[9]
- Principle II – Members should accept the obligation to act in a way that will serve the public interest, honor the public trust, and demonstrate commitment to professionalism.[10]
- Principle III – To maintain and broaden public confidence, members should perform all professional responsibilities with the highest sense of integrity.[11]
- Principle IV – A member should maintain objectivity and be free of conflicts of interest in discharging professional responsibilities. A member in public practice should be independent in fact and appearance when providing auditing and other attestation services.[12]
- Principle V – A member should observe the profession's technical and ethical standards, strive continually to improve competence and the quality of services, and discharge professional responsibility to the best of the member's ability.[13]
- Principle VI – A member in public practice should observe the Principles of the Code of Professional Conduct in determining the scope and nature of services to be provided.[14]

The AICPA code explains each of its principles in detail. They are similar to those in most professional codes – service to others, competency, integrity,

---

[8] AICPA Professional Code of Conduct, Preamble, Section 51.02.
[9] AICPA Professional Code of Conduct, Section 52, Article I.
[10] AICPA Professional Code of Conduct, Section 53, Article II.
[11] AICPA Professional Code of Conduct, Section 54, Article III.
[12] AICPA Professional Code of Conduct, Section 55, Article IV.
[13] AICPA Professional Code of Conduct, Section 56, Article V.
[14] AICPA Professional Code of Conduct, Section 57, Article VI.

objectivity and independence, professionalism (including continuing education), and accountability to the profession. Let's review each of the code principles more fully.

Principle I – Responsibilities

> In carrying out their responsibilities as professionals, members should exercise
> sensitive professional and moral judgments in all their activities.

This principle simply and clearly states that professional responsibilities require moral judgment, thereby equating professional behavior with moral
behavior. The interpretation of the principle reads as follows:

> As professionals, certified public accountants perform an essential role in soci-
> ety. Consistent with that role, members of the American Institute of Certified
> Public Accountants have responsibilities to all those who use their professional
> services. Members also have a continuing responsibility to cooperate with each
> other to improve the art of accounting, maintain the public's confidence, and
> carry out the profession's special responsibilities for self-governance. The collec-
> tive efforts of all members are required to maintain and enhance the traditions
> of the profession.[15]

This paragraph, which notes the essential role that CPAs play in society, has
great import. Accountants have a responsibility to "all those who use their
professional services." Here, again, is the anomaly we noted earlier. Most professionals' prime responsibility is to their clients. Accountants, however, who
play a critical role in the free-market system (see Chapter 2) by providing an
organization's financial picture, have numerous constituencies. Because the
scope of their responsibility extends to all those who use the information –
data that are essential to doing business – accountants have *prima facie* responsibilities beyond those to their clients or whoever pays them. Even though
Enron paid Arthur Andersen, for example, as an external auditor, Andersen
did not work for Enron. Andersen's primary responsibility was therefore to
the general public.

The first principle also indicates the responsibility to cooperate with fellow
professionals to maintain the integrity of the accounting profession. As we saw
in Chapter 4, one of the obligations of a professional is to the profession itself.
Specifically, the principle mentions three obligations: "to improve the art of

---

[15] AICPA Professional Code of Conduct, Section 52, Article I.01.

accounting, maintain the public's confidence, and carry out the professional responsibility for self-governance."

Although the code gives little guidance on the obligation to improve the art of accounting, it pays particular attention to the obligation to maintain the public's confidence in the profession and the obligation to self-governance. Chapter 6, which addresses the code rules, will explore these obligations more fully. For now, suffice to say that critics of the accounting profession – most of whom are accountants themselves – have maintained for years that accounting standards are inadequate for today's complex financial transactions. Recent accounting scandals have made their inadequacies only too clear. These events have also eroded the public's confidence in the profession. Thus, it is an ethical imperative that the profession carry out its responsibility for self-governance. It is arguable that the current practice of peer review is sufficient to fulfill that responsibility.

To meet the moral obligations, according to the first principle, accountants must "exercise sensitive professional and moral judgments." To do so, they must determine whether an activity harms others, is respectful of others and their rights, is fair, and is in accord with the commitments the accountants have made. Sensitive moral judgment is incompatible with selfish behavior. Thus, accountants are bound by the Golden Rule: Do unto others as you would have them do unto you.

Principle II – Serve the public interest

> Members should accept the obligation to act in a way that will serve the public interest, honor the public trust, and demonstrate commitment to professionalism.

In the interpretation of this principle, the code asserts that "acceptance of its responsibility to the public" is a "distinguishing mark of a profession."[16] That is a somewhat idiosyncratic view. As mentioned above, professions such as law and medicine – even, to an extent, teaching – are clearly client-oriented. Doctors and lawyers would likely indicate that their first – possibly only – obligation is to their patients or clients (subject only to the constraints of some higher, inviolable moral principle – for example, a lawyer cannot suborn perjury). A distinguishing mark, if not *the* distinguishing mark, of a public accountant, on the other hand, is that the accountant's primary obligation is to the public, and in a broader sense to the truth – the accuracy and veracity of the financial statements with which they deal.

---

[16]AICPA Professional Code of Conduct, Section 53, Article II.01.

The code spells out who is included in the public, naming "clients, credit grantors, governments, employers, investors, the business and financial community and others who rely on the objectivity and integrity of certified public accountants to maintain the orderly functioning of commerce."[17] This principle explains that the public nature of accounting is grounded in the social purpose of the orderly functioning of commerce. Ethical behavior is necessary to the public interest, which is defined as "the collective well-being of the community of people and institutions the profession serves."[18]

Conflicts of interest between clients and the public, or between employers and the public, are bound to occur. To resolve these conflicts, the code issues this mandate: "In discharging their professional responsibilities, members may encounter conflicting pressures from among each of those groups. In resolving those conflicts, members should act with integrity, guided by the precept that when members fulfill their responsibility to the public, clients' and employers' interests are best served."[19] The code states unequivocally that accountants must act with integrity (we will discuss Principle III, integrity, shortly). But what is remarkable is the assertion that fulfilling the responsibility to the public best serves the accountant's clients or employers.

Is it indeed true that clients' interests are always best served when accountants fulfill their responsibility to the public? Suppose a client's business will go bankrupt if the company cannot obtain a loan from the bank, and there will be no loan unless the accountant misrepresents the company's financial status. According to the code, good ethics is good business; when the accountant tells the truth, everyone will be better off, even if it does not look that way at first glance. But is that realistic? Whether it is or not, the precept is still a powerful normative principle in the heart of the code, one worth looking at, arguing for, and developing.[20] Those who rely on certified public accountants expect them to discharge their responsibilities with integrity, objectivity, due professional care, and a genuine interest in serving the public. These are the characteristics the code identifies and the public expects.

To be an AICPA member is to promise or contract to act on behalf of the public interest. All accountants who voluntarily accept membership in the AICPA commit themselves to honor this public trust. But does this commitment apply to accountants who are not AICPA members? We need to look at other grounds to establish nonmembers' responsibility to the public.

[17,18] AICPA Professional Code of Conduct, Section 53, Article II.01.
[19] AICPA Professional Code of Conduct, Section 53, Article II.02.
[20] cf. Ronald Duska, "Business Ethics, an Oxymoron or Good Business?" *Business Ethics Quarterly,* Vol. 10, No. 1.

Principle III – Integrity

> To maintain and broaden public confidence, members should perform all professional responsibilities with the highest sense of integrity.

In the interpretation of Principle II, the code calls for members to resolve conflicting pressures with integrity. Principle III specifies the requirements of that integrity.

The code defines integrity as follows: "Integrity is an element of character fundamental to professional recognition. It is the quality from which the public trust derives and the benchmark against which a member must ultimately test all decisions … [It] requires a member to be, among other things, honest and candid within the constraints of client confidentiality. Service and the public trust should not be subordinated to personal gain and advantage … [It] is measured in terms of what is right and just."[21]

This interpretation is quite general. It identifies integrity as "an element of character that is fundamental to professional recognition," and it maintains that "the public trust derives" from the recognition of this quality. It further identifies integrity as "the benchmark against which a member must ultimately test all decisions." None of this, however, tells us what integrity *is*.

Clearly, the decision to misrepresent a company's financial picture or to overlook some red flags in a company's financial statement violates an accountant's integrity. But what is the integrity being violated?

The obvious answer is that the misrepresentation involves dishonesty. Indeed, integrity is sometimes equated with honesty. But to stop at that meaning is not enough. Nor is it enough to avow that integrity entails subordinating personal gain and advantage to the public trust or doing what is right and just. Exactly what does all this mean? What sort of character does a person of integrity have?

We need further analysis. To understand integrity as an element of character we must consider what is called virtue or character ethics. (See Chapter 3 for a discussion of virtue ethics.) At its most basic, integrity is related to the word "integer," which refers to whole numbers. Thus, one definition of integrity is "the state of being whole, entire, or undiminished."[22] Integrity, therefore, means wholeness, the kind of wholeness referred to as "having it all together." But what does it take to have it all together? The primary definition of integrity is relevant: "adherence to moral and ethical principles; soundness

---

[21] AICPA Code of Ethics, Section 54, Articles III.01, III.02, and III.03.
[22] http://dictionary.reference.com/browse/integrity.

of moral character; honesty."[23] But these definitions, while instructive, are still rather vague.

Limiting the concept of integrity simply to being honest is analogous to describing Walt Disney's story of "Pinocchio"[24] merely as the tale of a boy whose nose grew when he lied. Certainly, the story tells us not to lie, just as integrity tells us to be honest. But honesty is not a synonym for integrity. Lying and dishonesty are merely symptoms of the lack of integrity, and identifying the lack of integrity only with lying does not embrace the core meaning, any more than Pinocchio's growing nose is the whole story of "Pinocchio."

What does the story tell us? Think back. Geppetto creates a special puppet, Pinocchio, who walks and talks by himself. But he is a wooden puppet, not a real boy. To be a real boy, Pinocchio must become morally complete. What does it take for Pinocchio to become "whole, entire, and undiminished" – that is, to achieve integrity – and become a real boy?

First, he must develop a conscience. Since puppets don't come equipped with consciences, he is given Jiminy Cricket. But Jiminy is external to Pinocchio. With Jiminy, Pinocchio hears from the outside what is right and wrong. The code of conduct, which Jiminy represents, is not yet part of Pinocchio. He needs to internalize that code. Similarly, just learning the rules of a profession is not enough. An accountant must internalize and live by those rules.

In his incomplete state, Pinocchio goes off to school. On the way, he meets Gideon and Honest John (who is anything but honest), who entice Pinocchio to join a puppet show. They promise him fame, convincing him that a puppet who can walk without strings and talk by himself will become an instant celebrity. Pinocchio soon learns, though, that celebrity and fame do not make him complete. As a matter of fact, celebrity and fame entrap Pinocchio when the puppet-master puts Pinocchio in a cage because he is too valuable to be set free.

Jiminy Cricket helps Pinocchio escape, only to see him lured to Pleasure Island, where he can engage in the self-centered pursuit of pleasure without restraint. Unrestrained pleasure, however, does not lead to his completeness either. Rather, it turns him into a jackass, including ears and a tail. With Jiminy's help, Pinocchio flees the island and returns to Geppetto's workshop.

Meanwhile, Geppetto, who had gone to sea to rescue Pinocchio from Pleasure Island, has been swallowed by a giant whale, Monstro. Pinocchio, with wisdom and self-control, devises a plan to rescue Geppetto. After the brave and selfless act of entering Monstro's belly, Pinocchio finally becomes a real boy. He is complete. He has integrity.

---

[23] http://dictionary.reference.com/browse/integrity.
[24] The original version was written in Italian by Carlo Collodi in 1881 and 1882 in serial form, and it differs somewhat from the Disney version. But the lessons still hold.

The story of Pinocchio illustrates that lying is only a symptom of the lack of integrity. People lie because they are self-absorbed. They lie to prevent unpleasantness, look better, avoid a harm, or gain an advantage. People with integrity do not need to lie, because their values are sound. Moreover, they have the wisdom to recognize that there is nothing for which they should compromise those values. Individuals with integrity have the courage to live with the consequences of the truth and the self-assurance to give others their due (justice) without unduly fearing for themselves.

Beginning with Plato and Aristotle, traditional ethical theories have placed a high emphasis on integrity, or wholeness. A person was not whole unless he or she possessed what were called the four cardinal virtues – wisdom, justice, temperance, and courage. The individual had integrity only if he or she had all four virtues; each virtue required the others.

We can readily apply the lessons of Pinocchio and traditional ethics to accounting. The accountant who is tempted to misrepresent a financial statement or to condone dubious accounting practices must undergo a transformation similar to Pinocchio's. To be a real professional, the accountant must acquire the virtues of wisdom, justice, self-control, and courage. The accountant must act with integrity, which is measured in the following terms:

> Integrity is measured in terms of what is right and just. In the absence of specific rules, standards, or guidance, or in the face of conflicting opinions, a member should test decisions and deeds by asking: "Am I doing what a person of integrity would do? Have I retained my integrity?" Integrity requires a member to observe both the form and the spirit of technical and ethical standards; circumvention of those standards constitutes subordination of judgment.[25]

This passage is subject to individual interpretation. It says, for example, that if there aren't any specific rules, standards, or guidance, or if there are conflicting opinions, a member should ask, "Am I doing what a person of integrity would do?" The answer should lead to doing what is right and just. Determining what is right and just, however, can be difficult. It seems, therefore, that we are caught in a vicious circle.

There may be a way out. One way is to use the Golden Rule to test the justice and rightness of an action. Propose a course of action and ask whether you would approve of that action if it were done to you. Generally, but not always, that is a reasonable test. At least it assures that you do not follow your interests exclusively and that you show concern for another's needs and dignity. Another test is to ask whether or not you can live with yourself after you make a certain decision. If you can't, the action will undermine your integrity.

[25] AICPA Professional Code of Conduct, Section 54, Article III.03.

Virtue Ethics driven system

*w/o moral courage, all else
doesn't matter*

This is another important aspect of the third principle: the explicit requirement that members "observe both the form and the spirit of technical and ethical standards." Circumventing those standards, the code says, means "subordination of judgment." In tax accounting, for example, bypassing the intent of the tax legislation is unethical. The invention of "black box" accounting – financial statements based on accounting methodologies so complex that numbers, even though they are accurate and legal, confuse rather than clarify – clearly violates the *spirit* of accounting standards, which were set up precisely to guarantee the public and other users accurate financial pictures. Restatements of revenues, inventory, and earnings, and the use of derivatives and off-the-books partnerships all circumvent the accountant's responsibility to present a company's financial status accurately. It is difficult to imagine, in the case of the KPMG tax dodges, for example, how an accountant could defend such behavior on the basis that no laws were actually broken, when the behavior clearly violated the spirit of the law.

Finally, Principle III says, integrity requires a member to observe the principles of "objectivity and independence and of due care."[26] Objectivity and independence are perhaps the most important of the principles in the AICPA code. We turn to that principle now.

Principle IV – Objectivity and independence

> A member should maintain objectivity and be free of conflicts of interest in discharging professional responsibilities. A member in public practice should be independent in fact and appearance when providing auditing and other attestation services.

"Objectivity," according to the code, "is a state of mind, a quality that lends value to a member's services."[27] Hence, objectivity is a virtue; it is a habit to be developed. The principle requires that the objective person be impartial, intellectually honest, and free of conflicts of interest. The code also makes this powerful statement: "Independence precludes relationships that may appear to impair a member's objectivity in rendering attestation services."[28] It is difficult to imagine that anyone could think that Arthur Andersen could "appear" to be objective with respect to Enron, when Andersen "depended on Enron for $52 million in fees, more than half of which, $27 million, was derived not from auditing its books, but from providing other services."[29]

---

[26] AICPA Professional Code of Conduct, Section 54, Article III.04.
[27,28] AICPA Professional Code of Conduct, Section 55, Article IV.01.
[29] "The Twister Hits," *The Economist* (Industry Overview), January 19, 2002, p. 59.

Achieving objectivity is not easy. Consider these two statements: "He believed because it was a fact," and "Because he believed, it was a fact." People, in general, often see things as they think they are or as they want them to be, rather than seeing them as they actually are. This also applies to accountants. If you believe that all the people in the company you are auditing are honest, you give them the benefit of the doubt and don't see things that a more skeptical auditor would see. It is interesting that the interpretation of the code thus cautions auditors to adopt a skeptical attitude.

Specifically, "the principle on objectivity imposes the obligation to be impartial, intellectually honest, and free of conflicts of interest."[30] We'll take a closer look at the obligations to be impartial and to be free of conflicts of interest.

To be impartial, AICPA members must try to remove their personal feelings and interests from any judgments or recommendations being made or any actions being taken. Members must detach themselves from the situation and look on it as a disinterested third party.

Moreover, the code prohibits conflicts of interest – not only real conflicts of interest but also appearances of a conflict. If the accountant is auditing a company in which she has stock and an unfavorable audit would decrease the stock's worth, for example, there is a conflict of interest. Similarly, if the accountant is consulting with one client and the advice would hurt another client, there is a conflict. Members should either avoid such conflicts or free themselves from them.

Also, a member who is overlooking discrepancies in an audit in order to secure a consulting job from the firm being audited faces a huge conflict of interest. The Sarbanes–Oxley Act addressed that conflict by prohibiting accountants from auditing clients with which they are engaged in other activities such as consulting.[31] Because consulting often yields larger financial benefits

---

[30] AICPA Code of Professional Conduct, Section 55, Article IV.01.

[31] AICPA Summary of Sarbanes–Oxley, Section 201: Services Outside the Scope of Practice of Auditors; Prohibited Activities. "It shall be 'unlawful' for a registered public accounting firm to provide any non-audit service to an issuer contemporaneously with the audit, including: (1) bookkeeping or other services related to the accounting records or financial statements of the audit client; (2) financial information systems design and implementation; (3) appraisal or valuation services, fairness opinions, or contribution-in-kind reports; (4) actuarial services; (5) internal audit outsourcing services; (6) management functions or human resources; (7) broker or dealer, investment adviser, or investment banking services; (8) legal services and expert services unrelated to the audit; (9) any other service that the Board determines, by regulation, is impermissible. The Board may, on a case-by-case basis, exempt from these prohibitions any person, issuer, public accounting firm, or transaction, subject to review by the Commission." (See Appendix A.)

to an accounting firm than auditing, this creates a huge temptation to "go soft" on the auditing, and makes the requisite skepticism difficult to achieve.

The code stresses the appearance of independence for AICPA members in public service (this does not apply to private service):

> For a member in public practice, the maintenance of objectivity and independence requires a continuing assessment of client relationships and public responsibility. Such a member who provides auditing and other attestation services should be independent in fact and appearance. In providing all other services, a member should maintain objectivity and avoid conflicts of interest.[32]

Although it is clear-cut that in performing attestation services, the accountant must be objective and independent, that may not be possible, some might argue, for internal auditors or management accountants. Yet the code does not make that distinction. In fact, it recognizes those different interests. "Members often serve multiple interests in many different capacities," the code states, but "must demonstrate their objectivity in varying circumstances."[33] It even describes the various functions AICPA members perform: "Members in public practice render attest, tax, and management advisory services. Other members prepare financial statements in the employment of others, perform internal auditing services, and serve in financial and management capacities in industry, education, and government. They also educate and train those who aspire to admission into the profession."[34] In spite of the different roles accountants play for different constituencies, the code demands objectivity: "Regardless of service or capacity, members should protect the integrity of their work, maintain objectivity, and avoid any subordination of their judgment."[35]

Just as the ideal researcher is motivated to search for true knowledge, the ideal accountant is motivated to present as true a financial picture as possible. Accountants cannot accomplish this if they subordinate their judgment to others, or if out of fear (note the need for courage) or greed (note the need for temperance), they tell the boss what the boss wants to hear. To maintain their integrity, accountants must, first and foremost, be true to themselves and their profession. Thus, the interpretation of Principle IV concludes with these strong words on the responsibilities of members not in public practice, who by nature of their job are not independent:

> Although members not in public practice cannot maintain the appearance of independence, they nevertheless have the *responsibility* to maintain

[32] AICPA Code of Professional Conduct, Section 55, Article IV.03.
[33–35] AICPA Code of Professional Conduct, Section 55, Article IV.02.

objectivity in rendering professional services. Members employed by others to prepare financial statements or to perform auditing, tax, or consulting services are charged with the same responsibility for objectivity as members in public practice and must be *scrupulous* in their application of generally accepted accounting principles and candid in all their dealings with members in public practice.[36]

Thus, we can conclude that *all* accountants – public and private – have one primary responsibility: to make their work as honest and true as possible. Anything short of that, for whatever reason, damages their integrity and their dedication to the goals of the accounting profession. Any unethical activity – even legal activities that violate the spirit of the code – is prohibited.

Principle V – Due care

A member should observe the profession's technical and ethical standards, strive continually to improve competence and the quality of services, and discharge professional responsibility to the best of the member's ability.

The principle of due care sets a very high bar for the accountant. The interpretation of the principle identifies the "quest for excellence" as the "essence of due care."[37] That excellence requires both competence and diligence. The accountant must perform to the best of her ability with a "concern for the best interest of those for whom the services are performed and consistent with the profession's responsibility to the public."[38]

Accountants attain competence through education and experience. First, they must learn the common body of accounting knowledge. To maintain a high level of facility and acumen, they must supplement this knowledge by a continual commitment to professional improvement. Due care further requires that when accountants recognize the limitations of their competence, they consult with others or refer a client to another who has the requisite competence. "Each member is responsible," according to the code, "for assessing his or her own competence – of evaluating whether education, experience, and judgment are adequate for the responsibility to be assumed."[39]

Diligence, which "imposes the responsibility to render services promptly and carefully, to be thorough, and to observe applicable technical and ethical

---

[36] AICPA Code of Professional Conduct, Section 55, Article IV.04.
[37,38] AICPA Code of Professional Conduct, Section 56, Article V.01.
[39] AICPA Code of Professional Conduct, Section 56, Article V.03.

standards,"[40] is another aspect of due care. To be prompt, careful, and thorough requires that an accountant "plan and supervise adequately any professional activity for which he or she is responsible."[41] Hence, sloppy planning that leads to less than competent service to clients can be characterized as unethical behavior – although some accountants might disagree that sloppiness can be considered an ethical dimension.

Principle VI – Scope and nature of services

> A member in public practice should observe the Principles of the Code of Professional Conduct in determining the scope and nature of services to be provided.

This principle ties all the principles together. It begins with professionalism: "The public interest aspect of certified public accountants' services requires that such services be consistent with acceptable professional behavior for certified public accountants. Integrity requires that service and the public trust not be subordinated to personal gain and advantage."[42] The principle also states, "Objectivity and independence require that members be free from conflicts of interest in discharging professional responsibilities. Due care requires that services be provided with competence and diligence."[43]

A member must decide in what circumstances to provide specific services by considering each of the six principles. The code notes, "In some instances, they may represent an overall constraint on the nonaudit services that might be offered to a specific client. No hard-and-fast rules can be developed to help members reach these judgments, but they must be satisfied that they are meeting the spirit of the Principles in this regard."[44] In other words, the prudent practitioner must apply the principle of scope and nature of services in the spirit of justice. To accomplish this, the code calls for AICPA members to do the following:

- Practice in firms that have in place internal quality-control procedures to ensure that services are competently delivered and adequately supervised.
- Determine, in their individual judgments, whether the scope and nature of other services provided to an audit client would create a conflict of interest in the performance of the audit function for that client.

[40] AICPA Code of Professional Conduct, Section 56, Article V.04.
[41] AICPA Code of Professional Conduct, Section 56, Article V.05.
[42,43] AICPA Code of Professional Conduct, Section 57, Article VI.01.
[44] AICPA Code of Professional Conduct, Section 57, Article VI.02.

- Assess, in their individual judgments, whether an activity is consistent with their role as professionals.[45]

The practical implications of this are monumental. It means that members should *not* practice in firms that do not have adequately supervised internal quality control procedures for competent services. Members must also be aware of and determine what other services for a client would create a conflict of interest. Finally, members must assess the propriety of their activities against what the true professional would do.

III Criticisms of the Code of Conduct

The code principles, taken as a whole, establish the framework for an accountant's ethical approach to the accounting profession. Critics say, however, that the principles have at least two insufficiencies: (1) they are too broad and amorphous; and (2) they lack sanctions.

The first principle, for example, says, "In carrying out their responsibilities as professionals, members [of the AICPA] should exercise sensitive professional and moral judgments in all their activities." That statement is too broad, critics contend, because no one acts as a CPA in *all* activities, and too amorphous because it does not specifically define "sensitive" professional judgments. A rejoinder, however, is that language is always general and in need of interpretation and that rules and interpretations of code principles address the lack-of-specificity problem. Furthermore, principles are meant to be inspirational; rules are meant to be concrete.

The second drawback to codes, overall, is that they are seldom enforced. And a code without enforcement may be worse than no code at all. To mitigate this deficiency in accounting codes, the Sarbanes–Oxley Act, in addition to establishing the Public Company Accounting Oversight Board, gave the SEC greater power to enforce standards. (We will examine these issues more fully in a later chapter.)

Nevertheless, despite these drawbacks, codes of conduct are tremendously important in establishing professional standards. Specific rules can clear up any vagueness in a code principle. Chapter 6 discusses the AICPA rules that clarify the principles in its code of professional conduct.

---

[45] AICPA Code of Professional Conduct, Section 57, Article VI.03.

Chapter Six

The Rules of the Code of Conduct

After presenting the principles, the AICPA Professional Code of Conduct examines the rules that govern those principles. The code states, "The bylaws of the American Institute of Certified Public Accountants require that members adhere to the Rules of the Code of Professional Conduct. Members must be prepared to justify departures from these Rules."[1] These rules are formally applicable only to members of the AICPA and people under members' control. If members violate the rules, they are subject to disciplining by the AICPA. Thus, it is necessary to review these rules to understand the AICPA's expectations regarding accountants' behavior.

The code breaks down the rules into five sections, as follows:

- Section 100 – Independence, Integrity, and Objectivity
- Section 200 – General Standards Accounting Principles
- Section 300 – Responsibilities to Clients
- Section 400 – Responsibilities to Colleagues
- Section 500 – Other Responsibilities and Practices

In most cases, the rule in each of the five sections is followed by interpretations of that rule, which address the acceptability of specific types of activities. Finally, under each of the sections, there are numerous specific ethics rulings. Over the years, as it has evolved, there have been many deletions and revisions to the code.

This chapter examines the rules of the AICPA code.[2]

---

[1] AICPA Code of Professional Conduct, Section 91.01.
[2] To examine the rules of the AICPA in full, go to www.aicpa.org.

Accounting Ethics, Second Edition. Ronald Duska, Brenda Shay Duska, and Julie Ragatz.
© 2011 John Wiley & Sons, Ltd. Published 2011 by John Wiley & Sons, Ltd.

I Section 100 – Independence, Integrity, and Objectivity

Rule 101 – Independence

This rule, which governs independence, reads, "A member in public practice shall be independent in the performance of professional services as required by standards promulgated by bodies designated by Council."[3]

Under the interpretation of Rule 101, the code specifies what bodies a member should consult:

> In performing an attest engagement, a member should consult the rules of his or her state board of accountancy, his or her state CPA society, the Public Company Accounting Oversight Board and the U.S. Securities and Exchange Commission (SEC) if the member's report will be filed with the SEC, the U.S. Department of Labor (DOL) if the member's report will be filed with the DOL, the Government Accountability Office (GAO) if law, regulation, agreement, policy or contract requires the member's report to be filed under GAO regulations, and any organization that issues or enforces standards of independence that would apply to the member's engagement. Such organizations may have independence requirements or rulings that differ from (e.g., may be more restrictive than) those of the AICPA.[4]

There is not time to examine all of these different standards. Therefore, we will focus on what Section 100 says about independence. In general, what does independence require?

The interpretation in the code does not specify what constitutes independence. Rather, it cites the threats to independence. Independence is considered to be impaired if the following transactions, interests, or relationships occur:

A   During the period of a professional engagement a covered member
   (1)   Had or was committed to acquire any direct or material indirect financial interest in the client.
   (2)   Was a trustee of any trust or executor or administrator of any estate if such trust or estate had or was committed to acquire any direct or material indirect financial interest in the client. ...
   (3)   Had a joint, closely held investment that was material to the covered member.

[3,4]AICPA Code of Professional Conduct, Section 101.01.

(4) … had any loan to or from the client, any officer or director of the client, or any individual owning 10 percent or more the client's outstanding equity securities or other ownership interests.

B During the period of the professional engagement, a partner or professional employee of the firm, his of her immediate family, or any group of such persons acting together owned more than 5 percent of a client's outstanding equity securities or other ownership interests.

C During the period covered by the financial statements or during the period of the professional engagement, a firm, or partner or professional employee of the firm was simultaneously associated with the client as a(n)

(1) Director, officer, or employee, or in any capacity equivalent to that of a member of management;

(2) Promoter, underwriter, or voting trustee; or

(3) Trustee for any pension or profit-sharing trust of the client.[5]

Not only can any of the above entanglements compromise an accountant's independence, but they can also jeopardize the accountant's integrity and objectivity by creating a real or perceived conflict of interest, a subject covered in the next rule.

Rule 102 – Integrity and objectivity

Rule 102 is a powerful governing rule in accounting ethics: "In the performance of any professional service, a member shall maintain objectivity and integrity, shall be free of conflicts of interest, and shall not knowingly misrepresent facts or subordinate his or her judgment to others."[6]

We have already discussed integrity at length in the previous chapter on code principles. But what about objectivity? Code principles impose the obligation on the accountant to be impartial, intellectually honest, and free of conflicts of interest. Objectivity, then, is the ability to stand back as a third-party observer, to set aside personal interests and appraise an issue on its own merits. Intellectual honesty requires looking at a situation from all possible perspectives.

Ethical theory gives us various ways to achieve objectivity – for example, Kant's universalizability principle, which asks, What if everyone did this? But the most common way in ethics to attain objectivity is to invoke the Golden

---

[5] AICPA Code of Professional Conduct, Section 101.01, Section 101.02.
[6] AICPA Code of Professional Conduct, Section 101.01, Section 102.01.

Rule: Do unto others as you would have them do unto you. Asking how you would like others to treat you enables you to abandon the doer's perspective of the action and adopt the receiver's perspective. By going outside of yourself to consider an issue, you become a detached, disinterested observer – that is, you become impartial and objective.

Misrepresentation

Rule 102-1 proscribes deliberate, knowing misrepresentations of facts. This is simply an appeal to the accountant's honesty. Misrepresentation is lying, and lying, as we discussed earlier in this book, is unethical. Although the code applies only to AICPA members, the spirit of this rule applies to all accountants. Thus, it prohibits auditors from misrepresenting a financial statement, tax accountants from misrepresenting income or assets, and management accountants from misrepresenting inventories. The accounting professional must be truthful; to misrepresent is to use the person to whom the misrepresentation is given merely as a means to the misrepresenter's end.

Conflicts of interest

Rule 102-2 describes a conflict of interest as a situation in which certain relationships impair objectivity. It is not advisable, for example, for doctors to diagnose their loved ones, or for business colleagues to become romantically involved with subordinates whose work they need to evaluate. Judges must recuse themselves if they have an interest in a case. Similar recommendations hold for accountants:

> A conflict of interest may occur if a member performs a professional service for a client or employer and the member or his or her firm has a relationship with another person, entity, product, or service that could, in the member's professional judgment, be viewed by the client, employer, or other appropriate parties as impairing the member's objectivity."[7]

An important element of this interpretation is that it goes beyond the mere existence of a conflict of interest. It even includes the *appearance* of a conflict, a distinction that has become highly contentious. Some think the mere appearance of a conflict is not enough to disqualify an accountant from performing an audit. Others insist that even the appearance of a conflict undermines the trust that the general public must have in the integrity of the accountant's work. The code interpretation agrees with

[7] AICPA Code of Professional Conduct, Section 101.01, Section 102.03.

this line of thought, directing members to avoid any situation that can be *viewed* by the client or other parties as impairing the member's objectivity.

As far back as the 1970s, the AICPA's Commission on Auditor's Responsibilities, usually known as the Cohen Report after its chairman, stated, "It is obvious the auditing firms' aspirations to maximize the number of well-paying clients provides them considerable interest in their clients' financial success."[8] The SEC's Theodore Levitt, more than a quarter of a century later, asserted, "It is not enough that the accountant in an engagement act independently ... For investors to have confidence in the quality of the audit, the public must perceive the accountant as independent."[9]

The code seems to concur with Levitt, although it may not appear so at first glance. Initially, the interpretation makes allowances for apparent conflicts of interest under circumscribed conditions: "If the member believes that the professional service can be performed with objectivity, and the relationship is disclosed to and consent is obtained from such client, employer, or other appropriate parties, the rule shall not operate to prohibit the performance of the professional service."[10]

The code warns, however, that disclosure and consent cannot eliminate independence impairments in all cases: "Certain professional engagements, such as audits, reviews, and other attest services, require independence. Independence impairments according to rule 101, its interpretations, and rulings cannot be eliminated by such disclosure and consent."[11]

The code presents several scenarios that could impair – or be seen to impair – objectivity:

- A member has been asked to perform litigation services for the plaintiff in connection with a lawsuit filed against a client of the member's firm.
- A member has provided tax or personal financial planning (PFP) services for a married couple who are undergoing a divorce, and the member has been asked to provide the services for both parties during the divorce proceedings.
- In connection with a PFP engagement, a member plans to suggest that the client invest in a business in which the member has a financial interest.

[8] The Commission on Auditors' Responsibilities, "Report, Conclusion and Recommendations", New York, 1978, p. 2.
[9] Stephen Cohn, "Auditing and Ethical Sensitivity," Brooklyn College, City University of New York.
[10,11] AICPA Code of Professional Conduct, Section 102.03.

- A member provides tax or PFP services for several members of a family who may have opposing interests.
- A member has a significant financial interest, is a member of management, or is in a position of influence in a company that is a major competitor of a client for which the member performs consulting services.
- A member serves on a city's board of tax appeals, which considers matters involving several of the member's tax clients.
- A member has been approached to provide services in connection with the purchase of real estate from a client of the member's firm.
- A member refers a PFP or tax client to an insurance broker or other service provider, which refers clients to the member under an exclusive arrangement to do so.
- A member recommends or refers a client to a service bureau in which the member or partner(s) in the member's firm hold material financial interest(s).[12]

Obligations to external accountants

Rule 102-3 enumerates the obligations of a member to his or her employer's external accountant, requiring members to "be candid and not knowingly misrepresent facts or knowingly fail to disclose material facts."[13] Hence, if there are irregularities, an accountant's obligation is to make them known.

Subordination of judgment

In Rule 102-4, the code prohibits members from subordinating their judgment to their supervisors'. It takes courage and self-control to disagree with a supervisor. Nevertheless, it is unethical to represent a company's financial situation in the way a supervisor wishes if the accountant's best judgment indicates that the representation is inaccurate or misleading. The accountant must use research and consultation to determine whether the supervisor's approach is acceptable under generally accepted auditing or accounting practices.

If a member and his or her supervisor have a dispute regarding the preparation of financial documents, the member should take the following steps:

> Under this rule, if a member and his or her supervisor have a disagreement or dispute relating to the preparation of financial statements or the recording of transactions, the member should take the following steps to ensure that the situation does not constitute a subordination of judgment:

---

[12] AICPA Code of Professional Conduct, Section 102.03.
[13] AICPA Code of Professional Conduct, Section 102.04.

(1)   The member should consider whether (a) the entry or the failure to record a transaction in the records, or (b) the financial statement presentation or the nature or omission of disclosure in the financial statements, as proposed by the supervisor, represents the use of an acceptable alternative and does not materially misrepresent the facts. If, after appropriate research or consultation, the member concludes that the matter has authoritative support and/or does not result in a material misrepresentation, the member need do nothing further.

(2)   If the member concludes that the financial statements or records could be materially misstated, the member should make his or her concerns known to the appropriate higher level(s) of management within the organization (for example, the supervisor's immediate superior, senior management, the audit committee or equivalent, the board of directors, the company's owners). The member should consider documenting his or her understanding of the facts, the accounting principles involved, the application of those principles to the facts, and the parties with whom these matters were discussed.

(3)   If, after discussing his or her concerns with the appropriate person(s) in the organization, the member concludes that appropriate action was not taken, he or she should consider his or her continuing relationship with the employer. The member also should consider any responsibility that may exist to communicate to third parties, such as regulatory authorities, or the employer's (former employer's) external accountant. In this connection, the member may wish to consult with his or her legal counsel.

(4)   The member should at all times be cognizant of his or her obligations under interpretation 102–3.[14]

Thus, the rule against subordination of judgment places a heavy responsibility on an accountant. If the member and his or supervisor cannot resolve their disagreement, even after taking the appropriate steps, the member may have to terminate his or her relationship with the supervisor.

Let's now move on to Section 200.

II Section 200 – General Standards Accounting Principles

Rule 201 – General standards

The first rule in Section 200, which reiterates the prescriptions under the principle of due care states, "A member shall comply with the following standards

---

[14]AICPA Code of Professional Conduct, Section 102.05.

and with any interpretations thereof by bodies designated by Council."[15] The rule lists four standards, as follows:

- *Professional Competence.* Undertake only those professional services that the member or the member's firm can reasonably expect to be completed with professional competence.
- *Due Professional Care.* Exercise due professional care in the performance of professional services.
- *Planning and Supervision.* Adequately plan and supervise the performance of professional services.
- *Sufficient Relevant Data.* Obtain sufficient relevant data to afford a reasonable basis for conclusions or recommendations in relation to any professional services performed.[16]

Rule 202 – Compliance with standards

Rule 202 reads, "A member who performs auditing, review, compilation, management consulting, tax, or other professional services shall comply with standards promulgated by bodies designated by Council."[17]

Several bodies determine technical standards. The Financial Accounting Standards Board (FASB) is designated to establish financial accounting principles for federal government entities. The Governmental Accounting Standards Board (GASB) is authorized to establish financial accounting and reporting standards for activities and transactions of state and local governmental entities. The AICPA, in accord with the Sarbanes–Oxley Act of 2002, recognizes the Public Company Accounting Oversight Board (PCAOB) as the body to set standards relating to the preparation and issuance of audit reports for entities within its jurisdiction. As of May 2008, and subject to review in 3 to five 5 years, the AICPA designated the International Accounting Standards Board (IASB) to establish professional standards for international financial accounting and reporting principles.

The AICPA, under Rule 201, names several committees and boards to promulgate technical standards: The Accounting and Review Services Committee is "designated to issue enforceable standards in connection with the unaudited financial statements or other unaudited financial information of a nonpublic company."[18] The Auditing Standards Board establishes standards for disclo-

---

[15] AICPA Code of Professional Conduct, Section 201.01.
[16] AICPA Code of Professional Conduct, Section 102.03.
[17] AICPA Code of Professional Conduct, Section 202.01.
[18] For complete information about the ARSC, go to www.aicpa.org.

sure of financial information not included in the PCAOB purview. The Management Consulting Services Executive Committee oversees rules governing consulting services. The Tax Executive Committee promulgates professional practice standards regarding to tax services. Finally, the Forensic and Valuation Services Executive Committee sets standards to govern those areas.[19]

Rule 203 – Accounting principles

The final rule in Section 200 deals with the use of generally accepted accounting principles (GAAP). The first part of the rule reads as follows:

> A member shall not (1) express an opinion or state affirmatively that the financial statements or other financial data of any entity are presented in conformity with generally accepted accounting principles (GAAP) or (2) state that he or she is not aware of any material modifications that should be made to such statements or data in order for them to be in conformity with generally accepted accounting principles, if such statements or data contain any departure from an accounting principle promulgated by bodies designated by Council to establish such principles that *has a material effect* on the statements or data *taken as a whole.*[20]

Thus, the rule enjoins a member from certifying that financial statements or data are in accord with GAAP if there is a departure from those principles that has a material effect on the statements or data. The rule then qualifies that prohibition with the following provision:

> If, however, the statements or data contain such a departure and the member can demonstrate that due to unusual circumstances the financial statements or data would otherwise have been misleading, the member can comply with the rule by describing the departure, its approximate effects, if practicable, and the reasons why compliance with the principle would result in a misleading statement."[21]

An accountant should follow GAAP, therefore, unless there is a reason to depart from those rules, and if so, the accountant must be prepared to justify the departure. Currently, there is a heated debate over whether GAAP affords

[19] ARSC, Appendix A: "Council Resolution Designating Bodies to Promulgate Technical Standards," as amended January 12, 1988; revised April 1992, October 1999, May 2004, October 2007, and May 2008.
[20,21] AICPA Code of Professional Conduct, Section 203.01.

sufficient tools to determine the worth of large corporations and whether techniques such as "pro forma" accounting and other valuation methods provide adequate information about a company's financial condition. There is a loud call to FASB for needed reform in these areas. (We will return to this issue later in the book.)

III Section 300 – Responsibilities to Clients

This brings us to the rules devoted to the accountant's responsibilities to clients. Section 300 focuses on the specific areas of confidentiality and contingent fees.

Rule 301 – Confidential client information

This rule is straightforward: "A member in public practice shall not disclose any confidential client information without the specific consent of the client."[22] Although the rule does not specify what is deemed confidential, such information would logically include income figures, debts, and information that is not part of the public record and that a third party has no legitimate claim to know.

An accountant can be relieved of the obligation of confidentiality in certain circumstances. The accountant must comply, for example, to a "validly issued and enforceable subpoena or summons," and must not "prohibit review of a member's professional practice."[23]

Rule 302 – Contingent fees

Rule 302, which is rather complex, concerns contingent fees. The rule prohibits members from accepting fees contingent upon audits or reviews of financial statements, or compilations of statements to be used by a third party that do not disclose a lack of independence. Hence, accountants who engage in "opinion shopping," or guarantee that their auditing will make the company look good – no matter how subtly they market these activities – are in violation of Rule 302. The rule also prohibits preparing original or amended tax returns for a contingent fee.

The code defines a contingent fee as follows: "[A] a contingent fee is a fee established for the performance of any service pursuant to an arrangement

---

[22,23] AICPA Code of Professional Conduct, Section 301.01.

in which no fee will be charged unless a specified finding or result is attained, or in which the amount of the fee is otherwise dependent upon the finding or result of such service."[24] Fees fixed by public authorities are not considered contingent in this area.

IV Section 400 – Responsibilities to Colleagues

Don't worry

The next section of the code is reserved for the accountant's responsibilities to colleagues. Whereas other professional codes exhort fellow professionals to encourage, aid, and mentor each other, and they delineate the responsibilities of self-policing, the AICPA code is currently silent in these areas. According to William Keenan, technical manager of the AICPA's professional ethics committee, "There is nothing in existence at present to be included in Section 400. I believe the section was reserved for addressing possible future rules and interpretations dealing with responsibilities to colleagues, but there is nothing in the offing at present and nothing to my knowledge that has been issued in the past in exposure draft form to the membership."[25]

Although Section 400 remains empty, there are obviously times when accountants must evaluate their responsibilities to their colleagues – how to handle situations in which other accountants commit illegal or unethical actions in pursuing their work, for example. Accountants must also consider their responsibilities to other professionals in multidisciplinary financial planning groups in which they participate. Throughout the course of this book, we will deal with specific issues as they arise.

V Section 500 – Other Responsibilities and Practices

The final section of the code details the accountant's other responsibilities and practices.

Rule 501 – Acts discreditable

Rule 501 says succinctly, "A member shall not commit an act discreditable to the profession."[26]

---

[24] AICPA Code of Professional Conduct, Section 302.01.
[25] E-mail communication to author, March 25, 2001.
[26] AICPA Code of Professional Conduct, Section 501.01.

The interpretation of this rule discusses when and to what extent requests for records by clients and former clients should be honored. In brief, the client is entitled to receive client-provided records, client records prepared by the member, or supporting records. The accountant can "charge the client a reasonable fee for the time and expense incurred to retrieve and copy such records and require that such fee be paid prior to the time such records are provided to the client; ... [p]rovide the requested records in any format usable by the client; and [m]ake and retain copies of any records returned or provided to the client."[27] The accountant is not obligated to return any working papers, which are the accountant's property.

The rule then lists the following types of discreditable acts:[28]

- discrimination and harassment in employment practices
- failure to follow standards and/or procedures or other requirements in government audits
- negligence in the preparation of financial statements or records
- failure to follow requirements or governmental bodies, commissions, or other regulatory agencies
- solicitation or disclosure of CPA examination questions or answers
- failure to file a tax return or pay tax liability
- failure to follow requirements of governmental bodies, commissions, or other regulatory agencies on indemnification and limitation of liability provisions in connection with audit and other attest services

Rule 501 also notes that if state laws and regulations impose obligations that are greater than the provisions in this interpretation, the accountant must comply with those laws and regulations.

Rule 502 – Advertising and other forms of solicitation

Rule 502 forbids a member in public practice "to obtain clients by advertising or other forms of solicitation in a manner that is false, misleading, or deceptive. Solicitation by the use of coercion, over-reaching, or harassing conduct is prohibited."[29] According to the code, prohibited activities are those that:

(1)   Create false or unjustified expectations of favorable results.
(2)   Imply the ability to influence any court, tribunal, regulatory agency, or similar body or official.

---

[27] AICPA Code of Professional Conduct, Section 501.02.
[28] AICPA Code of Professional Conduct, Sections 501.03–501.09.
[29] AICPA Code of Professional Conduct, Section 502.01.

(3) Contain a representation that specific professional services in current or future periods will be performed for a stated fee, estimated fee or fee range when it was likely at the time of the representation that such fees would be substantially increased and the prospective client was not advised of that likelihood.

(4) Contain any other representations that would be likely to cause a reasonable person to misunderstand or be deceived.[30]

Rule 503 – Commissions and referral fees

The first section of Rule 503 prohibits commissions, as follows:

> A member in public practice shall not for a commission recommend or refer to a client any product or service, or for a commission recommend or refer any product or service to be supplied by a client, or receive a commission, when the member or the member's firm also performs for that client.[31]

This section creates problems for accountants who undertake financial or estate planning for their clients. Given that an accountant is familiar with the client's financial affairs, it is argued, it is prudent for the accountant to perform financial or estate planning services, provided, of course, that the accountant is trained in and has the competence to offer such services. Because these services often involve brokering products for a commission, it only seems fair that the accountant be entitled to the commission on selling those products. In the section on standards of disclosure for permitted commissions, the code recognizes the potential conflict of interest that commission-based sales can generate:

> A member in public practice who is not prohibited by this rule from performing services for or receiving a commission and who is paid or expects to be paid a commission shall disclose that fact to any person or entity to whom the member recommends or refers a product or service to which the commission relates.[32]

Rule 503 also addresses referral fees:

> Any member who accepts a referral fee for recommending or referring any service of a CPA to any person or entity or who pays a referral fee to obtain a client shall disclose such acceptance or payment to the client.[33]

---

[30] AICPA Code of Professional Conduct, Section 502.03.
[31–33] AICPA Code of Professional Conduct, Section 503.01.

In short, if an accountant is receiving commissions or referral fees, he or she is obliged to disclose that fact to the client.

Rule 505 – Form of organization

The general precepts of the final rule of the code (Rule 504 has been deleted) are simple:

> A member may practice public accounting only in a form of organization permitted by law or regulation whose characteristics conform to resolutions of Council.
>
> A member shall not practice public accounting under a firm name that is misleading. Names of one or more past owners may be included in the firm name of a successor organization.
>
> A firm may not designate itself as "Members of the American Institute of Certified Public Accountants" unless all of its CPA owners are members of the Institute.[34]

There are, however, two applications of this rule that are complicated: applications to members who own a separate business and applications to alternative practices. For members who, either individually or collectively, own a separate business, all the principles and rules in the AICPA code apply to the member. Whether they apply to the firm itself in terms of referrals depends on the composition of the firm.

With regard to alternative practices, the code requires, as follows:

> … among other things, that a majority of the financial interests in a firm engaged in attest services (as defined therein) be owned by CPAs. In the context of alternative practice structures (APS) in which (1) the majority of the financial interests in the attest firm is owned by CPAs and (2) all or substantially all of the revenues are paid to another entity in return for services and the lease of employees, equipment, and office space, questions have arisen as to the applicability of rule 505.
>
> The overriding focus of the Resolution is that CPAs remain responsible, financially and otherwise, for the attest work performed to protect the public interest. The Resolution contains many requirements that were developed to ensure that responsibility. In addition to the provisions of the Resolution, other requirements of the Code of Professional Conduct and bylaws ensure that responsibility:

[34]AICPA Code of Professional Conduct, Section 505.01.

(a)   Compliance with all aspects of applicable state law or regulation
(b)   Enrollment in an AICPA-approved practice monitoring program
(c)   Compliance with the independence rules prescribed by Rule 101, Independence …
(d)   Compliance with applicable standards promulgated by Council-designated bodies … and all other provisions of the Code, including ET section 91, Applicability

Taken in the context of all the above-mentioned safeguards of the public interest, if the CPAs who own the attest firm remain financially responsible, under applicable law or regulation, the member is considered to be in compliance with the financial interests provision of the Resolution.[35]

To summarize, the rules of the code break down into five sections: (1) Independence, Integrity, and Objectivity, (2) General Standards Accounting Principles, (3) Responsibilities to Clients, (4) Responsibilities to Colleagues, and (5) Other Responsibilities and Practices. The rules are informed by the general principles of honesty, integrity and independence.

Upcoming chapters examine how the accountant fulfills his or her responsibilities in the various fields of accounting – auditing, financial or management accounting, and tax accounting. Chapter 7 looks at the auditing function.

[35] AICPA Code of Professional Conduct, Section 505.04.

Chapter Seven

The Auditing Function

"It's Enron and Arthur Andersen all over again. In the end, the firm [KPMG] acquiesced to what were just flat-out errors in the financial statements." (Lynn Turner, Former Securities and Exchange Commission Chief Accountant.[1])

"This is really the embryo of the credit crisis ... The theme of the report is how easily the loans were originated, how exceptions were made, how they used bad appraisals. There were no appropriate internal controls, and KPMG failed to look at these things skeptically." (Michael Missal, Court Examiner.[2])

In January 2007, "KPMG and New Century's own accountants stunned the company's board by revealing that the lender had incorrectly calculated the reserves for troubled home loans. That mistake was likely to cost New Century $300 million, wiping out profits from the second half of 2006."[3] A week later, New Century announced it would restate financials from the first three quarters of 2006. The market reaction to New Century's announcement was swift, and its stock price dropped significantly at the news. Shares dropped further when the company announced on March 2, 2007, that it would not file its 2006 annual report on time. This declaration placed additional financial pressure on the beleaguered mortgage lender, and on March 8, New Century stated that it had stopped accepting new loan applications. A few days later, the New York Stock Exchange delisted New Century Financial Corporation, and

---

[1] Nicholas Rummell, "KPMG Faces Fallout from New Century," *Financial Week*, March 31, 2008.
[2] Tiffany Kary, "New Century Bankruptcy Examiner Says KPMG Aided Fraud," www.Bloomberg. com, March 26, 2008.
[3] Vikas Bajaj and Julie Creswell, "A Lender Failed. Did Its Auditor?" *New York Times*, April 13, 2008.

Accounting Ethics, Second Edition. Ronald Duska, Brenda Shay Duska, and Julie Ragatz.
© 2011 John Wiley & Sons, Ltd. Published 2011 by John Wiley & Sons, Ltd.

on April 2, only 2 months after the restatement announcement, New Century filed for bankruptcy protection.[4]

The March 2008 report submitted by the court-appointed bankruptcy examiner chronicles the catastrophic failure of the company, once the second largest distributor of subprime mortgages. New Century originated, retained, sold, and serviced home mortgage loans designed for subprime borrowers. In 1996, the company originated more than $350 million in loans, and by 2005, subprime loan originations and purchases had grown to an astounding $56 billion. New Century's growth trajectory mirrored the growth of the subprime loan industry in the United States. Between 2001 and 2003, subprime loans accounted for only 8 percent of all residential mortgage originations, but by 2005, they had grown to 20 percent.

New Century retained KPMG as the company's auditor from its inception in 1995 until April 2007 when KPMG resigned. KPMG had several different engagement partners, with varying degrees of experience in the mortgage industry, heading the New Century account over the years. The examiner's report lists seven types of improper accounting practices not in conformity with GAAP. The practice that has garnered the most attention concerns the mistakes in calculating the repurchase reserve. New Century sold mortgages in loan pools to investors, primarily major financial intermediaries such as Goldman Sachs and JPMorgan Chase. New Century's loan purchase agreement required them to repurchase the loans if (1) they suffered an early payment default, (2) it was found that New Century had misrepresented their loans, or (3) if there was borrower fraud.[5] The problem, according to the examiner's report, was that New Century calculated the repurchase reserve incorrectly. Essentially, New Century used historical data about the rate of repurchases, which was inaccurate, and based its model on the incorrect assumption that all repurchases would be made within 90 days.[6]

The error was exacerbated by New Century's lack of reliable data on the numbers of repurchase claims it received, because repurchase claims where handled by different departments within the company. This led to a backlog of repurchase claims worth $188 million, which were unresolved in 2005. By 2006, the backlog had skyrocketed to $421 million as many borrowers

---

[4]Michael J. Missal and Lisa M. Richman, "New Century Financial: Lessons Learned," *Mortgage Banking*, October 2008, p. 48.

[5]Krishna Palpeu, Suraj Srinivasan and Aldo Sesia Jr., "New Century Financial Corporation," Harvard Business School Case Study. 9-109-034, October 23, 2008, p. 5.

[6]Krishna Palpeu, Suraj Srinivasan and Aldo Sesia Jr., "New Century Financial Corporation," Harvard Business School Case Study. 9-109-034, October 23, 2008, p. 8.

became delinquent within only a few months of taking out a loan.[7] New Century's reserves were seriously inadequate, as it had only $13.9 million set aside for repayment, which would cover a mere 3.5 percent of the repurchase claims.

Did KPMG fail? According to one report:

> "New Century's accounting methods let it prop up profits, charming investors and allowing the company to tap a rich vein of Wall Street cash that it used to underwrite more mortgages. Without the appearance of a strong bottom line, New Century's financial lifeline could have been cut even earlier than it was."[8]

The examiner's report did not find sufficient evidence to conclude that New Century had engaged in earnings management or manipulation, or that KPMG had engaged in intentional wrongdoing. The report did conclude, however, that KPMG failed to conduct its audits in accordance with professional standards:

> "Had KPMG conducted its audits and reviews prudently and in accordance with professional standards, the misstatements included in New Century's financial statements would have been detected long before February 2007. The 2005 (KPMG) engagement team, in particular, was not staffed with auditors with sufficient experience in the client's industry and/or relating to the particular tasks to which they were assigned. ... The team also consisted of auditors who were relatively inexperienced in the mortgage banking industry. The engagement team's lack of experience was compounded by the fact that New Century's accounting function was weak and led by a domineering and difficult controller."[9]

Lawsuits filed against KPMG in the matter of New Century allege that the engagement team dismissed the claims made by experts from KPMG's Structured Finance Group when they tried to call attention to the problems at New Century:

> When a KPMG specialist continued to raise questions about an incorrect accounting practice on the eve of the Company's 2005 Form 10-K filing, the lead KPMG audit partner told him: "I am very disappointed we are still discuss-

---

[7,8] Vikas Bajaj and Julie Creswell, "A Lender Failed. Did Its Auditor?" *New York Times*, April 13, 2008.

[9] Vikas Bajaj and Julie Creswell, "A Lender Failed. Did Its Auditor?" *New York Times*, April 13, 2008. www.nytimes.com/2008/04/13/business/13audit.html.

ing this. As far as I am concerned we are done. The client thinks we are done. All we are going to do is piss everybody off."[10]

Although KPMG may not have created New Century's problems, many claim that it turned a blind eye to what could be considered reckless and irresponsible business practices. More egregiously, KPMG continued to do so even when its own experts challenged New Century's accounting practices. The lawsuit alleges that KPMG's failings were motivated by a desire to appease a demanding client and to maintain a profitable relationship.

Not everyone, however, is convinced that KPMG should be held responsible for what is ultimately the failure of a risky and poorly conceived business strategy. David Aboody, an accounting professor at UCLA argued as follows:

> "I think it's a stretch to blame everything on the accounting profession ... What does the SEC want? Does it want an auditor who tries to predict the future? Or does it want an auditor to record what is clearly going on at the time?"[11]

Professor Aboody raises an interesting question: What does the public expect of independent auditors in a situation like New Century? If a company is engaged in risky and unsound business practices, it seems that the public expects the audit report to reflect this. This leads to another question: If auditors cannot provide the investing public with this information, if they cannot or will not sound the alarm about companies operating like New Century, then is the independent auditor of any use to the average – or even the sophisticated – investor?

The case of KPMG and New Century is only one example of the serious ethical pressures in the accounting profession today – risks and dangers to the integrity of the accounting practice created by conflicts of interest and the necessity to survive in a competitive market. To maintain profitable relationships with valued clients, the auditor can feel intimidated into approving inappropriately aggressive accounting treatments that can lead to financial statements that misrepresent the firm's economic substance.

It appears unlikely that an auditor will be able to maintain a client relationship if that client is given an unfavorable audit. The client might then shop for an audit firm that will provide a more lenient reading of the books. If the audit is inadequate, however, and people suffer from misinformation

---

[10] Marianne M. Jennings, "Of Candor and Conflicts: What Were We Thinking?", *CFA Institute Conference Proceedings Quarterly* March 2009, Vol. 26, No. 1: 29–39
[11] Vikas Bajaj and Julie Creswell, "A Lender Failed. Did Its Auditor?", *New York Times*, April 13, 2008.

that the accountants should have uncovered, the accounting firm might be sued, because auditors are expected to look out for the public interest before looking out for the client's interest. This responsibility reinforces the critical importance of the role the auditor plays in financial services.

As a result of the way financial markets and the economic system have developed, society has carved out a role for the independent auditor, one that is absolutely essential for the effective functioning of the economic system. If accounting is the language of business, it is the auditor's job to ensure that the language is used properly to communicate relevant information accurately – "to see whether the company's estimates are based on formulas that seem reasonable in the light of whatever evidence is available and that formulas chosen are applied consistently from year to year."[12] The lawsuits filed against KPMG in the matter of New Century Financial allege that the audit team failed to fulfill this obligation.

I The Ethics of Public Accounting

Usually, when people talk about the ethics of public accounting, they are discussing the responsibilities of the independent auditor. Auditing the financial statements of publicly owned companies is not the only role of an accountant, but in the current economic system, it is certainly one of the most important.

John Bogle, founder of The Vanguard Group, articulates it skillfully:

"The integrity of financial markets – markets that are active, liquid, and honest, with participants who are fully and fairly informed – is *absolutely central* to the sound functioning of any system of democratic capitalism worth its salt …

Sound securities markets require sound financial information. It is as simple as that. Investors require – and have a right to require – complete information about each and every security, information that fairly and honestly represents every significant fact and figure that might be needed to evaluate the worth of a corporation …

It is unarguable, I think, that the independent oversight of financial figures is central to that disclosure system. Indeed independence is at integrity's very core. And, for more than a century, the responsibility for the independent oversight of corporate financial statements has fallen to America's public accounting profession. It is the auditor's stamp on a financial statement that gives it its validity, its respect, and its acceptability by investors. And only if the auditor's work is

---

[12] *Encyclopedia Britannica*, Vol. 1, "Accounting."

comprehensive, skeptical, inquisitive, and rigorous, can we have confidence that financial statements speak the truth."[13]

As Bogle notes, a free market economy needs to base transactions and decisions on truthful and accurate information. In market transactions, a company's financial status is vital information on which a decision to purchase is based. The role of the auditor is to attest to the accuracy of the company's financial picture presented to whatever user needs to make a decision on the basis of that picture.

This function and responsibility is not new. It has recently come to the public's attention, however, with the eruption of the numerous accounting scandals that shocked investors, regulators, and politicians in 2002. Justice Warren E. Burger made this statement about the auditor's function and responsibility in the 1984 landmark Arthur Young case:

> Corporate financial statements are one of the primary sources of information available to guide the decisions of the investing public. In an effort to control the accuracy of the financial data available to investors in the securities markets, various provisions of the federal securities laws require publicly held companies to file their financial statements with the Securities and Exchange Commission. Commission regulations stipulate that these financial reports must be audited by an independent CPA in accordance with generally accepted auditing standards. *By examining the corporation's books and records, the independent auditor determines whether the financial reports of the corporation have been prepared in accordance with generally accepted accounting principles. The auditor then issues an opinion as to whether the financial statements, taken as a whole, fairly present the financial position and operations of the corporation for the relevant period.*[14]

Burger states the responsibility of the auditor clearly: to issue an opinion about whether the financial statement *fairly* presents the financial position of the corporation. Performance of this role, attesting that the corporation's financial positions and operations are fairly presented, requires that an auditor has integrity and honesty. Further, to ensure that an accurate picture has been presented, it is essential that the auditor's integrity and honesty is not jeopardized by the presence of undue influence. To bolster integrity and honesty, the auditor must have as much independence as possible. Those who need to make decisions about a company based on true and accurate information must be able to trust the accountant's pictures if the market is to function efficiently. Trust is eroded if there is even an appearance of a conflict of interest.

II Trust

We can understand why if we apply Immanuel Kant's first categorical imperative, the universalizability principle: "Act so you can will the maxim of your action to be a universal law." As we saw earlier (see Chapter 3 for a detailed discussion of Kant's ethical theories), to universalize an action, we must consider what would occur if everyone acted the same way for the same reason. As we learned earlier in this book, an individual generally gives a false picture to cause another party to act in a way other than the party would act if given full and truthful information. Suppose a CFO misrepresents his company's profits to obtain a bank loan, thinking that no loan would be forthcoming if the bank had the true picture. What would happen if this behavior were universalized – that is, if all individuals misrepresented the financial health of their companies when it was to their advantage to lie?   2 Results

Two things would happen. First, trust in business dealings that require information about financial status would be eroded. Chaos would ensue, because financial markets cannot operate without trust. Cooperation is vital, and trust is a precondition of cooperation. We engage in hundreds of transactions daily that demand trusting other people with our money and our lives. If misrepresentation became a universal practice, trust and, consequently, cooperation would be impossible.

Second, universalizing misrepresentation, besides leading to mistrust, chaos, and inefficiencies in the market, would make the act of misrepresentation impossible. Why? Because no one would trust another's word, and misrepresentation can occur only if the person lied to trusts the person lying. Prudent people do not trust known liars. Thus, if everyone lied, no one would trust another, and it would be impossible to lie. Universalized lying, therefore, makes lying impossible. Do we trust the defendant in a murder case to tell the truth? Do we trust young children who are concerned about being punished to tell the truth? Of course not. Once we recognize that certain people are unreliable or untrustworthy, it becomes impossible for them to misrepresent things to us, because we don't believe a word they're saying. Hence the anomaly: If misrepresentation became universalized in certain situations, it would be impossible to misrepresent in those situations, because no one would trust what was being represented. This makes the universalizing of lying irrational or self-contradictory.

The contradiction here, according to Kant, is a will contradiction, and the irrationality lies in simultaneously willing the possibility and the impossibility of misrepresentation, by willing out of existence the conditions (trust) necessary to perform the act. Face it, people who lie don't want lying universalized. Liars are free riders. Liars want an unfair advantage. They don't want others to lie – to act like the liars are acting. They want others to tell the truth and be trusting so that the liars can lie to those trusting people. Liars want the world to work one way for them and differently for all others. In short, liars want a double standard. They want to have their cake and eat it, too. Such a selfish, self-serving attitude is the antithesis of ethical.

If misrepresentation of an organization's financial situation were universal, auditing would become a useless function. Rick Telberg, in *Accounting Today,* claims this may have already happened. "CPA firms long ago became more like insurance companies – complete with their focus on assurances and risk-managed audits – than attesters,"[15] he says. The attitude precludes telling the public what a company's financial condition really is. Firms with this attitude just guarantee that the presentation won't be subject to charges of illegal behavior. These firms serve the client and not the public.

This points to another important aspect of trust. Only a fool trusts someone who gives all the appearances of being a liar. Only a fool trusts people who put themselves in positions where it is likely that their integrity will be compromised. These are the reasons why individuals take precautions against getting involved with anyone who gives even the appearance of being caught in a conflict of interest. Because trust is essential, even the *appearance* of an accountant's honesty and integrity is important. The auditor, therefore, must not only be trustworthy, but he or she must also appear trustworthy.

III The Auditor's Responsibility to the Public

The auditor's duty to attest to the fairness of financial statements imbues the accountant with special responsibilities to the public. As we saw in Chapter 4, these responsibilities give the accountant a different relationship to the client than those relationships in other professions. Justice Burger refers to this relationship in his classic statement of auditor responsibility:

> "The auditor does not have the same relationship to his client that a private attorney does ... who1 has a role as ... a confidential advisor and advocate, a loyal representative whose duty it is to present the client's case in the most

[15] Rick Telberg, "Editorial," *Accounting Today*, September 26, 1999.

favorable possible light. An independent CPA performs a different role. *By certifying the public reports that collectively depict a corporation's financial status, the independent auditor assumes a public responsibility transcending any employment relationship with the client.* The independent public accountant performing this special function owes ultimate allegiance to the corporation's creditors and stockholders, as well as to the investing public. This 'public watchdog' function demands that the accountant maintain total independence from the client at all times and requires complete fidelity to the public trust. To insulate from disclosure a CPA's interpretations of the client's financial statements would be to ignore the significance of the accountant's role as a disinterested analyst charged with public obligations."[16]

Given the sometimes opposing interests between the public and clients, it is clear that auditors face conflicting loyalties. To whom are they primarily responsible – the public or the client who pays the bill? Accountants are professionals and thus should behave as professionals. Like most other professionals, they offer services to their clients. But the public accounting profession, because it includes operating as an independent auditor, has another function. The independent auditor acts not only as a recorder, but also as an evaluator of other accountants' records. The auditor fulfills what Justice Burger calls "a public watchdog function."

Over time, the evaluation of another accountant's records has become a necessary component of capitalist societies, particularly the part of society that deals in money markets and offers publicly traded stocks and securities. In such a system, it is imperative for potential purchasers of financial products to have an accurate representation of the companies in which they wish to invest, to whom they are willing to loan money, or with whom they wish to merge. There must be a procedure to verify the truthfulness of a company's financial status. The role of verifier falls to the public accountant – the auditor.[17]

In their article, "Regulating the Public Accounting Profession: An International Perspective," Baker and Hayes reiterate the accountant's distinctive role:

"Other professionals, such as physicians and lawyers, are expected to perform their services at the maximum possible level of professional competence for the

[16] As quoted in Abraham J. Briloff, "Commentary: The 'Is' and the 'Ought,'" *Accounting Today*, September 6, 1999, p. 6.
[17] Interestingly enough, in Germany, where most capitalization is done through a bank and not through securities, the role of this public auditor is not as essential. The verification function is handled by the bank.

benefit of their clients. Public accountants may at times be expected by their clients to perform their professional services in a manner that differs from the interests of third parties who are the beneficiaries of the contractual arrangements between the public accountant and their clients. This unusual arrangement poses an ethical dilemma for public accountants."[18]

Although auditors' clients are the ones who pay the fees for the auditor's services, the auditor's primary responsibility is to safeguard the interest of a third party – the public. Because the auditor is charged with public obligations, he or she should be a disinterested analyst. The auditor's obligations are to certify that public reports depicting a corporation's financial status *fairly* present the corporation's financial position and operations. In short, the auditor's fiduciary responsibility is to the public trust, and "independence" from the client is fundamental in order for that trust to be honored.

As Justice Burger notes, the auditor's role requires "transcending any employment relationship with the client." Thus, dilemmas arising from conflicts of responsibility occur. We'll now examine the auditor's specific responsibilities.

IV The Auditor's Basic Responsibilities

We have seen that the auditor's first responsibility is to certify or attest to the truth of financial statements. But an auditor also has other responsibilities. A document known as the Cohen Report contains a comprehensive statement of an independent auditor's responsibilities. They are the same today as when the report was issued. We turn now to that report.

In 1974, the AICPA's Commission on Auditor's Responsibilities (the Cohen Commission) was established to develop conclusions and recommendations regarding the appropriate responsibilities of independent auditors. Another of the commission's tasks was to evaluate the public's expectations and needs and the realistic capabilities of the accountant. If disparities existed, the commission was to determine how to resolve them.

As we might expect, the report defined the independent auditor's main role as an intermediary between the client's financial statements and the users of those statements, to whom the auditor is accountable. Hence, the Cohen Commission made it clear that the auditor's primary responsibility is to the public, not to the client.

---

[18] C. Richard Baker and Rick Stephan Hayes, "Regulating the Public Accounting Profession: An International Perspective," from http://les.man.ac.uk/cpa96/papers.htm/baker2.htm, p. 9.

The commission also examined what auditors, given the restraints of time and business pressures, can reasonably be expected to accomplish. The report pointed out some areas that *are not* the responsibility of the independent auditor.

For example, some people erroneously assume that auditors are responsible for the actual preparation of the financial statements. Others wrongly believe that an audit report indicates that the business being audited is sound. Auditors, however, are not responsible for attesting to the soundness of the business. Recall that Professor Aboody made this point in reference to the KPMG/New Century Financial case earlier in this chapter. In most cases, management accountants prepare the financial statements, and it is management – not the auditor – who is responsible for them. (We will examine the management accountant's role in the next chapter.)

[margin note: Not Responsible]

Auditors are responsible for forming an opinion on whether the financial statements are presented in accord with appropriately utilized accounting principles. The traditional attest statement affirms that the financial statements were "presented fairly in accordance with generally accepted accounting principles." This is a controversial subject in the accounting ethics literature. In the 1960s, a committee of the AICPA raised the following questions about the fairness claim:

> "In the standard report of the auditor, he generally says that financial statements 'present fairly' in conformity with generally accepted accounting principles – and so on. What does the auditor mean by the quoted words? Is he saying: (1) that the statements are fair *and* in accordance with GAAP; or (2) that they are fair *because* they are in accordance with GAAP; or (3) that they are fair only *to the extent* that GAAP are fair; or (4) that whatever GAAP may be, the *presentation* of them is fair?"[19]

The Cohen Report recognizes that "fair" is an ambiguous word; hence, it is imprudent to hold auditors accountable for the fairness of the financial statements, if that means the accuracy of material facts. Rather, the responsibility of the auditors is to determine whether the judgments of managers in the selection and application of accounting principles was appropriate in the particular circumstance. Note that this differs from Justice Burger's opinion that the auditor attests to the "fairness" of the picture.

The Cohen Report would likely find Burger's viewpoint too rigid for three reasons: (1) In some situations, there may be no detailed principles

[19] Quoted in Abraham J. Briloff, *The Truth about Corporate Accounting*, Harpercollins, 1981, p. 6.

that are applicable; (2) in others, alternative accounting principles may be applicable; and (3) at times, the cumulative effects of the use of a principle must be evaluated. The report calls for more guidance for auditors in these three areas. Still, the idea prevails that "fairly" presented means that the report being audited will give a reasonable person an accurate picture of an entity's financial status. GAAP principles, however, can be used by artful dodgers to hide the real health or sickness of a company. Indeed, one accountant has suggested that accounting is an art, and a truly proficient artist can, by the skillful use of GAAP, make the same company look to be a dizzying success or a miserable failure. We will consider the "fairness" debate in the final chapter of this book. For now, let's return to the Cohen Report and its enumeration of auditors' responsibilities.

The evaluation of internal auditing control

The Cohen Report also discussed corporate accountability and the law, and it examined the auditor's duties regarding internal accounting control. Not only is the auditor responsible for attesting to the appropriateness of the financial statements, the commission said, but he or she is also responsible for determining whether the internal auditing system and controls are adequate. This necessarily leads to the conclusion that auditors have an obligation to examine the internal workings of the company's accounting procedures and safeguards. The issue of the appropriateness of internal controls at New Century Financial and KPMG's failure to challenge what it knew were faulty assumptions and inadequate policies were criticized in the examiner's report and cited as grounds for the lawsuit against KPMG.

But what specifically is an internal auditor to do? Briefly, the auditor is responsible for evaluating whether the management accountant is fulfilling his or her obligations, and for ascertaining the adequacy of and adherence to internal auditing controls. This subject is covered fully in the next chapter.

If material Responsibility to detect and report errors and irregularities

Another auditor responsibility, according to the Cohen Report, is to convey any significant uncertainties detected in the financial statements. Further, the report clarified the auditor's responsibility for the detection of fraud, errors, and irregularities. Consider the following situation, which is strikingly similar to the New Century/KPMG case:

> "Lawyers for the Allegheny health system's creditors have sued Allegheny's longtime auditors, PricewaterhouseCoopers, asserting that the accounting

firm 'ignored the sure signs' of the system's collapse and failed to prevent its demise.

The suit called PricewaterhouseCoopers 'the one independent entity that was in a position to detect and expose' Allegheny's 'financial manipulations.' Yet the system's financial statements audited by the firm 'consistently depicted a business conglomerate in sound financial condition,' even after Allegheny's senior officials were fired in 1998.

A spokesman for PricewaterhouseCoopers, Steven Silber, said, 'We believe this lawsuit to be totally without merit. We intend to defend ourselves vigorously and we're fully confident that we will prevail. Accounting firms are considered to be deep pockets and lawsuits happen to auditors with great frequency.'"[20]

What was PricewaterhouseCoopers' responsibility to detect and expose Allegheny's financial manipulations? How much time, effort, and money must be expended to identify the signs of a system's collapse? Does the public have a right to expect an audit to identify such matters? The responsibility to report errors and irregularities is one of the most serious – and confusing – to an auditor. In the first place, it seems to run counter to the accountant's responsibility of confidentiality that we examined in Chapter 6.[21]

John E. Beach in an article, "Code of Ethics: The Professional Catch 22," gives two examples of how the accountant's responsibility to the public can lead to a lawsuit if it conflicts with the responsibility to keep the client's affairs confidential:

> "In October of 1981, a jury in Ohio found an accountant guilty of negligence and breach of contract for violating the obligation of confidentiality mandated in the accountant's code of ethics, and awarded the plaintiffs approximately $1,000,000. At approximately the same time, a jury in New York awarded a plaintiff in excess of $80,000,000 based in part on the failure of an accountant to disclose confidential information."[22]

Without wrestling with this complex issue, which involves deciding when it is permissible for auditors to report certain of their client's inappropriate activities, suffice it to say that there is legal opinion that the duty of confi-

---

[20] Karl Stark, *The Philadelphia Inquirer*, "Lawsuit is filed against auditors for Allegheny", Section D, p. 1, Thursday, April 13, 2000.

[21] See Rule 301 – Confidential Client Information, AICPA Code of Professional Conduct, www.aicpa.org.

[22] John E. Beach, "Code of Ethics: The Professional Catch 22," *Journal of Accounting and Public Policy*, Vol. 3, 1984, pp. 311–323.

dentiality is not absolute, and "overriding public interests may exist to which confidentiality must yield."[23]

Now we turn to the auditor's most important obligation – the obligation to maintain independence.

V Independence

Thus far, we have discussed the responsibilities of the auditor. To meet those responsibilities, it is imperative that the auditor maintain independence. Let's look at Justice Burger's statement again:

> "… The independent public accountant performing this special function owes ultimate allegiance to the corporation's creditors and stockholders, as well as to the investing public. This "public watchdog" function demands that the accountant maintain total independence from the client at all times and requires complete fidelity to the public trust …"[24]

"Total independence" is the term that Burger uses. Obviously, an external auditor should be independent from the client. But must independence be total, as Justice Burger says? If so, what does total independence require? What does "complete fidelity to the public trust" require? We need to examine whether total independence is a possibility or even a necessity. How much independence should an auditor maintain, and how should the auditor determine that?

The AICPA Code of Professional Conduct recognizes two kinds of independence: independence in fact and independence in appearance. Independence in fact is applicable to all accountants. If the accountant's function is to render accurate financial pictures, conflicts of interest that cause incorrect pictures do a disservice to whoever is entitled to and in need of the accurate picture. Whether independence in appearance must apply to all accountants or only to independent auditors is an open question. Some contend that independence in appearance is applicable only to independent auditors.[25]

The Independence Standards Board (ISB) published "A Statement of Independence Concepts: A Conceptual Framework for Auditor Independence,"

[23] Appellate *Wagenheim, J.S. (Consolidated Services, Inc.) v. Alexander Grant & Co.,* 1983. 10th District, Court of Appeals, Ohio 3393.
[24] Abraham J. Briloff, "Commentary: The 'Is' and the 'Ought,'" *Accounting Today,* September 6, 1999, p. 6.
[25] cf. Philip G. Cottell Jr. and Terry M. Perlin, *Accounting Ethics: A Practical Guide for Professionals,* New York, Quorum Books, 1990.

one of the most thorough documents on independence ever prepared. The ISB was established in 1997 by Securities and Exchange Commission Chairman Arthur Levitt in concert with the AICPA. "The ISB was given the responsibility of establishing independence standards applicable to the audits of public entities, in order to serve the public interest and to protect and promote investors' confidence in the securities markets."[26] It acknowledged that "[t]he various securities laws enacted by Congress and administered by the SEC recognize that the integrity and credibility of the financial reporting process for public companies depends, in large part, on auditors remaining independent from their audit clients."[27]

The ISB originated from discussions between the AIPCA, other representatives of the accounting profession, and the SEC. However, as a result of the pressure that large accounting firms were exerting on the AICPA – for which independence might mean surrendering their lucrative consulting contracts with firms they audited – the ISB was dissolved in August 2001. Nevertheless, its findings are among the best resources for ethical responsibilities.

Shortly after the dissolution of the ISB, the fallout from the Enron/Andersen debacle occurred, and in the winter of 2002, the Big Five (now the Big Four since Andersen's fall) began separating their auditing and consulting functions. This separation was ultimately mandated, as we have discussed, by provisions of the Sarbanes–Oxley Act. Recent history has taught us that this independence is necessary.

John Bogle explains why eloquently:

"Our government, our regulators, our corporations, and our accountants have … properly placed the auditor's independence from his client at the keystone of our financial reporting system. And auditor independence has come to mean an absence of any and all relationships that could seriously jeopardize – either in fact or in appearance – the validity of the audit, and, therefore, of the client's financial statements. The auditor, in short, is the guardian of financial integrity."[28]

What did the proposed conceptual framework of the now-defunct ISB say about independence? The ISB board defined auditor independence as "freedom from those pressures and other factors that compromise, or can reason-

[26,27] John C. Bogle, "Public Accounting: Profession or Business?" The Seymour Jones Distinguished Lecture, Vincent C. Ross Institute of Accounting Research, New York University, October 16, 2000.

[28] Philip G. Cottell Jr. and Terry M. Perlin, *Accounting Ethics: A Practical Guide for Professionals*, New York, Quorum Books, 1990.

ably be expected to compromise, an auditor's ability to make unbiased audit decisions."[29] This, of course, does not mean freedom from all pressures, only those that are "so significant that they rise to a level where they compromise, or can reasonably be expected to compromise, the auditor's ability to make audit decisions without bias."[30] "Reasonably be expected" means based on rational beliefs of well-informed investors and other users of financial information.

For example, if I stand to gain from a company to which I give a favorable attestation because I am a shareholder, a reasonable person would be somewhat skeptical of my ability to be unbiased in that case. Similarly, if the company is planning to hire my accounting firm for extensive consulting work when it gets a loan from the bank, which is contingent on a favorable audit, a prudent person would doubt that I could perform an impartial audit. The doubt would arise, not because I am inherently a dishonorable person, but because human beings, in general, can be unduly influenced by such pressures.

What sorts of pressures are there? To begin, there are pressures that can stem from relationships such as family, friends, acquaintances, and business associates. Standards-setting bodies issue rules to limit certain activities and relationships that they believe represent "potential sources of bias for auditors generally."[31] Although some auditors may be able to remain unbiased in such situations, the rules apply to them as well, because "it is reasonable to expect audit decisions to be biased in those circumstances."[32] Accordingly, noncompliance with those rules might not preclude a particular auditor from being objective, but it would preclude the auditor from claiming to be "independent" at least in appearance, if not in reality.

Still, not every situation can be identified or covered by a rule. The absence of a rule dealing with a certain relationship, therefore, does not mean that the relationship does not jeopardize the auditor's independence if the audit decision could reasonably be expected to be compromised as a result. "Compliance with the rules is a necessary, but not a sufficient, condition for independence."[33]

The goal of independence, the report says, is "to support user reliance on the financial reporting process and to enhance management efficiency."[34] Hence, independence is an instrumental good, while the goal is management efficiency.

[29,30]"A Conceptual Framework for Auditor Independence," Independence Standards Board, November 2000.
[31,32]Independence Standards Board.
[33,34]"A Conceptual Framework for Auditor Independence," Independence Standards Board, November 2000.

The ISB delineated four basic principles and four concepts to use as guidelines to determine what interferes with or aids independence. The four concepts are:

- threats
- safeguards
- independence risk
- significance of threats/effectiveness of safeguards

Threats to auditor independence are defined as "sources of potential bias that may compromise, or may reasonably be expected to compromise, an auditor's ability to make unbiased audit decisions."[35] There are five types of threats to independence:

- self-interest threats
- self-review threats
- advocacy threats
- familiarity threats
- intimidation threats

In an article titled "Auditing and Ethical Sensitivity,"[36] Gordon Cohn discusses several other factors that jeopardize auditor independence. First, he considers the effect of family and financial relations on independence. Obviously, if the auditor is a relative of a client or maintains financial interests with a client, this could create a conflict of interest that affects the auditor's independence. Hence, the AICPA's rule of independence prevents someone being an auditor where such relationships exist. Even if the auditor could overcome the conflict of interest and his or her evaluation and attestations were impeccably honest, the public would be suspicious of the auditor's findings. As we have discussed before, it is important to avoid even the appearance of a conflict.

But there are other possible conflicts of interest that challenge the auditor. The problems with an auditor's independence, according to Cohn, arise from two places: The first is the actual or apparent lack of independence, and the second is the inefficient functioning of accounting firms.

---

[35]"A Conceptual Framework for Auditor Independence," Independence Standards Board, November 2000.
[36]Gordon Cohn, "Auditing and Ethical Sensitivity," forthcoming in *Outlook,* available at http://academic.Brooklyn.cuny.edu/economnic/cohn/ind.htm.

Concerning lack of independence, it is important to recognize that auditing firms have a strong stake in client retention and financial solvency, as was apparent in the New Century/KPMG case, among others. A claim can be made, therefore, that an "accountant's dependence on compensation from and gratitude to the client limits independence."[37]

Having other financial relationships with the client firm also puts a strain on the auditor's independence. The practice of opinion shopping indicates how far we are from actual independence. Opinion shopping – the act of searching for an auditor who will give a positive attestation, even if it is unwarranted – is simply bad. Any accountant or accounting firm that succumbs to that practice should immediately be ethically suspect.

On the other hand, defenders of the claim that auditors can remain independent, even when they are performing consulting or other services for a company, maintain that "the synergy between two functions assists the accounting firm to produce improved services in both areas."[38] Indeed, after 15 years of research, studies[39] found not one instance in which the values of the accounting firm's auditing department were compromised by performing management advisory services. Those findings have been challenged,[40] however, on the grounds that the AICPA's definition of independence is ambiguous, and that some cases in which an accounting firm's integrity was compromised are settled out of court and therefore not identified. The recent accounting scandals, as well as the Big Four's decision to limit their consulting roles for firms they are auditing, seem to weaken that argument.[41]

The second threat to auditor independence – inefficient functioning of accounting firms – raises this question: How much time and effort can and should be spent to determine the accuracy of presented data? Being skeptical takes time. Consider a teacher who suspects plagiarism. Think of how much time it takes to trace the possible sources of the plagiarized material. The same is true for the accounting firm that suspects discrepancies in a company's finances. If these discrepancies are overlooked, is it because of shortcomings in the accounting firm's structure or constraints of time and money?

---

[37] Gordon Cohn, "Auditing and Ethical Sensitivity," forthcoming in *Outlook,* available at http://academic.Brooklyn.cuny.edu/economnic/cohn/ind.htm.

[38] Gordon Cohn, "Auditing and Ethical Sensitivity," forthcoming in Outlook. available at http://academic.brooklyn.cuny.edu/economic/cohn/ind.htm

[39] S. R. Klion, MAS practice: are the critics justified? *The Journal of Accountancy*, Vol. 145(6), (1978) pp. 72–78.

[40] Roger W. Bartlett, A heretical challenge to the incantations of audit independence, *Accounting Horizons*, March 1991, pp.11–16.

[41] Jonathan D. Flatern, "Audit Firms are set to Alter Some Practice," Wall Street Journal, February 1, 2002.

VI Independence Risk

After examining the threats to independence, the ISB report outlines "controls that mitigate or eliminate threats to auditors independence."[42] These include "prohibitions, restrictions, disclosures, policies, procedures, practices, standards, rules, institutional arrangements, and environmental conditions."[43]

Another important concept is independence risk, which the report defines as "the risk that threats to auditor independence, to the extent that they are not mitigated by safeguards, compromise, or can reasonably be expected to compromise, an auditor's ability to make unbiased audit decisions. Simply, risk to independence increases with the presence of threats and decreases with the presence of safeguards."[44] The report also examines the significance of threats and the effectiveness of safeguards, noting, "The significance of a threat to auditor independence is the extent to which the threat increases independence risk."[45]

Because there will always be some bias and interest, and because no independence is absolute or total, it is necessary to assess the different levels of risk. For example, with the development of mutual fund investing, it is possible that an accountant's family members may hold stocks in companies the accountant is auditing. Or, given the number of sudden mergers (such as PricewaterhouseCoopers), there may be stock holdings in companies audited by a firm with which the accountant's own has recently merged. There must be ways to judge the seriousness and significance of such threats.

Recognizing that total independence is impossible, the report gives auditors a framework in which to evaluate whether the amount of independence they have will protect them from the risks that would jeopardize their judgment or audit. There are four basic activities, called principles, used to determine auditor independence. The first principle reads as follows:

> Principle 1. *Assessing the level of independence risk.* Independence decision makers should assess the level of independence risk by considering the types and significance of threats to auditor independence and the types and effectiveness of safeguards.[46]

To help with this assessment, the report suggests that auditors examine five levels of independence risk:

* no independence risk (Compromised objectivity is virtually impossible.)
* remote independence risk (Compromised objectivity is very unlikely.)

↳ mutual fund

[42–46]"A Conceptual Framework for Auditor Independence," Independence Standards Board, November 2000.

- some independence risk (Compromised objectivity is possible.)
- high independence risk (Compromised objectivity is probable.)
- maximum independence risk (Compromised objectivity is virtually certain.)

take a pass on that one

Although it is not feasible to measure any of these levels precisely, it is possible to associate a specific threat with one of the risk segments or to place it at one end of the continuum.

The remaining principles are as follows:

> Principle 2. *Determining the acceptability of the level of independence risk.* After assessing the level of risk the auditor needs to determine whether the level of independence is at an acceptable position on the independence risk continuum.
>
> Principle 3. *Considering benefits and costs.* Independence decision makers should ensure that the benefits resulting from reducing independence risk by imposing additional safeguards exceed the costs of those safeguards.
>
> Principle 4. *Considering interested parties' views in addressing auditor independence issues.* Independence decision makers should consider the views of investors, other users and others with an interest in the integrity of financial reporting when addressing issues related to auditor independence and should resolve those issues based on the decision makers' judgment about how best to meet the goal of auditor independence.[47]

The SEC released a "Revision of the Commission's Auditor Independence Requirements," effective February 5, 2001, which prohibits certain nonaudit services that impair auditors' independence. The release, which met with resistance from the accounting profession, was deemed necessary by Levitt of the SEC and those sympathetic with his position.

Because that position seems prophetic in the light of subsequent events, it is worth reviewing Bogle's defense of the SEC's recommendations. According to Bogle, the independence requirements that the SEC recommended ban "only those services which involve either a mutual or conflicting interest with the client; the auditing of one's own work; functioning as management or an employee of the client; or acting as the client's advocate."[48] Bogle rightly asserts that "it is unimaginable ... that any reasonable person could disagree *in the*

---

[47]"A Conceptual Framework for Auditor Independence," Independence Standards Board, November 2000.

[48]John C. Bogle, "Public Accounting: Profession or Business?" The Seymour Jones Distinguished Lecture, Vincent C. Ross Institute of Accounting Research, New York University, October 16, 2000.

abstract that such roles would threaten – or, at the very least, be perceived to threaten – the auditor's independence":[49]

Bogle fears that whereas the auditor's relationship to the client is one of a professional independently following the mandates of the profession, the role of consultant is:

> "a *business* relationship with a *customer* rather than a professional relationship with a client. Surely this issue goes to the very core of the central issue of philosophy that I expressed earlier: The movement of auditing from profession to business, with all the potential conflicts of interest that entails. So I come down with a firm endorsement of the *substance* of the proposed SEC rule, which would in effect bar such relationships."[50]

Nevertheless, Bogle recognizes that there is some merit to objections raised to the commission's recommendations:

> "Some arguments seem entirely worthy of consideration, especially those relating to technical – but nonetheless real – issues that engender unnecessary constraints on an auditor's entering into *any* strategic alliances or joint ventures, or that relate to the complexity in clearly defining 'material direct investment' or 'affiliate of the audit client' and so on."[51]

Still, there are objections Bogle sees as invalid and without merit. Again, in the light of subsequent events, Bogle's insights are remarkably astute:

> "But other opposition seemed to me to be rather knee-jerk and strident (rather like those debates I mentioned at the outset). No, I for one don't believe the SEC proposals represent 'an unwarranted and intrusive regulation' of the accounting profession. And, no, I for one do not believe that the new rules 'strait-jacket' the profession. And, yes, I do believe that the growing multiplicity of inter-relationships between auditor and client is a serious threat to the concept of independence, the rock foundation of sound financial statements and fair financial markets alike."[52]

But even considering recent accounting scandals, is it completely clear that the mere appearance of independence is necessary? After all, couldn't we argue that although there may seem to be a conflict, the accountant may have already resolved or avoided it? It is not the existence of a conflict of interest

[49–52] John C. Bogle, "Public Accounting: Profession or Business?" The Seymour Jones Distinguished Lecture, Vincent C. Ross Institute of Accounting Research, New York University, October 16, 2000.

that is the issue; it is whether or not the accountant can set it aside and do the right thing.

Lynn Turner, former chief accountant at the SEC, presented an extensive argument for the importance of appearing independent:

> "The SEC requires the filing of audited financial statements to obviate the fear of loss from reliance on inaccurate information, thereby encouraging public investment in the Nation's industries. It is therefore not enough that financial statements *be* accurate; the public must also *perceive* them as being accurate. Public faith in the reliability of a corporation's financial statements depends on the public perception of the outside auditor as an independent professional … If investors were to view the auditor as an advocate for the corporate client, the value of the audit function itself might well be lost."[53]

The accounting profession has long embraced the need for the appearance of independence. Statement on Auditing Standards No. 1 reads as follows:

> Public confidence would be impaired by evidence that independence was actually lacking, and it might also be impaired by the existence of circumstances which reasonable people might believe likely to influence independence … Independent auditors should not only be independent in fact, they should avoid situations that may lead outsiders to doubt their independence.[54]

Witnesses at the Commission's hearings on the auditor independence rule strongly endorsed the need for auditors to maintain the appearance of independence from audit clients. Paul Volcker, former chairman of the Federal Reserve Board, in response to a question about investors' perceptions of a conflict of interest when auditors provide nonaudit services, said, "The perception is there because there is a real conflict of interest. You cannot avoid all conflicts of interest, but this is a clear, evident, growing conflict of interest …"[55]

In addition, John Whitehead, former co-chairman of Goldman Sachs and a member of numerous audit committees testified as follows:

> "Financial statements are at the very heart of our capital markets. They're the basis for analyzing investments. Investors have every right to be able to depend

[53] Lynn E. Turner, "Current SEC Developments: Independence Matters," Chief Accountant, Office of the Chief Accountant, U.S. Securities and Exchange Commission 28th annual National Conference on Current SEC Developments , December 6, 2000.
[54] "Due Professional Care in the Performance of Work," PCAOB Standards, AU Section 230.07. http://www.pcaobus.com/standards/interim_standards/auditing_standards/au_230.html.
[55] Speech by SEC Staff: "Independence Matters." http://www.sec.gov/news/speech/spch445.htm.

absolutely on the integrity of the financial statements that are available to them, and if that integrity in any way falls under suspicion, then the capital markets will surely suffer if investors feel they cannot rely absolutely on the integrity of those financial statements."[56]

In 1988, three major accounting firms had petitioned the SEC to modify the independence rules and allow expanded business relationships with their audit clients; by 1989 all of the big accounting firms had applied for a modification. But in the wake of Enron/Andersen, the Sarbanes–Oxley Act tightened the independence rules.

On January 28, 2003, in response to the act, the SEC adopted amendments to strengthen requirements on requiring auditor independence. Rule 2-01 lays out four principles, which "focus on whether the auditor–client relationship or the provision of service (a) creates a mutual or conflicting interest between the accountant and the audit client; (b) places the accountant in the position of auditing his or her own work; (c) results in the accountant acting as management or employee of the audit client; or (d) places the accountant in a position of being an advocate for the audit client."[57]

Finally, Rule 2-10 prohibits certain specific relationships, including financial relationships, employment relationships, business relationships, relationships in which the audit firm performs nonaudit services to the client. Rule 2-10 also includes requirements regarding partner rotation and audit committee administration of the engagement.

The reasons to avoid even the appearance of a conflict of interest, which might affect auditor independence, are obvious. To make their best judgments, people need faith in the representations upon which they base those judgments. Representations made by accountants who have – even appear to have – conflicting interests do not inspire such faith.

People's thoughts govern their responses. If I think someone is angry, my response will be different from my response if I think the person is in pain. Similarly, if I trust someone, I will respond differently than if I suspect that individual. Thus, the appearance of dependence will have a major impact on the estimation of a financial entity's worth.

VII Professional Skepticism

extremly important

Independence is crucial because it is the auditor's responsibility to maintain professional skepticism. During workshops with accountants, we often ask

[56] Lynn E. Turner, "Current SEC Developments: Independence Matters."
[57] Brian Carroll, "Highlights of the New SEC Auditor Independence Rule," *The Attorney-CPA*, 2001, at http://findarticles.com/p/articles.

them how it is possible to be objective about a friend's income statements. Does it cloud their judgment? In establishing standards for auditors early in its existence, the Public Company Accounting Oversight Board (PCAOB) incorporated the AICPA's Auditing Standard No. 82, which called for due professional care. There are two key statements:

> Due professional care is to be exercised in the planning and performance of the audit and the preparation of the report.[58]
>
> Due professional care imposes a responsibility upon each professional within an independent auditor's organization to observe the standards of field work and reporting.[59]

In addition to possessing the requisite skills, the AICPA standards stipulate that auditors must maintain professional skepticism, arguably one of the auditor's most important responsibilities:

> Due professional care requires the auditor to exercise *professional skepticism*. Professional skepticism is an attitude that includes a questioning mind and a critical assessment of audit evidence. The auditor uses the knowledge, skill, and ability called for by the profession of public accounting to diligently perform, in good faith and with integrity, the gathering and objective evaluation of evidence.[60]

[handwritten margin note: what client says doesn't mean it's true]

Auditing Standard No. 82, approved by PCAOB as AU 230.07 provides further clarification of auditors' obligations. An auditor may not detect a material irregularity, for example, because generally accepted auditing standards do not require the authentication of documents, or there may be collusion and concealment. The auditor is not an insurer; nor does the auditor's report constitute a guarantee. The auditor, therefore, needs only to give reasonable assurance – that is, maintain a proper degree of professional skepticism.

To be appropriately skeptical, the auditor must consider factors that influence audit risk, especially the internal control structure. "The auditor's understanding of the internal control structure should either heighten or mitigate the auditor's concern about the risk of material misstatements."[61] The auditor should ask the following questions: Are there significant difficult-to-audit transactions? Are there substantial and unusual related-party transactions not

---

[58]"Due Professional Care in the Performance of Work," PCAOB Standards, AU Section 230.01.
[59]"Due Professional Care in the Performance of Work," PCAOB Standards, AU Section 230.02.
[60]"Due Professional Care in the Performance of Work," PCAOB Standards, AU Section 230.07.
[61]SEC – Accounting and Auditing Enforcement. July 17, 1997. http://www.sec.gov/litigation/admin/3-9347.txt.

in the ordinary course of business? Is there a sizable number of known and likely misstatements detected in the audit of prior period's financials from the previous auditor?

The auditor should review information about risk factors and the internal control structure by considering these issues: Are there circumstances that may indicate a management predisposition to distort financial statements? Are there indications that management has failed to establish policies and procedures to assure reliable accounting estimates by utilizing unqualified, careless, or inexperienced personnel? Are there symptoms of a lack of control, such as recurrent crises conditions, disorganized work areas, excessive back orders, shortages, delays or lack of documentation for major transactions? Are there signs of insufficient control over computer processing? Are there inadequate policies and procedures for security of data or assets? The auditor needs to determine the effects of any of these issues on the overall audit strategy. High risk ordinarily demands more experienced personnel and more extensive supervision. "Higher risk will also ordinarily cause the auditor to exercise a heightened degree of professional skepticism in conducting the audit."[62]

The following paragraph summarizes the responsibility of maintaining professional skepticism:

> An audit of financial statements in accordance with generally accepted auditing standards should be planned and performed with an attitude of professional skepticism. The auditor neither assumes that management is dishonest nor assumes unquestioned honesty. In exercising professional skepticism, the auditor should not be satisfied with less than persuasive evidence because of a belief that management is honest.[63]

VIII Reasonable Assurance

The final section of the standard on due care deals with reasonable assurance. It includes the following stipulations:

> The exercise of due professional care allows the auditor to obtain *reasonable assurance* about whether the financial statements are free of material misstatement, whether caused by error or fraud, or whether any material weaknesses exist as of the date of management's assessment. Absolute assurance is not

---

[62] SEC – Accounting and Auditing Enforcement. July 17, 1997. http://www.sec.gov/litigation/admin/3-9347.txt
[63] "Due Professional Care in the Performance of Work," PCAOB Standards, AU Section 230.09.

attainable because of the nature of audit evidence and the characteristics of fraud. Although not absolute assurance, reasonable assurance is a high level of assurance. Therefore, an audit conducted in accordance with the standards of the Public Company Accounting Oversight Board (United States) may not detect a material weakness in internal control over financial reporting or a material misstatement to the financial statements.[64]

The independent auditor's objective is to obtain sufficient competent evidential matter to provide him or her with a reasonable basis for forming an opinion. The nature of most evidence derives, in part, from the concept of selective testing of the data being audited, which involves judgment regarding both the areas to be tested and the nature, timing, and extent of the tests to be performed. In addition, judgment is required in interpreting the results of audit testing and evaluating audit evidence. Even with good faith and integrity, mistakes and errors in judgment can be made.[65]

Furthermore, accounting presentations contain accounting estimates, the measurement of which is inherently uncertain and depends on the outcome of future events. The auditor exercises professional judgment in evaluating the reasonableness of accounting estimates based on information that could reasonably be expected to be available prior to the completion of field work. As a result of these factors, in the great majority of cases, the auditor has to rely on evidence that is persuasive rather than convincing.[66]

Hence, we conclude that a prerequisite for an effective auditor is to maintain both the fact of independence and the appearance of independence. This allows the auditor to practice due care, which requires an attitude of professional skepticism. As a professional, the auditor has a duty to the public that he or she freely embraced in becoming a public accountant. Ethics demands nothing more than fulfilling that duty.

This concludes our discussion of the function and responsibilities of the auditor. We turn now to an examination of the role and responsibilities of the management accountant.

[64]"Due Professional Care in the Performance of Work," PCAOB Standards, AU Section 230.10.
[65]"Due Professional Care in the Performance of Work," PCAOB Standards, AU Section 230.11.
[66]"Due Professional Care in the Performance of Work," PCAOB Standards,, AU Section 230.12.

Chapter Eight

The Ethics of Managerial Accounting

"Senior executives at Fannie Mae manipulated accounting to collect millions of dollars in undeserved bonuses and to deceive investors, a federal report charged. On May 22, 2006, the government-sponsored mortgage company was fined $400 million.

The blistering report by the Office of Federal Housing Enterprise Oversight, the result of an extensive three-year investigation, was issued as Fannie Mae struggled to emerge from an $11 billion accounting scandal. Also Tuesday, the housing oversight agency and the Securities and Exchange Commission announced a $400 million civil penalty against Fannie Mae in a settlement over the alleged accounting manipulation."[1]

The Fannie Mae case is typical of the worst scandals in accounting history. This financial information is critical: How much is a company worth? What are its assets? What are its liabilities? What sorts of internal auditing procedures are in place? How do you know? It is the task of the financial accountant or the management accountant to determine those matters and to report them accurately, honestly, and transparently.

A management accountant or financial accountant works for a particular company, either as the chief financial officer or controller, as a line accountant performing any number of possible tasks, or even as a consultant doing specific jobs that contribute to the company's financial picture. Management accountants can operate as financial managers, accountants, or internal auditors, depending on their position in the company and the organization's size and nature. Accountants who work for a firm have many of the

[1]"Fannie Mae slammed with $400M Fine" by Gina Pace. CBS NEWS. Mat 23, 2006

Accounting Ethics, Second Edition. Ronald Duska, Brenda Shay Duska, and Julie Ragatz.
© 2011 John Wiley & Sons, Ltd. Published 2011 by John Wiley & Sons, Ltd.

sameobligations as other accountants, but their relationship to the firm gives them a different set of responsibilities from those of the auditor. The Independence Standards Board (ISB) clearly delineated the responsibilities of internal management, including internal management accountants, as compared to outside auditors:

> Management is responsible for the financial statements, and responsibility for the choices and judgments inherent in the preparation of those financial statements cannot be delegated to the auditor or to anyone else. Whatever the service being provided, the auditor must understand the level of management's expertise and must be satisfied that management has taken responsibility for the assumptions and judgments made during the course of the work, and for the results produced.[2]

The accountants within the firm, whether financial officers, valuations experts, or bookkeepers, have the duty to portray the firm's financial picture as correctly and truthfully as possible, even if it is detrimental to the company. Although management accountants have a responsibility to the firms that employ them, their overriding obligation is to disseminate the truth.

The "Standards of Ethical Conduct for Practitioners of Management Accounting and Financial Management," which is the Institute of Management Accountants' code of ethics, defines the scope of obligations: "Practitioners of management accounting and financial management have an obligation to the public, their profession, the organization they serve, and themselves, to maintain the highest standards of ethical conduct."[3]

In accord with the primary principle of this book, any accountant's first obligation is to do his or her job. For the management accountant, that is to aid in the accurate representation of a company's financial picture, including assets and liabilities, or to present the most reliable advice based on that picture to all those entitled to it.

It takes little imagination to see how the accountant can be influenced by factors other than accurate reporting. Consider the following story:

Gateway Officials Charged with Manipulating Earnings

The Securities and Exchange Commission last week charged three former Gateway executives with overstating revenue by $70 million by booking revenue as part of a deal with AOL.

[2] ISB Interpretation 99-1, "Impact on Auditor Independence of Assisting Clients in the Implementation of FAS 133 (Derivatives)."
[3] "Standards of Ethical Conduct for Practitioners of Management Accounting and Financial Management," at http://www.allbusiness.com/management/302465-1.html.

The former computer company executives, CEO Jeffrey Weitzen, CFO John Todd, and controller Robert D. Manza allegedly engaged in a "fraudulent earnings manipulation scheme "in 2000 as part of a program referred internally as the "DDS program," which stood for "deep, deep #$*@."

Gateway, which received $219.45 from AOL for every consumer who used the pre-loaded AOL software installed on Gateway computers, began booking revenues when the PCs were shipped, rather than when consumers actually signed up for AOL, even though many consumers didn't actually sign up for AOL.[4]

It is obvious why company executives act the way Gateway did. If they have a favorable quarterly retained earnings report, the value of the company stock goes up, the board is pleased, the bank is more likely to grant a loan, and prospective investors are attracted to the company. Last but not least, favorable reports have a positive effect on the president's year-end bonus. In short, painting such a favorable picture has many benefits.

If, however, the picture is a deliberate distortion, doesn't creating that picture constitute unethical behavior? Isn't the accountant either lying or complicit in telling a lie? Even if this behavior benefits the company – a big if – isn't it still unethical? Clearly, it is unfair to prospective investors, stockholders, and board members who need to make decisions about the company and are entitled to know its true financial condition.

Suppose, for example, the company CEO wants the accountant to paint as rosy a picture as possible to impress the board of directors who are considering renewing the CEO's tenure. Obviously, not complying with the CEO's request will jeopardize the accountant's position in the company. There is a great temptation, therefore, to follow the CEO's request. It is clear, however, that doing so violates ethical principles, specifically one of the standards in the code of ethics for managerial accounting – the responsibility to be objective.

Let's address the code provisions more specifically. The code presents four standards of ethical conduct,[5] which we can summarize as follows:

- *competence.* The management accountant must maintain an appropriate level of knowledge and skill; follow the laws, rules and technical standards; and prepare reports that are clear and complete based on reliable and relevant information after appropriate analysis.

[4,5] David A. Vise, "SEC Accuses Former Gateway Officials of Fraud," *Washington Post*, November 13, 2003, at www.washingtonpost.com/wpdyn/articles/A38287003Nov13.html.

- *confidentiality.* The management accountant must refrain from disclosure of confidential information except when authorized and legally obligated to do so.
- *integrity.* This standard requires the management accountant to avoid both actual and apparent conflicts of interest and to refrain from activities that would prejudice the accountant's ability to execute ethical duties. The accountant must refuse gifts and favors that could influence his or her actions, and should not subvert the organization's legitimate objectives. The standard further requires that the accountant admit to professional limitations, communicate favorable and unfavorable information, and refrain from behavior that would discredit the profession.
- *objectivity.* The central standard of the code is objectivity, which requires the management accountant to "communicate information fairly and objectively" and to "disclose fully all relevant information that could reasonably be expected to influence an intended user's understanding of the reports, comments, and recommendations presented."[6]

If the accountant in the example above complies with the CEO's request, can the accountant "communicate the information fairly and objectively"? We have already discussed the concept of "fair" in the previous chapter. But a brief review may be helpful. *Black's Law Dictionary* defines "fair" as "having the qualities of impartiality and honesty; free from prejudice, favoritism, and self interest; just; equitable; evenhanded; equal as between conflicting interests."[7] We can conclude, therefore, that the accountant above could not communicate the information fairly and objectively if it is presented as the CEO wishes. It would not be impartial; it would not be honest; it would not be free from favoritism or self-interest; it would not be even-handed or free from conflicts of interest. It fails on all counts to be fair. It also fails to disclose fully relevant information that could reasonably be expected to influence an intended user's understanding of the reports, comments, and recommendations.

We have repeatedly emphasized that appropriate full disclosure is required for informed consent in a market economy. If the distorted report is supposed to impress the board of directors, it may lead its members to make a recommendation on the CEO's tenure that it might not otherwise make. If the report is meant to impress the stock market, it, again, may cause activity that would probably not have resulted, had the report been more accurate. Obviously, there is a conflict of interest here between the management accountant's

[6] David A. Vise, "SEC Accuses Former Gateway Officials of Fraud," *Washington Post*, November 13, 2003, at www.washingtonpost.com/wpdyn/articles/A38287003Nov13.html.
[7] *Black's Law Dictionary*, 9th ed., Thomson West, 2009.

self-interest and the interests of others, including the CEO. But this example should also cause us to reflect on the constituencies other than the CEO or the company to which the management accountant is responsible.

When we examine the ethical requirements that the standards impose, we see that the basic function of accountants does not change from auditor to managerial accountants. Bill Vatter, in his introductory comments to *Managerial Accounting,* published in 1950, succinctly articulates this point:

> "One of the basic functions of accounting is to report independently on the activities of others, so that information concerning what has happened may be relevant and unbiased. The major function *served by both public and managerial accountants* is to use their independent judgment with complete freedom; thus they may observe and evaluate objectively, the fortunes and results of enterprise operations … This is a highly important aspect of accounting, and it is one of the reasons for the separation of the accounting function from the rest of the management process. The detached and independent viewpoint of the accountant must be kept in mind."[8]

Because of the management accountant's obligation to fair reporting, the accounting function should be kept separate from the rest of the management process. This is not only ethically sound but also managerially wise. To make decisions about a company, it is important, even for those within the company, to have as accurate a picture as possible of the company's financial condition. In the scenario above, it is in the CEO's interests (misguided, though they may be) to misrepresent that picture. Concealing the true picture of the company's worth is not, however, in the best interest of the company, the stockholders, or any one else. Hence, the accountant has a responsibility to the company and its stakeholders that should override the responsibility to do what the CEO asks.

We all remember the story "The Emperor's New Clothes," in which two weavers make the emperor a suit of cloth that is invisible to anyone deemed unfit or stupid. The emperor's sycophants pretend to admire his new outfit, afraid that telling him the truth – that he is naked – will put them in jeopardy. The health of a business enterprise depends on the truth. If the business is naked, it is best to know. That is the accountant's task. In some cases, meeting this responsibility may not win the accountant too many friends. In the long run, however, the management accountant does no one a favor by cooking the books. It is interesting to speculate, therefore, about why an internal accountant would misstate a company's financial picture.

[8] William J. Vatter, *Managerial Accounting* (New York: Prentice Hall), 1950, p. 8.

I Reasons Used to Justify Unethical Behaviors

A remarkable article by <u>Saul W. Gellerman</u>[9] gives <u>four rationalizations</u> that managers use to justify suspect behavior. Management accountants can use these rationalizations as guides to warn against misrepresenting financial statements.

My behavior is not actually illegal or immoral

The first reason (rationalization?) given for unethical behavior is "a belief that the activity is within reasonable ethical and legal limits – that is, that it is not 'really' illegal or immoral."[10] Ambiguous situations allow for a great deal of discretion in behavior. In "The Sherlocks of Finance," an article in *Business*, Daniel McGinn notes that forensic accountant Howard Schilit discovered that companies like United Health Care, 3M, and Oxford Health Plans used aggressive, although legal, accounting policies "that might camouflage a sagging business ... [and] distort the true financial condition of the company."[11] McGinn describes such policies as "window dressing":

> "Schilit specializes in flagging the frequent – and perfectly legal – gambit of "window dressing," which puffs up profits and revenues. He is not alleging fraud; indeed the accounting techniques he highlights are allowed under generally accepted accounting principles (GAAP). But GAAP rules are subject to wide interpretation – and companies have great leeway in choosing how conservatively or aggressively they account for financial transactions."[12]

The application of GAAP is more an art than a science, and there are clearly many opportunities to present financial statements in a favorable, rather than unfavorable, light, even in accord with GAAP. It may be, however, that such behavior violates the spirit, even though it is within the letter, of the law.

Keeping only within the letter of the law was also the *modus operandi* of the accountants at Enron. Douglas Carmichael, an accounting professor at Baruch College in Manhattan, described Enron's behavior: "It's like somebody sat down with the rules and said, 'How can we get around them?' They

[9,10] Saul W. Gellerman, "Why 'Good' Managers Make Bad Ethical Choices," *Harvard Business Review*, July 6, 1986, p. 88.
[11,12] Daniel McGinn, "The Sherlocks of Finance," *Newsweek*, Vol. 132(8), pp. 38–39.

structured these things (special purpose entities) to comply with the letter of the law but totally violated the spirit."[13]

Charles DiLullo, an accountant and accounting professor at The American College in Bryn Mawr, Pennsylvania, identifies eight ways to manipulate a financial statement:[14]

- recognition of revenues earlier than they should be recognized
- recognition of questionable revenues
- recognition of false revenues
- recognition of asset disposals or investment gains as either reductions in operating expenses or increases in operating revenues
- recognition of current operating expenses as being applicable to some prior period or being deferred to some future period
- failure to recognize or the inappropriate reduction of liabilities in the current year
- recognition of current revenues as being deferred to some future period
- recognition of future expenses as current operating expenses

Why would an accountant operate within the letter of the law, but avoid the spirit, to manipulate financial information? Usually, it is to take advantage of someone else. Using the justification, "But it's legal," indicates that the accountant was hesitant to perform the activity, probably because of doubts about its probity. We should be willing to ask, "Why do I hesitate to do this?" It is also helpful to follow the "sniff test" to determine if the activity is ethical. If something just doesn't smell right, perhaps the best ethical advice is to remember this maxim from Benjamin Franklin: "When in doubt, don't."

The actions are in the company's best interests

A second reason to justify unethical behavior, according to Gellerman, is "a belief that the activity is in the individual's or the corporation's best interests – that the individual would somehow be expected to undertake the activity."[15] The management accountant is an employee of the company and does not

[13]Douglas Carmichael, as quoted in "Shell Game: How Enron Concealed Losses, Inflated Earnings – and Hid Secret Deals from the Authorities," by Daniel Fisher in *Forbes*, January 7, 2002, p. 52.
[14]Charles DiLullo, "Ethics and Financial Statements," Class Notes, The American College, Bryn Mawr, PA.
[15]Samuel Gellerman, "Why 'Good' Managers Make Bad Ethical Choices," *Harvard Business Review*, July 6, 1986, p. 88.

work for an accounting firm. Consequently, he or she is expected to be loyal to the company that is paying his or her salary. This loyalty may appear to require doing things for the good of the company that the employee would not do as an objective outsider. Although it is only natural for the first loyalty to be to his or her firm, the managerial accountant's code of ethics requires objectivity and an obligation to the public.

Take the example of General Electric (GE), which, as of 2001, reported 101 straight quarters of earnings growth. But these results were based on the use of accounting tactics that obfuscated GE's true performance. According to Andy Serwer in *Fortune*, "GE uses gains and losses from certain businesses – particularly its financial services area, GE Capital – to offset gains and losses in other divisions, whether they ought to belong in that quarter or not … The problem: If GE ever stumbled and chose to hide a shortfall, some critics say, it could take many quarters for investors to find out. This kind of earnings management isn't illegal, maybe not even immoral. The concern, rather, is that it's not transparent."[16]

General Electric met or exceeded analysts' consensus earnings-per-share expectations for every quarter from 1995 to 2004. During 2002 and 2003, executives approved accounting techniques that did not comply with GAAP. The company was charged with violating accounting rules when it changed its original hedge documentation to avoid recording fluctuations in the fair value of interest rates swaps, which would have dragged down the company's reported earnings-per-share estimates.

On August 4, 2009, the SEC issued a complaint of accounting fraud charges against the company. General Electric had finally stumbled.

The complaint alleged four problems:

(1)   Beginning in January 2003, an improper application of the accounting standards to GE commercial paper funding program to avoid unfavorable disclosures and an estimated approximately $200M pretax charge to earnings.

(2)   A 2003 failure to correct misapplication of financial accounting standards to certain GE interest rate swaps.

(3)   In 2002 and 2003, reported end-of-year sales of locomotives that had not yet occurred in order to accelerate more than $370M in revenue. The idea was that GE could book the sales made to the financial institution in the current year, while they allowed their railroad customers to purchase the locomotives at their convenience some time in the future. The problem … was that the six transactions were not true sales, and

---

[16] Andy Serwer, "A Rare Skeptic Takes on the Cult of GE," *Fortune*, Monday, February 19, 2001.

therefore did not qualify for revenue recognition under GAAP. Indeed, GE did not cede ownership of the trains to the financial institution.

(4) In 2002, an improper change to GE's accounting for sales of commercial aircraft engines' spare parts that increased GE's 2002 net earnings by $585M.[17]

GE paid a $50 million fine and agreed to remedial action relating to its internal control enhancements.

As another example, Enron used the now infamous tactic of creating special-purpose entities to hide losses – likewise, a perfectly legal but dubious maneuver. The firm was skirting ethical territory, a strategy that can lead to unethical behavior justified in the name of firm loyalty. Moreover, the promise of a large bonus to make the figures come out right can incentivize such suspect ethical behavior.

There are two things wrong with this kind of behavior. First, acting unethically may *not* be in the company's long-term best interest. Firms that lie, withhold information, or defraud the consumer – thinking it is necessary for the company's benefit – are often exposed eventually. Second, such behavior uses other people for the company's own ends; in many cases, it actually hurts other people. In short, this behavior is often unfair or harmful – or both.

No one will ever find out

A third reason to justify unethical activity, Gellerman says, is "the belief that the activity is 'safe' because it will never be found out or publicized; the classic crime-and-punishment issue of discovery."[18] But look at Cendant, Lucent, Rite Aid, and Sunbeam. They did get caught cooking the books. In fact, the literature is full of stories about firms that did something nefarious, only to be caught in the long run – for example, the SEC's charge of fraud against Micro Strategy[19] and its litigation against W.R. Grace for abuse of materiality:

"In Litigation Release No. 16008, the SEC asserts that the numbers for Grace's Health Care Group for 1991 through 1995 were put together with the goal of misleading capital market participants. Specifically, it alleges that Grace's managers tucked some of the division's unanticipated earnings away in a cookie jar

---

[17] http://www.secactions.com.
[18] Samuel Gellerman, "Why 'Good' Managers Make Bad Ethical Choices," *Harvard Business Review*, July 6, 1986, p. 88.
[19] "Microstrategy Chairman Accused of Fraud by SEC" by Floyd Norris. New York Times. December 15, 2000.

for later. They then dipped into the jar for 1995's fourth quarter to get reported earnings closer to their target.

What they did was clearly wrong, even if the amounts were immaterial ...

If the Grace managers and the auditors convinced themselves that a little fraud was immaterial, they were disgracefully wrong!"[20]

But the Grace managers didn't expect to get caught. Note that defending an action because you think you will never get caught is a rationalization, not a justification. The first two of Gellerman's rationalizations attempt to justify questionable or suspect behavior. In the third rationalization, the behavior is clearly wrong.

The company will protect me

A final reason, according to Gellerman, for bad ethical choices is "a belief that because the activity helps the company, the company will condone it and even protect the person who engages in it."[21] The belief that the company will protect an employee who performs a disputable activity depends on the integrity of the company's leaders. If they are the type of leaders who excuse illegal or unethical activity, they will condone the accountant's loyalty. Be advised, however, that condoning lasts only as long as the unethical or illegal activity remains undiscovered. After that, the rats will desert the sinking ship, and the person who performed the unethical or illegal activity will be sunk, so to speak. It is important to recognize that if you are an accountant in a culture that expects, promotes, or encourages unethical behavior – even silently condones illegal activity – your integrity is in mortal danger. The best course of action is never to engage in such behavior, even if it means losing your job. Accountants have been fired many times. Fortunately, it is a profession with many opportunities.

II Blowing the Whistle

This brings up another issue: whistle-blowing. The "Standards of Ethical Conduct for Practitioners of Management Accounting and Financial Management" offer this advice:

---

[20] J. Edward Ketz and Paul B.W. Miller, "W.R. Grace's Disgraceful Abuse of Materiality," *Accounting Today*, May 24, 1999–June 6, 1999.
[21] Samuel Gellerman, "Why 'Good' Managers Make Bad Ethical Choices," *Harvard Business Review*, July 6, 1986, p. 88.

... When faced with significant ethical issues, practitioners of management accounting and financial management should follow the established policies of the organization bearing on the resolution of such conflict. If these policies do not resolve the ethical conflict, such practitioner should consider the following courses of action:

- Discuss such problems with the immediate superior except when it appears that the superior is involved, in which case the problem should be presented initially to the next higher managerial level. If a satisfactory resolution cannot be achieved when the problem is initially presented, submit the issues to the next higher managerial level ... Except where legally prescribed, communication of such problems to authorities or individuals not employed or engaged by the organization is not considered appropriate.
- Clarify relevant ethical issues by confidential discussion with an objective advisor (e.g., IMA Ethics Counseling service) to obtain a better understanding of possible courses of action.
- Consult your own attorney as to legal obligations and rights concerning the ethical conflict.
- If the ethical conflict still exists after exhausting all levels of internal review, there may be no other recourse on significant matters than to resign from the organization and to submit an informative memorandum to an appropriate representative of the organization. After resignation, depending on the nature of the ethical conflict, it may also be appropriate to notify other parties.[22]

In an episode of *Chicago Hope*, the television show about doctors at a Chicago hospital, a patient died in the recovery room after undergoing liposuction from a particularly greedy doctor, who would schedule two or three surgeries simultaneously. One of the ethical issues raised was what fellow doctors should do to prevent him from acting that way again. Doctors are professionals, and one of the ethical obligations of professionals is to police their professions.

Although not as dramatic, there is an analogous problem among accountants. Consider the following scenario: You are an accountant for a large insurance company. As you begin an internal audit of the company books, you discover that a manager was replacing virtually every policy that he had sold with his previous carrier – with no analysis, no 1035 exchanges, and no replacement forms. He was also writing smokers as nonsmokers. What should you do? Are you obliged to blow the whistle? Suppose company officials refuse to do anything about the manager's shady practices. Do you need to go further?

As we saw in Chapter 4, one of the necessary characteristics of professionalism, according to Solomon Huebner, founder of The American College, is as follows: "The practitioner should possess a spirit of loyalty to fellow practitioners, of helpfulness to the common cause they all profess, and should not allow any unprofessional acts to bring shame upon the entire profession."[23] If a professional should not allow unprofessional acts to bring shame on the profession, it follows that there may be a time when he or she is obliged to set aside loyalty to a fellow practitioner or company and blow the whistle.

In the context of business ethics, whistle-blowing is the practice in which employees who know that their company or a colleague is engaged in activities that (1) cause unnecessary harm, (2) violate human rights, (3) are illegal, (4) run counter to the defined purpose of the institution or the profession, or (5) are otherwise immoral, *inform* superiors, professional organizations, the public, or some governmental agency of those activities.

Two questions remain: When is it permissible to blow the whistle? And when is it an ethical obligation to blow the whistle?

There is a strong judgment against whistle-blowing. Early in life, we learned not to "tell on others." This behavior is characterized by such words as "finking," "tattling," "ratting," "stooling," or some other pejorative term. Not only do people hesitate to blow the whistle, therefore, but they also think its wrong. Note that in sports, from which the word derives, whistle-blowing is the function of a neutral referee who is supposed to detect and penalize the illicit behavior of players of both teams. In competitive team sports, it is neither acceptable nor ethically obligatory for a player to call a foul on teammates. Thus, whistle-blowing is viewed as an act of disloyalty, and there is a presumption against it. If the analogy holds, what is unacceptable in sports is also unacceptable in business – whistle-blowing is considered wrong.

In spite of our early training, however, there are times when whistle-blowing is acceptable. There is an ethical obligation for human beings to prevent harm in certain circumstances. If the only way to prevent harm is to blow the whistle, then whistle-blowing becomes an obligation. The obligation to prevent harm to the public overrides the obligation of loyalty to a person's profession or company.

When do such times occur? Whistle-blowing is an obligation when it is based on the following conditions:

[23] Solomon Huebner's "Characteristics of a Professional," from an address to Baltimore Life and New York Life Underwriters. WWW.theamericancollege.edu/assets/pdfs/how-the-life-insurance-salesman.pdf.

- *the proper motivation.* Whistle-blowing should be done from the appropriate moral motive – not from a desire to get ahead, for example, or out of spite. Unfortunately, business people often blow the whistle on another person simply because they think the other person has stolen some business away. The proper motivation for blowing the whistle is an illegal or immoral action.
- *the proper evidence.* The whistle-blower must be sure that his or her belief that inappropriate actions have occurred is based on evidence that would persuade a reasonable person.
- *the proper analysis.* The whistle-blower should act only after a careful analysis of the harm that can result from the inappropriate action. Questions to ask include the following: How serious is the moral violation? (Minor moral matters need not be reported.) How immediate is the moral violation? (The greater time before the violation occurs, the greater chance that internal mechanisms will prevent it.) Is the moral violation one that can be specified? (General claims about a rapacious supervisor, obscene bonuses, and actions contrary to public interest simply will not do.)
- *the proper channels.* Except in special circumstances, the whistle-blower should exhaust all internal channels before informing the public. The whistle-blower's action should be commensurate with his or her responsibility to avoid or expose moral violations. If there are personnel in the company whose obligation it is to monitor and respond to immoral and/ or illegal activities, it is their responsibility to address those issues. Thus, the first obligation of the potential whistle-blower is to report the unethical activities to those personnel. The whistle-blower should inform the general public only if the company does not act.

The conditions above speak to the acceptability of blowing the whistle. The next question is when it is morally required (obligatory) for a professional to blow the whistle on a fellow professional? In our society, there is a moral obligation to prevent harm. For example, if you see a small child drowning in a wading pool and no one is helping her, you have a moral obligation to prevent the child from drowning. We can refer to this example as we enumerate the four general conditions for this obligation, developed by John Simon, Charles Powers, and Jon Gunneman in *The Ethical Investor*.[24] The situation must meet all of these four conditions:

- *need.* The child will drown without help. Thus, there is a need. If there is no harm occurring or about to occur, there is no ethical obligation.

[24] John G. Simon, Charles W. Powers, and Jon P. Gunneman, *The Ethical Investor* (New Haven: Yale University Press), 1972.

- *capability.* Most people are capable of pulling a child out of a wading pool. If the child is drowning in a deep lake, however, a person who cannot swim lacks the capability to prevent harm in that situation and so is not obliged to save the child.
- *proximity.* Even though you did not cause the child to be in the wading pool, you have an obligation simply because you happen to be there. You are in a position to help because you are close by. You are not obligated to help everybody in the world. That brings us to the next condition.
- *last resort.* If the parents of the child are there and capable, saving the child is their responsibility. That is the division of responsibility that society establishes. Unless the parents panic or are otherwise unable to act, you are not responsible for the child. If however, everyone there panics and cannot act, you become the last resort. In your professional capacity, if you are the only one who knows of a colleague's unethical activity, you are the last resort for blowing the whistle. If the colleague's superior knows of the activity, it is his or her responsibility to stop it. If, however, the superior does not act, from whatever motive – whether it is dereliction or inability – you become the last resort, and the responsibility falls to you.

As it relates to whistle-blowing, we need to add to a fifth condition to the four developed by Simon, Powers and Gunneman. The fifth condition is the *likelihood of success.*

The whistle-blower should have some chance of success. If there is no hope in arousing societal, institutional, or governmental pressure, then the whistle-blower needlessly exposes himself or herself (and perhaps others to whom the whistle-blower is related) to hardship for no conceivable moral gain. The obligation arises from the duty to prevent harm. If no harm will be prevented and there is no other ground for the obligation, there *is* no obligation. If nothing is accomplished except bad feelings toward the whistle-blower, there is hardly an obligation to blow the whistle.

Hence, we can summarize the responsibility to blow the whistle as follows: If you are in a proximate position, you are capable of preventing harm (the need) without sacrificing something of comparable moral worth, and you are the last resort, it is more than acceptable to blow the whistle – you have an *obligation* to blow the whistle to prevent such harm.[25]

In the business world, in which companies and fellow practitioners are seen as a team, loyalty is expected and rewarded. Leaving the team to function as

[25] John G. Simon, Charles W. Powers, and Jon P. Gunneman, *The Ethical Investor* (New Haven: Yale University Press), 1972.

a detached referee – to blow the whistle – is viewed as disloyal and cause for punitive action. Whistle-blowing, therefore, requires moral heroism. It will not be easy, and the consequences can be dire. Nevertheless, given that society depends on whistle-blowers to protect it from unscrupulous operators, it is sometimes required. Sherron Watkins, vice president for corporate development at Enron, sent a letter to Kenneth Lay, Enron's chairman, in August 2001, questioning Enron's financial activities and reporting behaviors. Warning that improper accounting practices threatened to destroy the company, Watkins has emerged as a hero in the Enron debacle.

Professionals must accept that upholding the standards of their profession may require them to blow the whistle. Accountants have a fiduciary responsibility – an ethical obligation – to report certain illegal or potentially harmful activities. This obligation arises from the accountant's status as a professional and from the human duty to prevent harm under the conditions of need, proximity, capability, and last resort. If accountants are to be true professionals, there will be times when they will be obliged to blow the whistle, as difficult as that may be.

In conclusion, let us summarize the management accountant's responsibilities. The first responsibility is to do his or her job – that is, to execute whatever accounting function he or she was hired to perform. The second is to do so with objectivity, honesty, and integrity, overcoming temptations from business pressures and intimidation by leaders to tamper with the books. Finally, the management accountant may have the unfortunate and difficult responsibility to blow the whistle on wrongdoing, but only under the circumstances described above.

The next chapter examines the role of the tax accountant.

Chapter Nine

The Ethics of Tax Accounting

In 2005 KPMG was indicted for promoting abusive tax shelters. The Department of Justice and the Internal Revenue Service on August 29, 2005 reported that:

> "KPMG LLP (KPMG) has admitted to criminal wrongdoing and agreed to pay $456 million in fines, restitution, and penalties as part of an agreement to defer prosecution of the firm. In addition to the agreement, nine individuals-including six former KPMG partners and the former deputy chairman of the firm-are being criminally prosecuted in relation to the multi-billion dollar criminal tax fraud conspiracy. As alleged in a series of charging documents unsealed today, the fraud relates to the design, marketing, and implementation of fraudulent tax shelters."[1]

After that settlement with KPMG a subsequent indictment was issued against specific individuals and alleged:

> "that from 1996 to early 2004 the 19 defendants, KPMG, and others conspired to defraud the IRS by designing, marketing and implementing illegal tax shelters, and focusing on four shelters known as FLIP, OPIS, BLIPS and SOS. It is charged that this illegal course of conduct was approved and perpetrated at the highest levels of KPMG's tax management and involved numerous KPMG partners and other personnel.
>
> "The development and promotion of abusive tax shelters had a corrupting effect on the legal and accounting professions," said IRS Commissioner Mark

[1] http://www.usdoj.gov/opa/pr/2005/August/.

Accounting Ethics, Second Edition. Ronald Duska, Brenda Shay Duska, and Julie Ragatz.
© 2011 John Wiley & Sons, Ltd. Published 2011 by John Wiley & Sons, Ltd.

Everson. "Tax professionals should help people pay what they owe – not more, not less."

According to the charges, the alleged conspirators designed, marketed and implemented the shelters so that wealthy individuals who had large incomes or a large capital gain could eliminate all taxes on that income or gain by simply paying to KPMG all-in costs and fees of from 5–7% of the income or gain they wished to shelter. The shelters were marketed only to individuals who needed a minimum of $10 million or $20 million in losses, and according to the charges, the defendants and their co-conspirators filed and caused to be filed false and fraudulent tax returns that incorporated the phony tax losses. In addition, the defendants and their co-conspirators took specific steps to conceal the very existence of the shelters from the IRS and from IRS scrutiny by – among other things – failing to register the shelters with the IRS as required, and by fraudulently concealing the shelter losses and income on tax returns, according to the indictment.

The indictment also alleges that from 2002–2003, in response to the IRS examination of KPMG for failure to register tax shelters and related matters, certain of the defendants continued the fraud on the IRS by concealing KPMG's involvement and role in certain shelters; intentionally failing to produce documents that were called for by summonses issued by the IRS; and providing false and evasive testimony to the IRS regarding the nature and scope of KPMG's involvement with certain shelters. In addition, in connection with the investigation into tax shelters being conducted during the pendency of the IRS examination by a Senate Subcommittee, certain defendants provided false, misleading and incomplete information and testimony at a hearing and a false response regarding documents that were called for in a subpoena issued by the Senate, relating to the personal use of tax shelters by KPMG and certain KPMG partners.

'It is hard to imagine anything that can serve to undermine our voluntary system of taxation more than the crimes charged today, where so many professionals banded together with wealthy individuals to perpetrate this massive fraud on the tax system. This was an orchestrated case of deliberate tax evasion, and not legitimate tax planning. Professionals, including lawyers, accountants, bankers, so-called investment advisors and their firms – as well as taxpayers – should be on notice that the government will pursue even the most complicated tax-fraud schemes designed to help the wealthy evade paying their fair share.'[2]

An article in *Business Week* explains how the BLIPS – "Bond Linked Issue Premium Structures" – which were sold to at least 186 wealthy individuals and generated at least $5 billion in tax losses, worked.

[2]http://www.usdoj.gov/opa/pr/2005/October/05_tax_547.html.

"A client would borrow from an offshore bank to buy foreign currency from the same bank. Roughly two months later the client would sell the currency back to the lender, creating what the government contends was a phony tax loss that the client could then deduct from his capital gains and income from other investments."[3]

The AICPA's *Statements on Standards for Tax Services (SSTS)* along with the *Treasury Department Circular 230, Internal Revenue Code Section 6694,* and the PCAOB *Release No. 2008-003,* as well as the various Internal Revenue Code Sections (i.e. 6700, 7408, etc.) dealing with abusive tax shelters, all delineate enforceable standards by which the tax preparer must abide. The *Statements on Standards for Tax Services* were revised in November 2009, with an effective date of January 1, 2010. The revised SSTS are an attempt to clarify certain inconsistencies or anomalies that were contained in the original SSTS. This chapter will deal with the *Statements on Standards for Tax Services (SSTS)* in detail. The other standards are mentioned because the tax accountant must be aware and must comply with all standards. Since the published standards are revised and updated on a regular basis, it is the tax accountant's responsibility to remain current with these standards.

The tax accountant has several responsibilities to the public, through the government. First, the tax accountant has an obligation not to lie or be party to a lie on a tax return. Second, "the signature on a tax return is a declaration under penalties of perjury that to the best of the preparer's knowledge, the return and accompanying schedules and statements are "true, correct, and complete".[4] Consequently, there is a responsibility to both the client and the public to be forthright and not to be complicitous in a client's attempt to deceive even if that means breaking off a relationship with the client.

Why that's the case is clearly laid out in the AICPA's Statement on Standards for Tax Services[5] No.1, numbers 10 and 11.

10. Our self-assessment tax system can only function effectively if taxpayers report their income on a tax return that is true, correct and complete. A tax return is prepared based on a taxpayer's representation of facts, and the taxpayer has the final responsibility for positions taken on the return ...
11. In addition to a duty to the taxpayer, a member has a duty to the tax system. However it is well-established that the taxpayer has no obligation to pay more

[3] Inside the KPMG Mess, *Business Week,* September 1, 2005.
[4] Evelyn C. Hume, Ernest R. Larkins, and Govind Iyer "On Compliance with Ethical Standards in Tax Return Preparation," *Journal of Business Ethics,* Vol. 18 (1999), pp. 229–238, (p. 237).
[5] *Statements on Standards for Tax Services.* November 2009. American Institute of Certified Public Accountants, New York. Sections 1-10, 1-11.

taxes than are legally owed, and a member has a duty to the taxpayer to assist in achieving that result …

Number 11 clearly spells out the fact that tax accountants have a duty not only to their clients but also to the system. The client's duty is to pay the taxes they legally owe, no more, no less. The taxpayer has the final responsibility for the representation of the facts and for the positions taken on the return, but the accountant has the responsibility to point out to the client what is legally owed and not owed, and the responsibility not to go along with a client who wants to take advantage of the tax system.

These responsibilities flow from the nature of the tax system. The tax system, which depends on self-assessment to function effectively, needs everyone to give honest assessments and pay their fair share of taxes.

Some might object that such a position is naïve, since certain taxes are unfair. Didn't the founding fathers of the United States refuse to pay taxes, which they deemed unfair, because they were taxes established without representation in an undemocratic fashion? One could adopt a position such as that to rationalize cheating the government on taxes. However, in spite of the fact that the founding fathers made such an argument, in a democratic society such a move is filled with peril. Fairness is a notoriously ambiguous concept and in applying it to the evaluation of tax burdens the most prudent course is probably that of adhering to what the society, following its due process of passing determining legislation, decides is fair. The founding fathers of the United States did not rail against taxes, the argument was against taxation without representation. If everyone decided not to pay what is owed there would be chaos in the government. Hence, there should be general agreement to comply with current tax laws, and if one thinks such laws are unfair, to work through the proper procedures to change them.

Not only is working within the system called for, we would claim that the tax accountant should be ruled by the spirit of the law and not just the letter of the law. Still we recognize that this goes against what may be the prevailing business culture to get away with paying as little tax as possible. Consider the following:

> "In 1993, Goldman Sachs & Co. invented a security that offered Enron Corp. and other companies an irresistible combination.
>
> It was designed in such a way that it could be called debt or equity, as needed. For the tax man, it resembled a loan, so that interest payments could be deducted from taxable income. For shareholders and rating agencies that would look askance at overleveraged companies, it resembled equity …

With corporate bookkeeping now under scrutiny, the story of this flexible financial instrument shows how such accounting gimmickry gained acceptance."[6]

We want to argue that such an approach goes against the general tenor of the code of ethics of the accounting practice, and goes against the spirit of the laws that are behind the tax structure of the market economy. The tax laws were developed with certain purposes in mind, certain objectives that were deemed desirable by duly elected officials. Now in any law there are loopholes that can be exploited to take advantage of the loopholes. But applying the Kantian universalizability principle we see that if everyone exploited the loopholes the system would not accomplish what duly elected officials thought we needed to accomplish, and indeed might collapse. It is only because most people abide by the spirit of the law and don't exploit the loopholes that the laws continue to function. Those who exploit the loopholes are *free riders* who take advantage of others. That is patently unfair.

Those would seem to be the general ethical considerations that underlie the standards put forward by the Tax Executive Committee of the AICPA in the *Statements on Standards for Tax Services*. It is interesting to note the opening paragraph of the work: "Standards are the foundation of a profession. The AICPA aids its members in fulfilling their ethical responsibilities by instituting and maintaining standards against which their professional performance can be measured."[7] The best indication of the ethical standards that should be met by a tax accountant is found in these standards.

There are seven standards presented in the Statements on Standards for Tax Services. As found in the explanation sections, the following summarize the central themes of each standard:

lower std than services   *substantial authority)*

(1) A member should not recommend a tax return position unless it has a realistic possibility of being sustained on its merits.
(2) A member should make a reasonable effort to obtain from the taxpayer the information necessary to answer all questions on tax returns.
(3) A member may rely on information furnished by the taxpayer or third parties without verification. However a member should not ignore the implications of information furnished and should make reasonable inquiries if the information appears to be incorrect, incomplete or inconsistent either on its face or on the basis of other facts known to a

Cannot turn a blind eye to the obvious

[6] John D. McKinnon and Greg Hitt, "How the Treasury Department Lost a Battle Against a Dubious Security", *The Wall Street Journal*, February 4, 2002.
[7] *Statements on Standards for Tax Services*. November 2009. American Institute of Certified Public Accountants, New York. Preface-1.

member. Further, a member should refer to the taxpayer's returns for one or more prior years whenever feasible.

(4)   Unless prohibited by statute or by rule, a member may use the taxpayer's estimates in the preparation of a tax return if it is not practical to obtain exact data and the member determines that the estimates are reasonable based on the facts and circumstances known to the member.

(5)   A member may recommend a tax return position or prepare or sign a return that departs from the treatment of an item as concluded in an administrative proceeding or court decision with respect to a prior return of a taxpayer. However, the member should consider whether the standards in SSTS No. 1 are met.

(6)   A member should inform the taxpayer promptly upon becoming aware of an error in a previously filed return or upon becoming aware of a taxpayer's failure to file a required return. A member should recommend corrective measures to be taken.

(7)   A member should use professional judgment to ensure that tax advice provided to a taxpayer reflects competency and appropriately serves the taxpayer's needs.[8]

Let's look at a scenario:

"One of your most important clients has strongly suggested that you change the treatment of an item on his income tax return. You believe that the treatment of the item suggested by the client will materially understate the client's correct tax liability. Further, there is no reasonable basis for the change. You have basically two choices: (1) You could refuse to change the item. (2) You could agree to change the item as suggested by the client. Would you agree to change the item?"[9]

According to the standards, it would be unethical to capitulate to the client's request to materially understate the client's correct tax liability, since in signing a return you are attesting that the return is true, correct, and complete. To sign it would be to engage in lying and that is a clear-cut ethical violation.

But there is an area of tax accounting that is not so clear-cut and is problematic. It is the area where there is exploitation of the tax system. Standard 1 states that "A tax accountant should not recommend a position that 'exploits'

---

[8] *Statements on Standards for Tax Practice.* November 2009. American Institute of Certified Public Accountants, New York. Sections 1-5a, 2-2, 3-2, 4-2, 5-4, 6-4, 7-2.
[9] Evelyn C. Hume, Ernest R. Larkins, and Govind Iyer "On Compliance with Ethical Standards in Tax Return Preparation," *Journal of Business Ethics*, Vol. 18 (1999), pp. 229–238, (p. 237).

the IRS audit selection process." But what exactly counts as exploiting? What is the ethics of engaging in tax dodge schemes, and are there other areas where the accountant can help the client exploit the tax system and avoid paying his or her fair share of the tax burden?

Consider the following scenarios:

(1) You assured your client that a particular expenditure was deductible only to find out later that it was not. However, it is unlikely the item will be detected by the IRS. Do you tell your client about your mistake and change the form, or do you let it stand as it is?

(2) You discover that the client's previous year's return, which someone else prepared, listed a deduction $3000 in excess of the actual expenditure. The mistake was not intentional and the IRS will probably not detect the error. Should you correct the error, costing your client additional liability? What if you prepared the return the previous year so that the mistake was yours?

(3) You are preparing a tax return for a very wealthy client, who can provide you with excellent referrals. You have reason to think the client is presenting information that will reduce his tax liability inappropriately. Should you inquire about the veracity of this information or just prepare the tax form with the information as given?[10]

(4) The accounting firm you work for sells tax savings strategies to clients, demanding a 30% contingency fee of the tax savings plus out of pocket expenses. The company will defend its "strategy" in an IRS audit, but not in court, and refund a piece of the fee if back taxes come due.[11] Is what your company doing acceptable? What obligation do you have?

What do you do in these cases? In making a decision about the appropriateness of these activities, particularly the fourth case, it is important to keep in mind the SSTS statement, "Our self-assessment tax system can only function effectively if taxpayers report their income on a tax return that is true, correct and complete." This position is eloquently stated in Justice Burger's opinion in the landmark Arthur Young case.[12]

---

[10] These three are adapted from Evelyn C. Hume, Ernest R. Larkins, and Govind Iyer "On Compliance with Ethical Standards in Tax Return Preparation," *Journal of Business Ethics*, Vol. 18 (1999), pp. 229–238.

[11] Abraham Briloff, "The Is and the Ought" *Accounting Today*, September 26, 1999, p. 6,

[12] *United States vs. Arthur Young and Co., et al*, 104 S. Circular 465 US 805, 11984.

"Our complex and comprehensive system of federal taxation, relying as it does upon self-assessment and reporting, demands that all taxpayers be forthright in the disclosure of relevant information to the taxing authorities. Without such disclosure, and the concomitant power of the government to compel disclosure, our national tax burden would not be fairly and equitably distributed."

A system that depends on self-assessment and reporting puts one in mind of the type of operation which makes golf such an honorable game. The rules of golf exist, and if something happens, for example if a ball moves upon address, it is incumbent on the golfer to penalize herself one stroke. Taxation is similar. It depends largely on self-assessment and reporting. In that context the fair thing for everyone to do is to police themselves. Our society is based on a large honor system and will work best when most people abide by that honor system. As we noted, those who take advantage of the system are free riders.

There are those who would like to insist that Justice Burger rightly indicates that the success of the scheme rests, not so much on honor as on the concomitant power of the government to compel disclosure. But this does not mean that because the government does not apprehend people it is OK to try to ignore elementary fairness in meeting one's tax burden. That is why as SSTS No. 1, 7.a. states, "A tax accountant should not recommend a position that 'exploits' the audit selection process of a taxing authority" and SSTS No.1, 7.b. adds, "or serves as a mere 'arguing' position." Even though some insist that from Justice Burger's perspective, such schemes as the last may be within the letter of the law, they are certainly not within the spirit of the law, which necessarily requires our national tax burden be fairly and equitably distributed.

What we may have here is a continuum between clearly unethical and illegal practices, practices that may be legal but are unethical, and practices which are ethically acceptable as well as legal.

If one takes the characterization of these moves by accounting firms as "hustling," "improper" and "schemes," or "abusive", it is clear that at least from some perspectives the accounting firms are doing something ethically questionable if not downright unethical.

Of course defenders of such practices will argue that these activities are necessary given the competition of the marketplace. Some will argue, as did Oliver Wendell Holmes, that we should not pay one iota more than the law allows. Still, every law, being composed by human beings, will probably have a loophole that can be exploited. We would argue that there is something contrary to fairness and the public welfare in attempting to circumvent the obvious purpose of a specific law to give one's client an edge in getting out of paying one's fair share of the taxes.

Indeed it can be objected that many taxes are not ethically proper. Nevertheless, many are and their spirit should be met in the interest of fair play. For those that can be shown to be unfair, the answer is not to circumvent the law, but to change it. Taxation, as much as one does not like it, is the human invention that centralizes the sharing of the expense of performing government functions in a fair and equitable manner. To view accounting as a profession best employed in dodging those expenses is a distortion of the role of the accountant.

In 1999 David A. Lifson, former chair of the Tax Executive Committee of the American Institute of Certified Public Accountants (AICPA), made the following statement in testifying to congress.[13] It indicates the AICPA view of the ethics of tax shelters.

> "We (the AICPA) strongly oppose the undermining of our tax system by convoluted and confusing tax sophistry. Clearly, *there are abuses* and they must be dealt with effectively. However, we have a complex tax system and believe that taxpayers should be entitled to structure transactions to *take advantage of intended incentives* and to pay no more tax than is required by the law. Drawing this delicate balance is at the heart of the issue we are addressing today."

Clearly this is a call to determine the "spirit of the law", by referring to the "intended incentives" that the legislature has provided. But to abuse the law by seeking out loopholes, eventually undermines the essential system of taxation.

It is imperative to strike a balance in distinguishing between those individual accountants or accounting firms taking advantage of intended incentives and those abusing loopholes to take advantage of the system itself. Such an operation may be legal, but it is hardly ethical. It may strictly comply with the law, but for an organization like the government to run efficiently, more than minimal compliance is required.

Let's call this the Lifson Principle, and see what implications it has for accountants and their clients. "Taxpayers should be entitled to structure transactions to *take advantage of intended incentives* and to pay no more tax than is required by the law." The presence of the word "should" and the word "entitled" in the principle clearly make it an ethical principle. According to the principle, taxpayers have the ethical right to take advantage of *intended* incentives, and one could add that their accountants or accounting firms would be remiss in their responsibility to their clients if they did not take full advantage of the intended incentives. But by implication, Lifson is suggesting that there is something ethically problematic about taking account of *unintended* incentives, and this is precisely the kind of operation that Burger and Briloff are objecting to on the part of individual accountants and accounting firms.

As Lifson says, "We strongly oppose the undermining of our tax system by convoluted and confusing tax sophistry. Clearly, *there are abuses* and they must be dealt with effectively." The tax system can be and is abused by accountants and accounting firms using tax avoidance schemes.

Implicit in all of this is a recognition of the responsibility of the accountant and firms to uphold the soundness of our tax system – to draw the delicate balance between intended tax advantages and loopholes which undermine the system.

But we have a cultural problem. Will such an interpretation of the responsibility of tax preparers fly? If you hire a tax accountant, what sort do you want, one who finds the loopholes or one who having found them tries to convince you it would be ethically unwarranted to take advantage of them. No one likes taxes, yet if no one pays taxes government cannot operate.

> "The Treasury Department, the ABA and others say shelters cause harm far beyond the initial loss of revenue. When one firm uses a shelter successfully, its competitors will feel pressure to try it, too, or be left at a disadvantage.
>
> In addition, individual taxpayers, who have to pay more as others succeed in paying less, become contemptuous of the tax system and more inclined to try tax avoidance maneuvers of their own. 'If unabated, this will have long-term consequences to our voluntary tax system far more important than the revenue losses we currently are experiencing in the corporate tax base.'"[14]

Obviously what is needed in the popular culture is a sea change in attitude, where the ethical responsibility to support the legitimate purposes of government overrides the individual interest of paying as little support as possible, even less than one's "fair share". Accountants and accounting firms need to recognize their responsibility to the society at large, even where this might be at the expense of their client. But of course this will probably damage them in the competitive race for clients. Who will pay for an accountant who up front indicates they may not take all the deductions "you can get away with?"

To think this would be voluntarily practiced is naïve in the extreme. If it were we would need no sanctions by the IRS to compel compliance with the

[14] Albert B. Crenshaw, "When Shelters Aren't Aboveboard: IRS, Hill Step up Efforts as *Improper Deals to Help Firms Cut Taxes Rise*," *The Washington Post*, November 23, 1999, p. E01.

tax code, not to mention the spirit of the tax code. Treasury Department Circular 230 would never need to be established. Nevertheless, absent the threat of the IRS one could argue that the accountant has an ethical obligation to temper his aggressive tax scheming on behalf of his client for the sake of the general welfare.

But why would a client, who is solely self-interested, hire an accountant or firm who he knew would not save him every penny possible? Such a client would not. I want my tax accountant to save me as much money as possible. Nevertheless, there are people who put a constraint on that imperative – as long as it is no more nor less than my fair share. If we assume the client shares the same ethical values as the accountant or the firm there will be a happy marriage of honorable people not taking unfair advantage.

Perhaps the way to convince skeptics that such a constraint is necessary is to imagine what would happen if waste disposal firms operated in the same solely self-interested way? I will dispose of your industrial waste in the cheapest way possible, even if it means harming the environment, as long as it is within the letter, but not the spirit, of the law. The quest for profit forces all sorts of ethical shortcuts, but if such harming is not acceptable for waste disposal firms, why is it acceptable for accounting firms to harm people by taking their money?

Clearly accountants and their companies need to insist, because of their professionalism, on following the ethical path. In an interesting article "The Tax Adviser", Yetmar, Cooper, and Frank, address two questions. What helps Tax Adviser's be ethical and what challenges their ethics?

The leading helps are personal moral values and standards plus a culture in the firm which does not encourage compromising ethical values to achieve organizational goals- – a strong management philosophy that emphasizes ethical conduct and clear communication that such ethical behavior is expected. In the situations described above even in the face of a loss of a client, the accountant would do what's right. The threat of losing one's license for unethical conduct is a factor, but it is not ranked as the primary factor.

As to what challenges ethical conduct, the following were mentioned high on the list: the complexity and constantly changing nature of the tax laws; scarcity of time to practice due diligence; keeping current with increasingly complex tax laws; pressure from clients to reduce their tax liability; and client's lack of understanding regarding accountant's professional responsibilities and potential penalties for both the tax practitioner and the taxpayer. So complex tax laws and unethical demands of clients are some of the biggest potential challenges to ethical behavior on the part of tax accountants.

The authors conclude their study by stating the following:

First, business can encourage ethical behavior by refraining from pressuring managers and employees to compromise their personal values. Second, businesses should ensure that managers are equipped not only to deal with their own ethical dilemmas, but also those encountered by their subordinates. Professional associations have an opportunity to help prepare their members holding managerial positions in business to meet these responsibilities.[15]

Defenders of such practices as hustling tax shelters will argue that these activities are necessary given the competition of the marketplace. But as Telberg suggests, if accountants are willing to go along with such pressures, "then the profession's entire system and philosophy of independence will need rethinking."[16]

But why if the government makes the tax laws can't they plug the loopholes? Why should it be the responsibility of the accountants and accounting firms? What is their role to be in this tax crisis? The suggestion would be to take the standards seriously and review the policy of profit by any means legally possible. A great deal would be accomplished if there were voluntary compliance with the spirit of the law by the larger accounting firms. Nevertheless there will be a great deal of pressure exerted on accountants who consider themselves professionals and take their obligations to the public seriously to capitulate to the demands of their companies. This raises the age-old problem for a professional who is an employee. Does one have a responsibility to the profession before the responsibility to the company for which one works? As small entrepreneurial practices are absorbed by larger firms, as happens not only in accounting, but in medicine, law, real estate, financial services, and elsewhere, this becomes more and more a crucial problem where the individual's ethics are compromised by the company's policies.

We will conclude this chapter by noting other standards that appear in the SSTS.

Standard Statement No. 1. Tax return positions

Statement 1, 5.a. States that "A member should not recommend a tax return position or prepare or sign a tax return taking a position unless the member has a good-faith belief that the position has at least a realistic possibility of being sustained administratively or judicially on its merits if challenged." [17]

---

[15] Scott Yertmar, Robert Cooper, and Garry Frank, "Practice and Procedures: Ethical Helps and Challenges", *The Tax Adviser*, February 1999, p. 114.

[16] Rick Telberg, Editorial, *Accounting Today*, September 26, 1999.

[17] *Statements on Standards for Tax Services*. November 2009. American Institute of Certified Public Accountants, New York. Section 1-5a.

The preparer is advised to avoid recommending or signing a return which reflects a positon that the preparer knows, "exploits the audit selection process of a taxing authority, or … serves as a mere arguing position advanced solely to obtain leverage in a negotiation with a taxing authority."[18] However, the preparer can advise a position that has a realistic possibility of being in conformity with existing law. But the realistic possibility is less stringent than the "substantial authority standard" which is a position defended by recognized authorities. It is also less stringent than the "more likely than not" standard, but more stringent than the "reasonable basis" standard in the Internal Revenue Code.

What is a reasonable basis? According to the IRC section 1.6662-3(b) (3) "The reasonable basis standard is not satisfied by a return position that is merely arguable or that is merely a colorable claim. If a return position is reasonably based on one or more of the authorities set forth in Sec. 1.6662-4 (d) (3) iii, the return position will generally satisfy the substantial authority standard. Authorities include but are not limited to applicable provisions of the IRC and other statutory provisions, regulations, proposed or final, rulings, treasury department explanations, court cases, congressional intent, general explanations prepared by the joint committee on taxations, private letter rulings, technical advice memoranda, general counsel memoranda, cases, and revenue rulings. However, conclusions reached in treatises, legal periodicals, legal opinions, or opinions rendered by tax professionals are not authority.

The realistic possibility standard, as set out by the AICPA in Statement 1, 5a, lies between the reasonable basis and substantial authority standards. The long and the short of this means that the professional tax accountant ought to look at the intention of the laws and take only those positions that can be upheld by some authority. It will not do to take a position to save substantial money for the client if there is no reasonable basis on which to base the return, with the anticipation that if detected and fined the penalties will be minimal, and the risk of penalty is well worth the frivolous claim.

Standard Statement No. 2. Answers to questions on returns

This statement is nonproblematic and prescribes the following: "A member should make a reasonable effort to obtain from the taxpayer the information

---

[18] *Statements on Standards for Tax Services.* November 2009. American Institute of Certified Public Accountants, New York. Section 1-7a-b.

necessary to provide appropriate answers to all questions on a tax return before signing as preparer."

Standard Statement No. 3. Certain procedural aspects of preparing returns

A preparer can rely on the good faith of the client to provide accurate information in preparing a tax return, but "should not ignore the implications of information furnished and should make reasonable inquiries if the information appears to be incorrect, incomplete or inconsistent." Here the obligation to the tax system is clear. The preparer will sign the statement attesting that the information contained therein is true, correct, and complete to the best of the preparer's knowledge. Consequently, if the preparer concludes because of an inconsistency that the information can't be correct or complete, the preparer has an obligation not to sign the return.

Standard Statement No.4. Use of estimates

This is another nonproblematic standard. A preparer may use the taxpayer's estimates if it is not practical to obtain the exact data and if the preparer determines the estimates are reasonable, based on the preparer's knowledge.

Standard Statement No.5. Departure from a previous position

Here again is a rather technical standard. As provided in SSTS no. 1, *Tax Return Positions,* "a member may recommend a tax return position or prepare or sign a tax return that departs from the treatment of an item as concluded in an administrative proceeding or court decision with respect to a prior return of the taxpayer."

Standard Statement No. 6. Knowledge of error

What needs to be done when a preparer becomes aware of an error in a taxpayer's previously filed tax return? The member should "inform the taxpayer promptly" and "recommend the corrective measures to be taken." If in preparing the current year's return the preparer discovers that the taxpayer has not taken appropriate action to correct an error from a prior year, the preparer needs to decide whether to continue the relationship with the taxpayer. This withdrawal should occur if the taxpayer is unwilling to correct the error, if the error has a significant effect on the return.

Standard Statement No. 7. Form and content of advice to taxpayers

This is a new statement added in 2009 which requires "a member … to use professional judgment to insure that tax advice … reflects competence and appropriately serves the taxpayer's needs." The communication of tax advice should also "comply with relevant taxing authorities standards."[19] This recalls the criteria of professionalism we saw in Chapter 4 as well as the notion that the tax accountant has a responsibility not only to the client but also to the taxing authority.

In the light of the standards it becomes fairly clear what our obligations are in the case of the three scenarios that we looked at earlier.

- You assured your client that a particular expenditure was deductible only to find out later that it was not. However, it is unlikely the item will be detected by the IRS. Do you tell your client about your mistake and change the form, or do you let it stand as it is?

Clearly you need to tell your client of the error and recommend that it be reported to the IRS.

- You discover that the client's previous year's return, which someone else prepared, listed a deduction $3000 in excess of the actual expenditure. The mistake was not intentional and the IRS will probably not detect the error. Should you correct the error, costing your client additional liability? What if you prepared the return the previous year so that the mistake was yours?

This situation is covered in Statement 6. You need to advise the taxpayer of the error. It is the taxpayer's responsibility to decide whether to correct it, but if the taxpayer does not choose to correct it, the accountant needs to reconsider whether to continue the relationship with that client. There are laws of privileged communication that affect this situation.

- You are preparing a tax return for a very wealthy client, who can provide you with excellent referrals. You have reason to think the client is presenting information that will reduce his tax liability inappropriately. Should

---

[19] *Statements on Standards for Tax Services.* November 2009. American Institute of Certified Public Accountants, New York. Section 7-2.

you inquire about the veracity of this information or just prepare the tax form with the information as given?[20]

Clearly, as pointed out in Standard 3, the accountant cannot ignore this. The accountant needs to attest to the veracity of the statements. The accountant should encourage his client to prepare the form accurately or consider terminating the relationship with the taxpayer.

---

[20] These three are adapted from Evelyn C. Hume, Ernest R. Larkins, and Govind Iyer "On Compliance with Ethical Standards in Tax Return Preparation," *Journal of Business Ethics*, Vol. 18 (1999), pp. 229–238.

Chapter Ten

Ethics Applied to the Accounting Firm

In 1997, the Subcommittee on Reports, Accounting, and Managing of the United States Senate Committee on Governmental Affairs (the Metcalf Committee) released a report titled "The Accounting Establishment," in which it expressed deep concern about "improving the professionalism and independence of auditors":

> "The committee is also committed to *fair* [Italics added] competition as a basic principle of the Nation's economic system. The benefits derived from professional self-regulation carry with them a corresponding responsibility of self-restraint from engaging in activities that detract from professional ideals. The subcommittee firmly believes the important function of independently auditing, publicly owned corporations should be and is financially rewarding and personally satisfying in its own right without any need for engaging in activities that *appear* (italics added) to detract from professional responsibilities."[1]

Whether the regulatory scrutiny worked during the 1970s to the 1990s is a matter for dispute. A series of high-profile corporate accounting "frauds that auditors missed at companies including Cendant, Sunbeam and Livent occurred. Public shareholders lost hundreds of millions of dollars in these cases, and confidence in accountants was shaken."[2]

---

[1] As quoted in Abraham Briloff, *The Truth about Corporate Accounting*, Harper and Row, 1980, p. 149.

[2] Gretchen Morgensen, "S.E.C. Seeks Increased Security And New Rules for Accountants," *New York Times*, May 11, 2000. Section C, p. 1, col. 2.

Accounting Ethics, Second Edition. Ronald Duska, Brenda Shay Duska, and Julie Ragatz.
© 2011 John Wiley & Sons, Ltd. Published 2011 by John Wiley & Sons, Ltd.

[In] January [1999], partners and employees at PricewaterhouseCoopers were found by the S.E.C. to have routinely violated rules forbidding their ownership of stock in companies they were auditing. The investigation found 8,064 violations at the firm, which then dismissed five partners. Pricewaterhouse said at the time that it did not believe that the integrity of any audit had been compromised by the violations.[3]

The role Arthur Andersen played in the Enron collapse led *Business Week* to author a special report called "Accounting in Crisis." According to the article:

"As shocking as Enron is, it's only the latest in a dizzying succession of accounting meltdowns, from Waste Management to Cendant. Lynn E. Turner, former chief accountant for the SEC and now a professor at Colorado State University, calculates that in the past half-dozen years investors have lost close to $200 billion in earnings restatements and lost market capitalization following audit failures. And the pace seems to be accelerating. Between 1997 and 2000 the number of restatements doubled, from 116 to 233."[4]

These inappropriate behaviors by accounting firms led to the passage of the Sarbanes–Oxley Act (SOX), which set limitations on what accounting firms are able to do. We will discuss SOX later in this chapter. For now, we ask these questions: What is going on in the accounting establishment today? Is the general tenor of what is happening ethically acceptable?

It is important to ask what brought about the accounting scandals, and whether or not those practices still exist in the profession. Critics of the direction that accounting is taking claim that it has ceased to be a profession and is driven by the profit motive. John C. Bogle, former CEO of the Vanguard Group and former member of the now defunct Independence Standards Board, contends that the accounting profession, rather than remaining an honorable profession where members look out for clients and the public, got involved in the enterprise of business, where its main concern is fidelity not to its various trusts but to the bottom line. Such critics insist that, just as commercialization is infecting professions like medicine, teaching, and law, profit-motivated business interests are interfering with accountants' professional responsibilities and corrupting their behavior. This tension between the demands of professionalism and the demands of business has created an identity crisis in the industry today.

We examine that crisis in this chapter.

[3] Gretchen Morgensen, "S.E.C. Seeks Increased Security And New Rules for Accountants," *New York Times*, May 11, 2000. Section C, p. 1, col. 2.
[4] Nanette Byrnes, Mike Mcnamee, Diane Brady, Louis Lavelle and Christopher Palmeri, "Accounting in Crisis," *Business Week*, January 28, 2002, pp. 44–48.

I Accounting as a Business

An old adage says that there is no such thing as business ethics. A more sophisticated version of the adage claims that business ethics is an oxymoron like military intelligence or jumbo shrimp. Sometimes, these quips are the self-righteous condemnation of business by anti-business academics or artists, who rarely engage in business (or so they think). They maintain that business activity is banal. Their attitude goes as far back as ancient Greek philosophers, who asserted that to engage in business activities is to do something illiberal. For philosophers such as Plato and Aristotle, business was not a worthy pursuit for a free human being. Academic and artistic elitists who assume that viewpoint today have a negative opinion of business and deplore the concern with materialistic goods and conspicuous consumption that business creates.

Sometimes, criticisms of business ethics are delivered by businesspeople simply to rationalize their own unethical business behavior. They fail to see that the majority of business dealings are ethical; if they weren't, business as we know it would cease to function. Criticism also comes from individuals who recognize that there *is* ethical behavior in business but bemoan the lack of it from their competitors.

Our contention – in spite of the seemingly unchecked greed of Enron and similar cases – is that ethics is essential for business to run smoothly. And what holds for business in general holds for accounting specifically.

Consider what it would mean if a businessperson really believed there was no such thing as business ethics. He would think it's okay to be dishonest in his dealings with you, to sell you a faulty product to make his company more money, or to tamper with the books if it helps the bottom line.

Now ask that businessperson this question: If he really thinks acting unethically is all right, why would he tell you that? If someone says, "I cheat all the time," I would be a fool to trust that person. Clever cheats keep silent about their dealings. A person who truly believes that there is no ethics in business is really just unscrupulous – and foolish enough to reveal it. Don't deal with foolish and unscrupulous people.

The claim that there is no such thing as business ethics is indefensible. Furthermore, it is outmoded and has outworn its usefulness, if it ever had any. Good business ethics is generally good business. When good ethics is not good business – situations that occur but rarely – then business interests should capitulate to ethical interests. For example, in a situation where doing the ethical thing will jeopardize profit, a businessperson with integrity will defer the pursuit of profit to do what is right.

If, however, it is nonsense to claim that business ethics is an oxymoron, it is important to ask why such nonsense occurs in the first place. Nonsense or not, this attitude has become part of our cultural fiber and is used to justify (rationalize) a lot of unethical behavior. Recognizing why the attitude has developed may help us to understand the dilemma between professionalism and profit that besets the accounting industry today. The attitude arises, we believe, from a mistaken, but widely held, consensus that the purpose, nature, and responsibility of business are to maximize profit or shareholder value.

To the extent that an accounting firm is a business, it falls under the profit-maximizing rubric. But when an accounting firm sees itself *primarily* as a business, making a profit overrides its main function of attesting to the truth and correctness of financial statements. The movement in accounting from auditing and attesting functions to management consulting changed it from a profession dedicated to public services to a business committed to maximizing partner or shareholder wealth. How did this ideal develop, and is it defensible?

II The Social Responsibility of Business

The contemporary idea of business as a social institution developed from the perception that its fundamental concern is to make a profit. Consider this statement by Milton Friedman:

> The primary and only responsibility of business is to use its resources and engage in activities designed to increase its profits so long as it stays within the rules of the game, which is to say, engages in open and free competition without deception and fraud."[5]

This principle refocused business's primary purpose from generating products and services (for example, attest and audit in accounting) to accumulating money. In doing so, promoters apparently forgot Friedman's constraints about staying within the rules of the game and avoiding deception and fraud. The generation of products and services was displaced as business's chief purpose and became merely instrumental to making a profit. This puts the cart before the horse. Let's see how.

This concept that the primary function of business is profit making has its roots in a reading (we would argue an incomplete reading) of the 18th century classic *The Wealth of Nations* by Adam Smith. (Also see Chapter 3 for more material on Adam Smith.) Smith introduced the model of the rational maximizer – a person concerned with increasing his or her own utility – and

[5] Milton Friedman, "The Social Responsibility of Business is to Increase Its Profits", *The New York Times Magazine*, September 13, 1970.

sees humans as motivated by self-interest. He notes, "It is not from the benevolence of the butcher, the brewer, or the baker, that we expect our dinner,
but from their regard to their own interest."[6]

Smith's genius was maintaining that it is the pursuit of self-interest that
makes commerce and society flourish by setting up free markets. He gave
currency to the belief that the entire society will be better off if each businessperson pursues his or her own interest – that is, if we leave the market forces
alone, people's pursuit of their individual interests will make the entire society
flourish. In arguing this, he refers to the "invisible hand," which describes the
self-regulating nature of the economy:

> "As every individual, therefore, endeavors as much as he can both to employ his
> capital in the support of domestic industry, and so to direct that industry that
> its produce may be of the greatest value, every individual necessarily labors to
> render the annual revenue of the society as great as he can. He generally, in-
> deed, neither intends to promote the public interest, nor knows how much he
> is promoting it, and by directing that industry in such a manner as its produce
> may be of the greatest value, he intends only his own gain, and he is in this, as
> in many other cases, led by an *invisible hand* to promote an end which was no
> part of his intention. Nor is it always the worse for society that it was no part
> of it. By pursuing his own interest he frequently promotes that of the society
> more effectually than when he really intends to promote it. I have never known
> much good done by those who affected to trade for the public good. It is an
> affectation, indeed, not very common among merchants, and very few words
> need be employed in dissuading them from it."[7]

Milton Friedman and other contemporary followers of Smith claim that
the success of our economic system can be attributed to this philosophy. When
we let business worry about nothing but profit, competition is created, more
goods are produced, and the entire society enjoys a higher standard of living.
The fact that the economic system of capitalism has led to the production of
more goods and services than any other economic system in the history of
mankind – and the highest material standard of living for more people – is
the evidence for the invisible hand argument.

The Utilitarian structure of the argument is simple enough to see. (See
Chapter 3 for a discussion of utilitarianism.) The practice of self-interested
pursuits is justified because of the good that will accrue to society in adopting
a profit-oriented system. In short, the greatest good for the greatest number
will be served if the market, driven by self-interest, is allowed to operate. Look

---

[6,7] Adam Smith, *The Wealth of Nations*, ed. Edwin Canan, New York, Random House, 1937.

out for your own concerns and society, as a whole, will benefit. That is probably true, most of the time.

If, however, we forget that the goal of pursuing our own interests is to make the society better off, a problem arises. Societal benefit is the end that justifies the pursuit of profit. The pursuit of profit cannot stand as an end in itself. The unconstrained and exclusive pursuit of self-interest can hurt others. Thus, it is not always true that self-interested pursuits make the society better off. When these activities are at others' expense, what is the proper thing to do? Pursue profits, or not hurt others? If societal benefit justifies self-interest, what happens when there is no benefit? At those times, the self-interested pursuit must be constrained. According to Smith, the pursuit of self-interest is justified only so long as it does not violate the laws of justice:

> "Every man is left perfectly free to pursue his own interest, his own way, and to bring both his industry and capital into competition with those of any other man, or order of men, as long as he does not violate the laws of justice."[8]

Because business was constructed by society, we must assume that it was constructed to benefit society – no society or group would create a social institution to harm itself. Rather, institutions are created and approved to the extent that they promote some good for the society or group. The purpose of any societally constructed system or institution, therefore, has to be an end that is compatible with some social good, which may or may not be compatible with an individual's interest. For example, our society does not sanction the manufacture and distribution of heroin or the production of pornographic films that exploit children, because society does not regard these activities as having any redeeming social value.

It follows, then, that society instituted (or should have instituted) business to help itself (society) develop and survive. Business, including its practices and rules, was created to benefit society. If the business is harmful to society, society should modify it or close it down. Hence, the assertion is made, from Adam Smith on down, that a competitive, profit-motivated free-enterprise system is an effective *means* to bring about a laudable goal – benefits to society.

Our somewhat regulated capitalist economic system is permitted because it is productive. Although it is not the only way to produce goods and services, it is the most efficient. This capitalist system centers on rules governing the distribution of profits. Profits are utilized to motivate or incentivize the entrepreneur. But profits are not the be all and end all. They are merely the

---

[8] Adam Smith, *The Wealth of Nations*, ed. Edwin Canan, New York, Random House, 1937.

means to achieve the purpose of business, and as the means, they should not usurp the ultimate goal of business.

The view that business's primary responsibility is to maximize profits confuses the self-interested motive and incentive for doing business – profit making – with the purpose of business – the generation of goods and services. Turning the means – self-interested motivation – into the purpose opens a Pandora's box. The legitimization of a self-interested means unleashes what theologians call "greed." The rational maximizer can become a greedy, grasping, acquisitive, profit-motivated, bottom-line-oriented entrepreneur who feels no responsibility to the public welfare. The benefits of utilizing the profit motive are obvious; so are the undesirable externalities.

There is a counter argument to Friedman's stance. If the purpose of business is to provide goods and services and the motive is to make a profit, management's responsibility is not simply to pursue profits, but to pursue them as regulated by the demands of the public interest. Although determining the extent of all those demands is beyond the scope of this discussion, it is clear that legislation requiring audits of publicly held corporations has the public purpose of ensuring that financial statements are accurate and useful to those who need them. Thus, auditing firms are incentivized by making money, but their purpose is to serve the public. Public accountants, fulfilling their public auditing role, have a purpose given to them by the government. They are watchdogs of the financial systems. That is their role and responsibility.

We see, then, that if we confuse the purpose of an activity or practice with the motives for performing it and thereby reduce the former (purpose) to the latter (motive), there are no theoretical grounds for legitimate ethical restraints on business (other than those required by a Kantian formalism). Conversely, if we construe business as an artifact created for the sake of society, specifically for the sake of the production of goods and services, we have grounds for constraints when its operations fail to fulfill its purpose or violate the demands of justice. An ethical business fulfills its purposes and betters society through production of goods and services. An ethical accounting firm fulfills its purpose by being faithful to the needs of society, for which it has been given a specific mandate.

Is this a mere semantic quibble between motives and purposes? We think not. The meaning of the word "purpose" encompasses the "what for" of an activity. Purposes direct us to an activity's goal. Goals, however, are not motivating forces. Motivating forces are the psychological "whys" for doing things. They are not necessarily self-justifying, and they must be constrained by purposes. To confuse a purpose with a motive is like confusing the purpose of a train – to get people from place to place – with what drives the train – the engine. The engine is analogous to the motive, because it moves the train.

From a societal point of view, then, the purpose of business is to produce and distribute goods and/or services, not to benefit the producer. Society certainly needs to incentivize and motivate producers, but that is always for a further purpose. Clarifying the distinction helps us to identify greed not as the ultimate driving force of business, but as a force that does not fulfill – and often frustrates – its purpose.

Motives are not the same as purposes. Furthermore, there can be many motives for the same action. For example, the purpose of giving to charity is to help the poor. But I may not be the least bit interested in helping the poor when I give to charity. I may do so simply to impress my friends. Hence, there is a social (outside) view of the purpose and a personal (inside) view of the motive. If giving to charity not only satisfies my motive but also rewards me, I'll be even more inclined to do so. But whether or not I donate to charity, there is still the need for charity. Similarly, the purpose of business is not to benefit me. It is not to make a profit. If doing business rewards me with a profit, I will be inclined to participate in it, but the purpose of business – why society allows it to exist in its profit-oriented form – is to provide goods and services.

There are all sorts of ways to make money, and wanting to make money is certainly okay as a motive, but the purpose of the practice of accounting is not to make money, any more than it is in the practice of medicine. Medicine's purpose is to minister to the sick. Auditing's purpose is to ensure that financial statements are accurate. Thus, social practices have their own purposes, independent of the motives of the persons engaged in the practices. Therefore, our motives for doing something may or may not accord with the activity's purpose.

A recurrent theme of this book is that it is important, from an ethical standpoint, to be clear about something's purpose. Knowing its purpose gives us a standard by which to judge it. Just as we judge a knife by how well it fulfills its purpose – to cut – we can judge a business by how well it fulfills its purpose. If its purpose is to make a profit, then a business that keeps generating healthy profits is a good business, no matter how it helps or hurts people. But if the purpose of business is to provide goods and services, and it is for that purpose that society allows businesses to exist, then we cannot judge a business simply on how much profit it generates. We must consider how good its products or services are. A good business is one that provides acceptable goods and services to the benefit of society. Making a profit may be a necessary condition for business to survive, and it is certainly a motive for doing business, but it is not its primary purpose.

III Good Ethics is Good Business

How do we motivate ethical behavior? Current thinking, encouraged by a shared ethical concern, has been to try to conflate the purpose and motives of business. Hence, the maxim, "Good ethics is good business." Consider the following:

> Although behaving ethically should be an end in itself, there also are valid business reasons for doing what's right. If you look closely at examples of unethical business behavior, you discover two things: the company derives only short-term advantages from its actions, and over the longer term, skimping on quality or service doesn't pay. It's not good business.[9]

Good business is like that of Johnson and Johnson, who:

> "… immediately took its pain reliever, Tylenol, off the market when faced with claims of product tampering. J&J knew the decision would be costly in dollars, but refused to put a price tag on its integrity. Some thought their sales could never recover, but the company ended up reinforcing its strong market leadership."[10]

Let's explore how the maxim that good ethics is good business applies to the accounting profession.

To begin, good ethics affects the good name of the company and builds trust. It is obvious that to cut corners for short-term gain will only erode the company's reputation. An accounting firm that cannot be trusted is useless, because people depend on the firm and individual accountants to provide them with accurate pictures of organizations' financial status.

Next, a firm that treats its clients or customers well and fairly should see a positive effect not only on its sales but also on its employees. Business ethicist Archie Carroll describes what happens to companies motivated only by greed:

> "If Management is actively opposed to what is regarded as ethical, the clear implication is that management knows right from wrong and chooses to do wrong. Thus, it is motivated by greed. Its goals are profitability and organizational success at almost any price. Immoral management does not care about others' claims to be treated fairly or justly."[11]

[9,10] Thomas G. Labrecque, "Good Ethics Is Good Business," *USA Today Magazine*, May 1990, p. 21. Copyright 1990 by Society for the Advancement of Education.
[11] Archie Carroll, "In Search of the Moral Manager," *Business Horizons*, March/April 1987, p. 8.

Employees are aware when a company is greedy, and that greed, that uncaring search for profit, erodes their morale and loyalty as they realize that it is their company's only motivation. If the company puts its customers second, behind profit, where does it put its employees?

Being ethical has another more subtle benefit for managers, as Kenneth Lux points out in an article in *Business Ethics*:

> "From the self-interest doctrine we inherit the picture of the businessman or woman as only greedy. This is exemplified by Dickens' portrayal of Scrooge, which is just one among scores of such portraits. But the real story may be rather different. The book that is the foundation of modern management theory, *The Human Side of Enterprise*, by Douglas McGregor (1960), recognized the virtues of the businessperson, as well as the economic value of those virtues. All contemporary business texts (which are distinguished, ironically, from economic texts) of any influence reflect the same humanistic values that McGregor recognized and advocated."[12]

The benefit, then, is that managers in ethical companies are allowed to let their humanism show. We don't have to act like Scrooge to achieve business success. In fact, our society today is saying that the cynical phrase to justify unethical behavior, "That's just business," is no longer acceptable. When ethical behavior overrides business greed, managers do not have to live in two worlds – one, their humanistic ethical world, and the other, their ruthless business world. Managers do not need to check their ethics at the door when they come to work.

Thus, there is a fourfold motivation for ethical behavior. Ethical behavior leads to (1) long-term profits for the company, (2) personal integrity and satisfaction for the individuals engaged in business, (3) honesty and loyalty from the employees, and (4) confidence and satisfaction from the customer. Corporations should behave ethically, in part because it will have good consequences for the company. Arthur Andersen's collapse because of its role in the Enron debacle attests to the dangers of profit-driven motivation. Ethical behavior in business is an idea whose time has come.

Still, as David Vogel points out, ethics and profit do not always go hand in hand.[13] Sometimes, management will have to choose between what is right and what is lucrative. By and large, however, it is more prudent to be ethical

---

[12] Kenneth Lux, quoted in *Business Ethics*, May/June 1991, p. 30.
[13] David Vogel, "Ethics and Profits Don't Always Go Hand in Hand", Los Angeles Times, December 28, 1988. articles.latimes.com/1988-12-28/local/me-870_1_corporate-ethics.

than not. When the right choice is the nonprofitable one, we would hope that business would make the ethical decision because it has responsibilities over and above making a profit.

IV Ethical Responsibilities of Accounting Firms

What is the ethical responsibility of business in general and of accounting firms in particular?

Businesses, through their owners and managers, enter into relationships with individuals and groups; relationships involve responsibilities. These relationships become the basis of the ethical obligations between the business and its stakeholders.

Certainly, an accounting firm must make some profit or increase the value of the business or partnership, but there are limits on profit making. To be sure, no firm – accounting or otherwise – can stay in existence without attention to the bottom line, but an accounting firm has other responsibilities beyond profit.

Accounting is a service industry that came into existence to benefit its clients and the public. Hence, harming its clients or the public in the name of profit violates its explicit purpose. Accounting firms have specific functions, which society has licensed. The chief function is to provide information about a company's financial situation. Another is to attest to the accuracy of that information. Thus, a good accounting firm should present as clear a picture as possible of an organization's financial condition, and/or attest to the fairness of that picture. Any practice that violates that purpose contradicts the firm's very essence.

V The Accounting Profession in Crisis

The Arthur Andersen/Enron fiasco has made it abundantly clear that it is naïve to think that accounting firms are not manipulated by the profit motive. There are troubles in the profession and among firms. The pressure to maximize profits has placed the contemporary accounting profession in crisis.

But we knew this even before Enron imploded. Abraham J. Briloff, the perennial scold of the accounting profession, in a 1999 article in *Accounting Today*, pointed to the gap between the "is" of the accounting profession and the "ought" of the accounting profession – what accountants do as opposed to what they ought to do.[14] In an editorial on the same page of that publication, Rick Telberg lamented a move by KPMG to merge with Cisco Systems, because it jeopardized the independence of the Peat Marwick branch of the corporation.[15] In *Forbes* magazine, Jane Novack condemns Deloitte and Touche's "hustling" tax strategies.[16]

Defenders of these practices argue that they are necessary, given the competitive marketplace. If, however, accountants comply with such pressures, Telberg says, "the profession's entire system and philosophy of independence will need re-thinking."[17]

We repeat Telberg's pessimistic words, quoted in the beginning of this book:

> "In fact we are probably past the time when independence mattered. CPA firms long ago became more like insurance companies – complete with their focus on assurances and risk-managed audits – than attesters. Auditors are backed by malpractice insurance in the same way that a re-insurer backs an insurance company, so they have become less like judges of financial statements than underwriters weighing probabilities.
>
> Some in the profession have even argued that auditors should function less like ultimate arbiters of fact and financial reality, and be allowed, instead, to function more like investment bankers, and provide only "due diligence." So that CPAs, who once valued fairness and truthfulness in financial reporting, would then promise little more than nods and winks, all beyond the reach of meaningful oversight."[18]

If every auditor or attestor acted as Telberg describes, the audits and attestations would be worthless. There would still be a use for accountants as tax preparers and financial reporters, but the audit function – the heart of the accounting profession – would be rendered virtually useless by misuse. We could, of course, concede that the accountant's function is simply to do what is required for a company to flourish monetarily. But that would be to view profit maximization as the only purpose of business. It would mean the absence of ethics.

Do Telberg's words signal the demise of accounting? Hardly. Telberg fails to take into account that the economic system would still need truthful and ac-

---

[14] Abraham J. Briloff, "Commentary: The 'Is' and the 'Ought,'" *Accounting Today*, September 6, 1999, p. 6.

[15] Rick Telberg, "Editorial Opinion: Truth? Or Consequences," *Accounting Today*, September 6, 1999, p. 6.

[16] Jane Novack, "The Hustling of X-Rated Shelters," *Forbes*, December 14, 1998.

[17,18] Rick Telberg, "Editorial Opinion: Truth? Or Consequences." *Accounting Today*, September 6, 1999, p. 6.

curate audited reports so that financial operations could continue effectively. Thus, even if the delivery of these reports is not profitable and accounting firms eliminate the audit function to maximize their own profits, there will still be a large accounting task. Someone will step into the gap to perform the service. New firms will arise, and the people in them will be subject to the same ethical requirements as today's professional auditor, while the auditor will be just another management consultant with accounting expertise. The names may change, but the function, and hence the ethical responsibilities, will remain.

Whatever form accounting takes, the biggest challenge will be to remain professional. That means, as we have emphasized throughout this book, putting the interest of clients, and especially the public, above considerations of self-interest.

Just before the Enron/Andersen collapse, John Bogle wrote an article that is remarkably prophetic, aptly named "Public Accounting: Profession or Business?" It is so perceptive, it deserves to be liberally quoted. In it, Bogle identifies the main factors pushing accounting away from the dedication to its professional goals into the arena of a profit-maximizing operation.[19] He observes that there are numerous issues that pressure accountants and accounting firms to put profit maximization ahead of professionalism, citing these five as the most important:

- adequacy of GAAP
- earnings management
- accounting for stock options
- overly aggressive tax shelters
- alternative business structures

Let's examine each of the five issues more fully.

Adequacy of GAAP

The first issue deals with generally accepted accounting principles, or GAAP. Accountants must examine the adequacy and hidden assumptions of the accounting principles they are using. These principles have ethical implications with respect to the accountant's obligation to give true and accurate pictures. Bogle asks these questions:

---

[19] John C. Bogle, "Public Accounting: Profession or Business?" The Seymour Jones Distinguished Lecture, Vincent C. Ross Institute of Accounting Research, New York University, October 16, 2000.

"Can the accounting principles that have served the Old Economy so well over so many years properly be applied to the New Economy? … Clearly, many, indeed most, New Economy companies are valued at staggering – even infinite – multiples of any earnings that GAAP could possibly uncover.

So while that seemingly omnipotent master, "the stock market," may be telling the profession that the 1930s-based model of reporting doesn't work any more, please don't write off too hastily the possibility that the *model* may be right and the *market* wrong. And don't forget that no matter what "the market" may say today, its level on future tomorrows well down the road *will* – not *may* – be determined by earnings and dividends. Nonetheless, a re-examination of today's basic accounting principles should be a high priority. And let the chips fall where they may."

There is a general reluctance in the accounting profession to develop principles to predict and internalize externalities and to engage in enterprises such as social audits. The reason for this reluctance is clear. Both of those procedures could have a substantial negative impact on the bottom line, and what company wants an accountant who costs them profits? The Sarbanes–Oxley Act, the proposed shift to International Financial Reporting Standards (IFRS), and the principles-versus-rules debate – coupled with attempts to understand the causes of the financial crisis of 2008–2009 – are forcing these issues to the forefront.

Earnings management

The second issue Bogle identifies, earnings management, is the diplomatic term for the possible tampering of the books. One particularly skeptical accountant was known to tell his students, "You can show anything you want using accounting principles." Whether or not that is correct, it is true that an accountant can manage the picture of the earnings. Hence, Bogle notes that, "we live in a world of managed earnings, where steady earnings growth of at least a 12 percent level if possible, is desired and above all don't fall short of earnings expectations." as follows:

"If all else fails, obscure the real results by merging, taking a big one-time write-off, and relying on pooling-of-interest accounting (although that procedure will soon become unavailable). All of this creative financial engineering apparently serves to inflate stock prices, enrich corporate managers, and to deliver to institutional investors what they want."

But, according to Bogle, "if the stock market is to be the arbiter of value, it will do its job best if it sets its valuations based on accurate corporate financial reporting and a focus on the long-term prospects of the corporations it values."[20]

"... There is a 'numbers game' going on, and *pro forma* operating profits permeate financial statements. *Pro forma* seems to mean, in an Alice-in-Wonderland-world, whatever the Corporation chooses it to mean. But I hope that the accounting profession will get involved before the coin of the realm – earnings statements with integrity – is further debased."[21]

Accounting for stock options

Bogle then examines the issue of accounting for stock options. Quoting Warren Buffet he asks, "if options *are* compensation, why aren't they charged to earnings? And if options *aren't* compensation, what are they?" Bogle thinks the profession ought to be more aggressive in answering that question. The fact that financial statements place of options in a sort-of "no man's land" in which options are not treated as compensation is an issue.

"The question of accounting for stock options will rise to even greater importance as corporations whose stocks have faltered – even plummeted – in the recent market decline re-price their options. I hope that FASB interpretation 44 on re-pricing underwater options will help to deal with this issue."[22]

Overly aggressive tax shelters

The fourth issue that Bogle addresses is one we discussed in the previous chapter – overly aggressive and potentially illegal tax shelters. Bogle states that "... it must be clear that any firm that helps develop such schemes or opines on their purported validity wins favor with the client involved, and runs a heavy risk of compromising its independence."[23] Firms that game the system to develop such tax shelters are not fulfilling their public purpose and hence are acting unethically.

The KPMG scandal reminds us of how right Bogle was. Still, tax abuses go on.

[20-23] John C. Bogle, "Public Accounting: Profession or Business?" The Seymour Jones Distinguished Lecture, Vincent C. Ross Institute of Accounting Research, New York University, October 16, 2000.

Alternative business structures

The fifth issue that Bogle raises is how accounting firms' independence, both now and in the future, will withstand the conflicts of interest generated by newly evolving forms of structure. Bogle notes that the simple partnership model is "being supplanted by alternative business structures." For example a group of smaller attest firms get "consolidated through the sale of their non-audit practice to a third party (in a private or public offering) with the audit practice retained by the partners." There is another "roll up" model where firms are united under a single umbrella through combination and then sale of their non-audit businesses to a third party or the public. Bogle asserts that:

> "when CPA firms – whose integrity and independence are their stock in trade – are in fact principally investment advisory firms offering financial products sponsored by their parents, a whole other set of questions about the meaning of *professional responsibility* come to the fore."[24]

We witnessed the problems that mergers and acquisitions caused for PricewaterhouseCoopers and Lybrand. We also saw how its merger with KPMG and involvement with Cisco Systems jeopardized Peat-Marwick's independence. It remains to be seen how effective the Sarbanes–Oxley Act has been in addressing the independence issue. There is a serious concern about the overwhelming size of corporations that need to be audited and the Big Four accounting firms that must cope with those oversized corporations. Perhaps, rather than too big to fail, companies are now too big to audit.

Bogle notes that the way attest firms respond to independence issues, if they do, will "shape the future of the profession." He concludes with the following remarks:

> "I am confident that if financial market participants come to understand that the independent oversight of financial figures plays a critical role in our system of disclosure, that independence is at the core of integrity, and that the integrity of our financial markets is essential to their well-being, the age of professional accounting too will shake off today's challenges and return to its roots."[25]

In summary, the accounting profession and accounting firms are facing enormous changes in structure and operations. There is an ever-expanding

[24,25] John C. Bogle, "Public Accounting: Profession or Business?" The Seymour Jones Distinguished Lecture, Vincent C. Ross Institute of Accounting Research, New York University, October 16, 2000.

gap between what is the case and what ought to be the case. But the fact that accountants everywhere are looking at and evaluating that gap gives us hope for the future. The struggles over the issues above merely confirm the necessity of being ethical in accounting. In these changing circumstances, however, it is not always easy to figure out how to accomplish that.

These concerns were heightened by the unprecedented, unacceptable behavior of so many accounting firms. Huge scandals, though, often give rise to serious reforms. The Sarbanes–Oxley Act was enacted; public regulatory bodies were formed. Fair value was examined because of the 2008–2009 economic crisis, and globalization forced the accounting community worldwide to consider developing one set of standards – the International Financial Reporting Standards. (We will examine some of these issues in the afterword.) Thus, even the crisis in the accounting profession has a silver lining. We might conclude, therefore, that the accounting profession is not so much in crisis as in the midst of substantial change. These are the first steps.

In this book, we have tried to provide the tools to evaluate what the accountant ought to do – that is, to determine the accountant's responsibilities. We have examined the various functions an accountant performs, considered the specific responsibilities of those functions, and discussed how these responsibilities can be performed with honesty and integrity. We have not studied all the possible functions of the accountant. We have concentrated on the three main ones – auditing, managerial accounting, and tax accounting. The approach, however, is the same for all accounting activities: Look at the purpose of the activity, and judge how well that purpose is being fulfilled. Also look at the relationships involved in that function, and determine what ethical responsibilities those relationships involve.

Afterword

Current Debates on Accounting Issues

I Fair Value and Principles vs. Rules

There are a number of issues that affect the public good, the service of which is the main concern of many accounting practices. Two of the main problems being addressed today are:

(1) Whether Fair Value Accounting is the best procedure for helping the public, and
(2) Whether the public would be better served with a principles-based or rules-based approach to valuation?

These topics are not resolved and require constant attention as they will affect the perception and the action of the accounting profession for years to come. We address them in this afterword recognizing that they are in an incredibly fluid state.

Did fair value exacerbate the financial crisis?

A letter from the American Banking Association to FASB, November 13, 2008 stated:

> "However, there has been and continues to be much controversy over recording losses that are based on the market's perception of value (fair value)

Accounting Ethics, Second Edition. Ronald Duska, Brenda Shay Duska, and Julie Ragatz.
© 2011 John Wiley & Sons, Ltd. Published 2011 by John Wiley & Sons, Ltd.

which often results in recognizing losses that exceed credit losses or recognizing losses for instruments that have experienced no credit problems and are performing in accordance with their terms. The erosion of earnings and capital due to the market's perception of losses or due to a lack of liquidity that drives values lower is misleading to investors and other users of financial statements."

This quote frames the ethical question underlying the debate over the implementation of fair value accounting. Does the fair value model have the capacity to substantially harm society through undermining the financial system? If it does, then this harm would present a moral dilemma in which decision makers would be required to balance the good of transparency and disclosure against the potential harms a fair value model would present. While it is certainly not possible to resolve this issue in this brief examination, it is instructive to consider not only the arguments made on both sides, but also to investigate how these arguments implicitly, and at times, explicitly make use of moral language and refer to moral values.

In 2007, the over-heated housing market began to cool down as adjustable rate loans moved upwards and the supply of new homes began to rapidly outpace demand. Facing mortgage payments they could no longer afford at the new, higher rates, many home owners began to miss payments and default on their mortgages. This was devastating for the individual families and communities involved while having other effects on the economy. As the foreclosure rate rose, the value of mortgage backed securities, made up of tranches of these individual mortgages, plummeted in value. In late 2007, the market became aware that several powerful financial intermediaries were deeply exposed to the collapse of the housing market because of their substantial holdings in these mortgage-backed securities. Realizing their exposure to these so-called "toxic assets," the financial firms attempted to sell them. Trading securities are required to be marked-to-market every financial period, unless those securities are marked as "being held to maturity." These "held-to-maturity" assets are only required to be marked-to-market if the decline in the market price is "other than temporary." As the rates of defaults and foreclosures climbed precipitously, it became increasingly difficult to contend that the decline in the market was "temporary" and it was painfully obvious that the value of the mortgage backed securities had suffered tremendous losses and that these "toxic assets" would not regain their original value in the near future.

The declines in the housing marketing had a depressing effect on the larger economy, since many consumers tightened their belts as their home values decreased and their mortgage payments increased. This decline caused problems for many financial institutions were left holding the depressed mortgage based securities on their books. These losses reduced the amount of capital and many firms were compelled to bring their "toxic" assets to market in an attempt to raise cash to shore up their declining capital reserves. But no one was buying.

The former CEO of American International Group (AIG), Martin Sullivan, was particularly vocal about the role he believed fair value accounting played in the demise of his company. Sullivan, in a conference call with AIG investors, "blamed a large part of the company's recent $11 billion write down of debt securities on FAS 157 ... and (claimed) that the write down under pre FAS 157 accounting might have been closer to $900 million."[1] The difficulties got worse for AIG when they were forced to set aside a large amount of reserves for their potential losses. This was devastating, as Sullivan admits, "Suddenly, a company with a trillion dollars of assets was reporting unrealized losses on its income statement that ultimately climbed into the tens of billions."[2]

The American Banking Association (ABA) also voiced concern over the harmful effects of FAS 157. According to the ABA, fair value permits the low values established by only a handful of transactions to depress values for all instruments, even where the underlying risk of default has not changed and the entity holding the instrument plans to hold it longer while waiting for the market to recover. This leads to an "unrealized loss" which can increase volatility and decrease available capital. One practitioner noted that, "an unrealized loss is one that you may still have the chance to recover. The company may say, 'I plan to hold the asset a long time and I'm convinced that the decline in value is temporary, so why record the loss now and in the next period record the gain? Isn't that introducing unnecessary volatility to my earnings?'"[3]

Thus we see that the opponents of fair value claim that if the financial institutions would not have been forced to mark these mortgage backed securities to market, that is, if they could have treated these assets as being "held-to-maturity", there would not have been a "fire sale." That fire sale essentially dumped the securities on the market causing an over-supply, which forced the prices of the securities lower and lower in what has been called a "death spiral." Quite simply, opponents contend, by being forced to act as hypothetical sellers in a depressed market, they were compelled to become actual sellers, which unnecessarily depressed the market even further.

---

[1] Tammy Whitehouse, "Fair Value Debated," *Compliance Week*, March 25, 2008.
[2] James Bandler and Roddy Boyd, "Ex AIG Brass Tries to Shift Blame," *CNN Money/Fortune.com*, October 7, 2008.
[3] Tammy Whitehouse, "Struggling on Values, Banks Fire at FAS 157," *Compliance Week*, September 16, 2008.

The question is would the devastating consequences of the deflating of the housing bubble been avoided if fair value was not applied? Was the "volatility the result of fair value accounting? Or did the new approaches to measuring fair value simply give investors a better view of trouble that had been there all along?"[4]

Defenders of fair value accounting argue that opponents are guilty of "blaming the messenger" when they already had a valuation model responsible for their failed and excessively risky business strategy. The Center for Audit Quality, in a statement with the Council of Institutional Investors claimed that:

> "Suspending fair value accounting during these challenging economic times would deprive investors of critical financial information when it is needed most. Fair value accounting with robust disclosures provides more accurate, timely, and comparable information to investors than amounts that would be reported under other alternative accounting approaches. Investors have a right to know the current value of an investment, even if the investment is falling short of past or future expectations."

In short, supporters of the fair value approach argue that fair value did not create the conditions which ultimately led to the financial crisis. Rather, lending institutions and financial intermediaries brought about the circumstances which ultimately led to their losses (and, in some cases, their demise) through aggressive positions in "toxic assets", risky business strategies and inappropriate reserves. It was fair value accounting that revealed the extent of their exposure to the decline in the housing market and gave investors and regulators the information each needed to act to protect their interests.

As to Sullivan's attempt to deflect claim, defenders of fair value ask: "… a big question: How is it that the management of AIG, long one of the top 10 derivative trading houses globally, was not closely focused on the risk a ratings downgrade posed to its $500 billion credit swap portfolio?"[5] According to defenders of fair value, the real cause of the failure of AIG was that Sullivan gambled that the market for securitized bonds would hold up.

This leads to the question of the worth of fair value accounting.

---

[4]Tammy Whitehouse, "Struggling on Values, Banks Fire at FAS 157," *Compliance Week*, May 20, 2008.
[5]James Bandler and Roddy Boyd, "Ex AIG Brass Tries to Shift Blame," *CNN Money/Fortune.com*, July 10, 2008.

II Fair Value Accounting

Warren Buffet said, "You get into a lot of trouble when you start putting fictitious numbers on value".[6] That sums up the general feeling on the topic of fair value accounting. But what is this fair value? The classic definition of market fair value is the amount for which an asset could be exchanged, or a liability settled, between knowledgeable, willing parties in an arm's length transaction. The Financial Accounting Standards Board in 2006 redefined fair value as: "… the price that would be received to sell an asset or price to transfer a liability in an orderly transaction between market participants at the measurement date."[7]

As we have seen fair value accounting raises interesting questions about the process by which accountants (and nonaccountants) determine the value or worth of a particular asset. There are many ways of determining the value of an object, but mostly people tend to believe that the worth of an object is determined by its value relative to other objects, namely, what it can be traded or sold for in a free and open market.

The debate may appear simple but it is not.

Defenders of fair value believe that if we don't allow the market to ascribe value to assets and liabilities, there is no other method to assess value. They insist that the fair value method provides the consumers of financial information what they need to make decisions regarding their interactions with a company. Consumers have a right to the sort of information provided by a form of fair valuation. They think that even though valuing assets in illiquid markets may be difficult, accountants have always been called upon to exercise professional judgment and apply assumptions to unclear cases. They warn that allowing managers to determine the value of assets and liabilities compromises the quality of information because managers might manipulate valuations in self-serving ways that are not in the interest of the consumer.

Opponents of fair value object that its use is not appropriate under certain market conditions, for example, when the market for a particular object is compromised or illiquid. They assert that the fair value approach undermines the stability and integrity of the financial system as it did in the crises of 2008 and 2009. This lack of stability threatens the financial health of market participants, and jeopardizes the well being of all members of society. Since they believe these harms can be avoided through the adoption of an alternative

---

[6]Charlie Rose Show (Transcript) October 2, 2008. www.bloomberg.com/apps/news?pid= newsarchives&sid=ah6TxCqMJaLU.
[7]Financial Accounting Standards Board, SFAS No. 157, Section 5.

form of valuation, without compromising the ability of accountants to provide an accurate picture of the underlying economic health of the corporation,
fair value accounting should be jettisoned.

On the surface, it does not seem that the debate about the fair value method
of valuation is the subject of accounting ethics, but if one of the chief ethical
responsibilities of an accountant is to give as accurate a picture as possible of
the financial state of an enterprise, it is important to determine what means
are most apt to bring about that result. We indicated earlier hat ethics has to
do with the evaluation of individual actions, institutions, and systems. If a
discussion leads us into the area of public policy, then we echo Aristotle who
said individual ethics is incomplete without an evaluation of the society in
which those individuals live. For him that was the science of politics.

History of fair value accounting

While the debate over the appropriateness of fair value has recently become
highly publicized, it is important to note that the use of fair value in financial
reporting is not new. Fair value has its roots in the "efficient market revolu-
tion" of the 1960s. The concept of the efficient market is based on the prem-
ise that the markets accurately reflected economic reality and therefore that
market prices would provide the most correct estimation of the value of an
asset or liability.

The Savings and Loan crisis in the 1980s reaffirmed the importance of fair
value accounting. Supposedly, the actions of the so-called "zombie lenders,"
who did not mark their assets and liabilities to the market, exacerbated the
harmful consequences of their risky lending decisions. Because these economic losses were allowed to remain unrecognized, bank regulators and other
actors were unaware of the extent to which these banks had been compromised. The lack of regulatory intervention encouraged the risky behavior of
the thrifts, behavior that included the exploitation of deposit insurance and
in some cases fraud.[8]

In 1991, partially in response to the Savings and Loan Crisis, the Financial Accounting Standards Board (FASB) instituted fair value accounting for
financial instruments. While there has certainly been debate regarding how
best to implement fair value, the underlying need for a system that determines
values based on market prices went relatively unchallenged.[9]

---

[8]Stephen Ryan, "Fair Value Accounting: Understanding the Issues Raised by the Credit Crunch."
Council of Institutional Investors, July 2008.
[9]Justin Fox, "Suspending Mark-to-Market is for Zombies," *The Curious Capitalist, Time
Magazine*, October 1, 2008.

History of FASB Action on Fair Market Issues		
FAS 105	Disclosure of Off Balance Sheet Risk and Market Risks of Instruments	1990
FAS 107	Requirements for Disclosure of Fair Value	1991/1993
FAS 115	Accounting for Certain Investments in Debt and Equity Securities	1993/1994
FAS 123	Stock-Option Accounting	
FAS 130	Reporting Comprehensive Income	1997/1998
FAS 133	Accounting for Derivative Instruments and Hedging Activities	1998/2000
FAS 141	Business Combinations	2001
FAS 142	Goodwill and Other Intangible Assets	2001
FAS 143	Asset Retirement Obligations	
FAS 155	Accounting for Certain Hybrid Financial Instruments – an Amendment of FASB Statements FAS 133 and 140	2006
FAS 157	Fair Value Measurements	2006
FAS 159	The Fair Value Option for Financial Assets and Financial Liabilities-Including an Amendment of Statement No. 115	2007

Fair value statements from FASB

The Financial Accounting Standards Board first addressed Fair Market Value in 1990. It last addressed it in January of 2009. The single biggest adjustment to the use of fair market values came in 2006 with Statement No.157, Fair Value Market Measurements. The FASB's move toward an expansion of the fair value model was motivated by residual issues from the S&L crisis issues, technology advances, the increased complexity of transactions, and the public demand for increased accounting transparency.

No.157 Fair Market Measurements
SFAS 157 was designed to accomplish the following objectives:

(1) Provide a framework for fair value measurements
(2) Change the definition of fair value
(3) Elaborate on the concept of market participants
(4) Introduce the concepts of principle market and most advantageous market
(5) Introduce the fair value hierarchy
(6) Introduce the concept of defensive valuation

SFAS 157 applies to financial assets of all publicly-traded companies in the United States as of November 15, 2007. It also applies to nonfinancial assets and liabilities that are recognized, or disclosed, at fair value on a recurring basis. Beginning in 2009, the standard applies to other nonfinancial assets and other accounting items that require or permit fair value measurements, except share-based payment transactions, such as stock option compensation. As we noted, SFAS 157 did not institute fair value; it merely clarified and provided greater guidance as to how particular financial instruments should be valued under certain market conditions.[10]

The fair value hierarchy (see table below) is an attempt to differentiate different levels of assets, from those with observable market prices to those which lack observable market prices. The hierarchy is one of the most commented upon developments of SFAS 157 as well as being at the heart of the debate concerning whether or not fair value exacerbated or caused the financial crisis of 2008. Even though there are three distinct levels, FASB mandates that, "in all levels of the fair value hierarchy the objective remains the same – a current exchange price for the asset or liability."[11]

Asset Description	Description
Level 1 Assets	Have an active market with observable market prices. Include publically traded securities that have a quoted price and are actively traded on a national securities exchange.
Level 2 Assets	Lack a directly observable market price; these assets are valued using inputs from observable market prices of similar assets.
Level 3 Assets	Lack observable market prices for the asset or similar assets or the market is illiquid. Pricing these assets is a more involved process that involves relying on the holder's (or managers') forecast of expected cash flow, based on its own assumptions. Valuing Level 3 assets involves using "unobservable inputs."

Challenges to SFAS 157

Besides the general objections to fair value accounting, there are specific challenges to SFAS 157, particularly the difficulty determining the hierarchy level

[10] Linda MacDonald, "Don't Bury Fair Value Accounting Just Yet," *Portfolio.com*, October 7, 2008.
[11] Robert H. Herz and Linda A. McDonald, "Some Facts about Fair Value," *Understanding the Issues*, Financial Accounting Standards Board, May 2008. www.fasb.org/articles&reports/uti_fair_value_may_2008.pdf.

(1, 2, or 3) of a particular asset or liability. The SEC and FASB have been unwilling to establish distinct definitions for asset classes. In a press release, the SEC stated: "the determination of fair value often requires significant judgment. In some cases, multiple inputs from different sources may collectively provide the best evidence of fair value … the weighting of the inputs in the fair value estimate will depend on the extent to which they provide information about the value of an asset or liability and are relevant in developing a reasonable estimate."[12]

The bottom line is that while a quoted market price in an active market for an identical asset is the most representative of fair value, when these inputs are not available, it is necessary for accountants to use their best judgment as to what combination of inputs and assumptions are most likely to generate the most representative valuation.[13]

III Arguments For and Against the Fair Value Approach

While we have looked briefly at the reasons for and against the fair value approach, a more thorough investigation should be helpful.

Disadvantages of fair value accounting

Opponents of fair value accounting, as defined in SFAS 157, offer a series of reasons why it is not appropriate.

(1) Unrealized gains and losses which are recognized within a fair value approach, will remain unrealized. Thus, fair value creates a false perception of great volatility. "Much of the volatility washes out over time such that earnings increases and decreases from fair value adjustments have zero effect on cash in most instances. This is misleading for going concerns."[14] In other words, fair value creates inappropriate highs and lows in the balance sheet which do not reflect the underlying economic health of the corporation.

(2) Different types of financial assets are not amenable to fair valuation. Thus a manager will be compelled to value those assets on the basis of

---

[12] SEC PR September 30, 2008 http://www.sec.gov/news/press/2008/2008-234.htm.

[13] Tammy Whitehouse, "FAS 157 and FAS 141R: Tricky Combination for Non Financials", *Compliance Week*, September 16, 2008.

[14] Bob Jensen, "Bob Jensen's Summary of Accounting History and Theory," Trinity University of San Antonio, http://www.trinity.edu/rjensen/theory.htm.

their "exit values" that does not reflect real differences in how corporations intend to use or disperse assets. "There is a vast difference between
valuing assets for the purpose for which they were acquired and valuing
them as though they would or could be liquidated."[15]

(3)   The information provided to the investing public through the fair
value approach offers a "snap shot" of the financial affairs of a corporation but this information is too time-sensitive. In other words, since
values of assets and liabilities are tied to the markets and the markets
respond on a daily (or even hourly basis) to changes in the economic
environment. The information received by consumers may be outdated
and unhelpful.

Robert Pickel, CEO of the International Swaps and Derivatives Association in New York states, "mark-to-market gives a real time picture of
a firm's exposures, but the average company releases its financial statements several weeks after the reporting data … there are question marks
over how meaningful that real-time information is to investors when
it merely provides a snapshot of a firm's position in markets that can
change quickly."[16]

(4)   Firms reporting unrealized losses under fair value accounting may pro-
voke a negative "feedback loop" which creates further deterioration in
market prices and could undermine the integrity of the financial system.
In times of economic downturn, fair value accounting forces all companies within an industry to recognize losses at the same time. This can
seriously impair their capital and trigger the fire sales of assets, assets that
were intended to be held or used by the corporation. This is precisely
what many opponents of fair value accounting believed occurred during
the financial crisis of 2008.

(5)   Inconsistency in the manner in which fair value is applied, both in terms
of which corporations choose to use fair value and also the manner in
which value is ascertained for particular assets and liabilities, particularly
those assets which are classified as Level 2 or Level 3 assets and therefore
rely on the use of unobservable inputs and assumptions. According to
an article in the *Economist:* "Different banks can hold the same assets at
different values … at the end of 2007, Western banks carried about half
of their assets at fair value, but the dispersion was wide; 86% at Goldman
Sachs to 27% at Bank of America."[17]

---

[15] Alfred King, "Determining Fair Value," *Strategic Finance*, January 2009, p. 32.
[16] Justin Wood, "A Fairwell to History," *CFO Europe Magazine*, November 29, 2004.
[17] "All's Fair," *The Economist*, September 18, 2008.

Advantages of fair value accounting

On the other hand, defenders of fair value take issue with the objections offered above and believe that there are important advantages to be gained from adopting and, in some cases, expanding, fair value.

(1)   Fair value accounting is not a new development. The transition from historical cost accounting to a fair value approach was undertaken because it was believed that such a shift would benefit the market through providing better information to end-users of financial statements. Fair value accounting gives better information because it makes changes in value, which result from changes in the level of risk, apparent.

Bob Jensen stated: "One of the major reasons for the FASB push to fair value instruments is the booking of alterations in value caused by changes in credit risk ... fair value accounting immediately recognizes changes in credit risk. Historical cost accounting only recognizes such changes in risk if the likelihood of actual default reaches a certain threshold ... Fair value accounting makes it more difficult to overvalue investments in cases of increased credit risk of creditors."[18]

In other words, fair value accounting enables investors to know and understand the level of risk they are exposed to at a given moment in time, important information for both consumers and regulators. The disclosure of this information also compels firms to respond to the level of risk by increasing capital and diversifying holdings.

David Tweetie, the Chairman of the IASB believes in the superiority of the fair value approach: "Without fair-value accounting, investors would not now be realizing the true worth of the mortgage-backed securities that have led to the write-downs at various firms. The use of fair value forces the true downsides of a company's investment – such as securities tied to bad lending practices – to come to fruition."[19]

What's more, David Bianco argues that volatility revealed through fair value valuation is an important piece of information for investors as it puts them on notice that "staying power" may be required while the market corrects itself.[20]

(2)   A second defense of fair value accounting is that it is a method necessary to maintain the trust and confidence of the investing public. Simply put,

---

[18] Robert E. Jensen, "Fair Value Accounting in the USA," at http://citeseerX,ist.psuedu/viewdoc/download?doi=10.1.1.161.3740 [p. 315].

[19] Sarah Johnson, "The Global Fair Value Fight," *CFO.com*, June 10, 2008.

[20] David Bianco, "Don't Blame Fair Value Accounting." *FRM UBS Investment Research*, March 17, 2000. Please see http://www.complianceweek.com/s/documents/UBSFAS157.pdf.

there is an "expectations gap" between the accounting industry and their clients and the investing public and society in general. Cost accounting is an abstract approach that simply does not resonate with most nonpractitioners. Most people believe that a thing is worth what it can be bargained, traded, or sold for and that the value of a thing should be closely bound up with this fact. Investing consumers need to have confidence that accounting models will reveal information about what is important to them in making their decisions and they believe they have a right to this information. When companies which have historically been provided with a "clean bill of health" from their audit firm collapse in a spectacular and devastating fashion, members of the investing public lose faith in both the integrity of the audit firm and the soundness of their audits. Hence the advantage of fair value accounting is that it contributes to the maintenance of trust in the accounting industry to provide useful information to members of the investing public.

Tom Reason in *CEO Magazine* wrote "I think it is hard to argue with the conceptual merits of fair value as the most relevant measurement attribute … Certainly, to those who would say that accounting should better reflect the true economic substance, fair value of – or marking to market – assets and liability whenever it can be reliably determined."[21]

(3)   The final defense of fair value is a denial of the claim that the fair value leads to heavy corporate losses. Even though Martin Sullivan, the former CEO of AIG, complained about the role of mark-to-market accounting in his companies' demise, defenders of fair value believe that AIG benefitted in some ways from the fair value standard. They argue that as a company's fortunes decline, so does the value of their liabilities, which actually can result in a profit (or at least, less of a loss).

Political postscript

On September 30, 2008, a group of congressmen and women led by Chairman Barney Frank, in a letter to SEC Chairman, Christopher Cox, requested that he suspend the use of mark-to-market accounting and "replace it with a form of mark to *value* that more accurately reflects the true value of the asset." While the legislators concede that the mark-to-market system can "raise important red flags, in an illiquid market it has become counter-productive and is simply making the situation worse."

[21] Tim Reason, "Questions of Value" *CFO Magazine*, February 1, 2003. http://www.cfo.com/article.cfm/3008070?f=related.

Robert Denham, the Chairman of the Financial Accounting Foundation (FAF), responded with a sharp defense of the independence of FAF, the private sector organization responsible for the oversight of the FASB. Denham wrote:

"Effective accounting standards are achieved only when the standard-setting process is independent and free of undue political influence ... We are very concerned about the current efforts of some to legislate the suspension of one of FASB's standards, Statement 157 on fair value measurements. We believe that any legislative effort to overturn a FASB standard will greatly undermine legislative confidence ... If congress sends the message that special interests are able, through legislation, to overturn expert accounting judgment arrived at through an open and thorough due process, necessary and timely improvements in financial reporting will likely become impossible and the best interests of participants in the capital markets will not be served."

In October 2008, the Emergency Economic Stabilization Act of 2008 (EESA) also known as the "The Bailout Act" was passed. Section 132 of EESA gave Congress the authority to suspend the use of fair value accounting under SFAS 157. In addition, Section 133 required the SEC to conduct a study of fair value accounting as stipulated in SFAS 157. Congress even called on the SEC to "review the process used by the Financial Accounting Standards Board in developing accounting standards."

This is a much broader mandate than just studying a single accounting standard. On December 30, 2008, the SEC issued a report to Congress pursuant to the requirements of the EESA (Report and Recommendations Pursuant to Section 133 of the Emergency Economic Stabilization Act of 2008: Study on Mark-To-Market Accounting). The SEC report concluded that "fair value accounting did not appear to play a meaningful role in bank failures occurring during 2008".[22]

However, the report did note that "fair value requirements should be improved through the development of application and best practices guidelines for determining fair value in illiquid and inactive markets."[23] The principle cause of concern seems to be that since FSP FAS 157-3 ("Determining the Fair Value of a Financial Asset When the Market for that Asset Is Not Active") which was released on October 10, 2008, requires that the market participant

---

[22] Securities and Exchange Commission: Report and Recommendations Pursuant to Section 133 of the Emergency Economic Stabilization Act of 2008: Study on Mark-To-Market Accounting.
[23] Financial Accounting Standards Board, "Board Meeting Handout: Proposed FSP FAS 157-x, *Determining Whether a Market is Not Active or a Transaction is not Distressed*. March 16, 2009. http://www.fasb.org/board_handouts/03-16-09.pdf.

liquidity risk must be considered (of which there is no better indicator than the last transaction price), it is difficult for reporters to use their judgment in valuing these Level 3 type assets. On February 18, 2009 additional application guidance to address concerns was added to FASB's agenda.

On April 2, 2009 FASB voted to relax fair value accounting rules by allowing companies to use "significant judgment" in determining the prices of some investments on their books, including mortgage backed securities. The FASB determined that since banks rely on competitors' asset sales to help determine the fair market value of similar securities they hold on their own books, this could lead to a presumption that all securities sales are "distressed" unless evidence proves otherwise. The conclusion was that banks should only disregard transactions that are not orderly, including situations in which the "seller is near bankruptcy" or needed to sell the assets to comply with regulatory requirements.

IV Summary

Should accounting standards be viewed as a fiscal policy tool to stimulate or moderate economic growth, or rather as a means of producing neutral and objective measurements of the financial performance of public companies? The value of independent standard setting is greatest when the going gets tough. The more serious the stresses on the market, the more important it is to maintain independence. Conrad Hewitt, a former chief accountant at the SEC who stepped down in January 2009, said representatives from the ABA, American International Group Inc., Fannie Mae and Freddie Mac all lobbied him over the past two years to suspend the fair-value rule. Executives "would come to me in the afternoon with the argument, 'You've got to suspend it,'" Hewitt said, the SEC, which oversees FASB, would reject their demands, and "the next morning their lobbyists would go to Congress," he said.

At any rate, this discussion leaves us with the following questions to pursue:

(1) Did the reliance on fair value make it impossible to accurately value (and therefore establish appropriate risk protection) certain financial instruments, such as mortgage backed securities?

(2) Does the use of mark-to-market lead to a "snowball" effect in which the "fire-sales" of one company inappropriately diminish the value of all other companies who hold this asset?

(3) Does the use of mark-to-market lead to excessive "unrealized" losses that are never realized?

V Principles vs. Rules

There is another debate going on in accounting circles, and this is the result of two factors, globalization and the push for the use of a unified set of accounting principles.

The Principles Rules Debate

"Rules-based systems encourage creativity (and not the good kind) in financial reporting. They allow some to stretch the limits of what is permissible under the law, even though it may not be ethically or morally acceptable. A principles-based system requires companies to report and auditors to audit the substance of the transaction; not merely whether they can qualify as acceptable under incredibly complex or overly technical rules ... a rules based system allows managers to ignore the substance and instead ask, 'Where in the rules does it say that I can't do this?" Full Page Advertisement, PriceWaterhouseCoopers, *Wall Street Journal* April 2003.

VI Introduction

The accounting scandals that were the impetus for the establishment of Sarbanes–Oxley Act of 2002 forced politicians, regulators and industry practitioners to investigate the causes of these unfortunate events. While blame certainly fell on a number of the particular individuals and firms involved, the number and scale of these scandals, as well as their devastating consequences, convinced some that a more systematic solution was needed. Many asked the question whether there was a problem with the form of the accounting standards that rendered them more susceptible to abuse?

While a few unscrupulous individuals and firms were responsible, perhaps a deeper explanation of the accounting scandals which threatened not only the integrity of the accounting industry, but the entire financial world could be found in the system which allowed those people to benefit through a sort of "gaming of the rules." Ray Ball notes that,

"A rule checking mentality seems to have crept over the accounting profession, including FASB, audit firms, researchers, and educators. Under this narrow world view, financial reporting requirements are embodied in rules, not principles, and compliance with rules-based GAAP is sufficient."[24]

[24]Ray Ball, "Market and Political/Regulatory Perspectives of the Recent Accounting Scandals," *Journal of Accounting Research*, Vol. 47, No. 2, May 2009, p. 283.

Concerns about the appropriateness of so called "Rules Based Standards" were reinforced by the expressed commitment on the part of Financial Accounting Standards Board (FASB) and the Securities and Exchange Commission (SEC) to work towards a convergence of Generally Accepted Accounting Principles (GAAP) with the standards promulgated by the International Accounting Standard Board (IASB), generally referred to as IFRS (International Financial Reporting Standards). The IFRS are founded on a "principles-based" approach to standard setting. These twin factors, the aftermath of the accounting scandals at the beginning of the decade and the move to establish greater harmony between GAAP and IFRS, has led to reflections on the advantages and disadvantages of a principles-based approach to standard setting.

Two questions arise. First, what is a principles-based approach and is the GAAP model a principles-based or rules-based approach? Second, which model *should* FASB and the SEC adopt? The first question is important since before any determination can be made about which model, or combination thereof, will be best for society, it is helpful to understand the state of affairs under which we are currently operating.

VII Isn't GAAP Already Principles Based?

In spite of most people believing that GAAP is a rules-based approach, the SEC maintains that at least in part it is already a "principles based" approach. The SEC states the following,

> "many contend that U.S. GAAP provides an example of a rules-based approach to standard setting. However, we do not fully agree. While we agree that certain standards do suffer from the short-comings of a rules-based approach, many others are closer to the kind of principles-based approach we prescribe herein."[25]

The FASB's promulgation of the Statements of Financial Accounting Concepts (SFAC) seems to reinforce this view. These Concept Statements are intended to:

---

[25]"Final Report: Conference on Federal-State Securities Regulation U.S. Securities and Exchange Commission," 450 Fifth Street, N.W. Washington, DC 20549, 2003. www.sec.gov/info/smallbus/ffedst2003.htm.

"set forth objectives and fundamentals which will be the basis for development of financial accounting and reporting standards. The objectives identify the goals and purposes of financial reporting. The fundamentals are the underlying concepts of financial accounting."[26]

Concept Statements create a Conceptual Framework which FASB claims is "a coherent system of interrelated objectives and fundamentals that is expected to lead to consistent standards and that prescribes the nature, function and limits of financial accounting and reporting." While the establishment of objectives and fundamental concepts may not directly resolve financial accounting and reporting problems, "objectives give direction, and concepts are tools for solving problems." The FASB adds that the objectives and fundamental concepts will aid in the development and revision of standards by, "providing the Board with a common foundation and the basic reasoning to consider the merits of alternatives."

It is not only the development of a Conceptual Framework which provides evidence for a principles based model of standard setting, but the content of these statements as well. In particular, *SFAC No. 2* states "the quality of reliability and, in particular, representational faithfulness leaves no room for accounting representations that subordinate substance to form."[27] Reliability is defined by FASB as the "quality of information that assures that information is reasonably free of error and bias and faithfully represents what it purports to represent." In short as objective and truthful a picture as possible. Of course as FASB notes, that reliability exists in degrees.

Representational Faithfulness is defined as "correspondence or agreement between a measure or description and the phenomenon that it purports to represent." This reminds one of the old philosophical definition of truth as the correspondence between thought and reality. This is all important because the main goal is the usefulness of the information.

---

[26] Financial Accounting Standards Board, *Statement of Financial Accounting Concepts (SFAS) No. 2*, 1980.

[27] Reliability is defined by FASB as the "quality of information that assures that information is reasonable, free or error and bias and faithfully represents what it purports to represent." The FASB notes that reliability exists in degrees and is assessed based on the extent to which the accounting description or measurement is verifiable and representationally faithful. Representational faithfulness is defined as "correspondence or agreement between a measure or description and the phenomenon that it purports to represent."

The Conceptual Framework elevates *decision usefulness* as the chief purpose of financial reporting.[28] *Decision usefulness* is determined by the *relevance, reliability and comparability* of the information presented in the financial statement. To be relevant, information must be capable of "making a difference in a decision by helping users to form predictions about the outcomes of past, present and future events or to confirm or correct expectations."[29] Reliability refers to "the faithfulness with which it purports to represent what it purports to represent, coupled with an assurance for the user, which comes through verification, that it has that representational quality."[30] In Comparability is, "the quality or state of having certain characteristics in common ... Clearly, valid comparison is possible only if the measurement used – the quantities or ratios-reliable represent the characteristic that is the subject of comparison."[31]

The Financial Accounting Standards Board established *relevance* and *reliability* as a primary decision-specific qualitative characteristics and *comparability* as a secondary qualitative characteristic.[32] Thus it is clear that for FASB *decision usefulness* is the "guiding principle" of current accounting standards, and that usefulness is determined by *relevance*, *reliability*, and *comparability* of the data use. These are the principles used by the standard setters in order to ensure that the purpose of financial reporting is achieved. It would follow that any manipulation such as we looked at in the chapters on auditing, managing, and taxation would violate the principles. Thus using GAAP to obfuscate or manipulate would be unethical.

A second argument for the position that United States currently operates within a principles-based framework comes if we examine the language of the standard unqualified US audit report. The independent auditor is charged to:

> Present fairly, in all material respects, the financial position of the company at year end, the results of operations, and its cash flows, in conformity with generally accepted accounting principles.

---

[28]"The FASB's conceptual framework is predicated on the fundamental notion that the information provided through financial reporting should be useful to investors." (SEC, 2003). The SEC is referring to the FASB's *Statement of Financial Accounting Standards No. 1* "Objectives of Financial Reporting by Business Enterprises," November 1978.

[29] FASB, *Statement of Financial Accounting Concepts (SFAS) No. 2*, 1980, paragraphs 46–47.

[30] FASB, *Statement of Financial Accounting Concepts (SFAS) No. 2*, 1980, paragraph 59.

[31] FASB, *Statement of Financial Accounting Concepts (SFAS) No. 2*, 1980, paragraph 115.

[32] Final Report: Conference on Federal-State Securities Regulation U.S. Securities and Exchange Commission," 450 Fifth Street, N.W. Washington, DC 20549, 2003. www.sec.gov/info/smallbus/ffedst2003.htm.

This language has been in place since 1939. Some commentators point out that the two key phrases in this statement, *present fairly* and *in conformity with generally accepted accounting principles*, are not synonymous. In other words, merely acting in accordance with GAAP does not entail that the accounting professional has, in fact, provided a *fair presentation* of the financial position of the firm in question. It is indeed the case that one can use GAAP rules to manipulate. Like most rules, clever people can violate the spirit of the law by playing with the letter of the law. But if present fairly is the important thing, it demands a use of GAAP to provide reliable and relevant information. If this is the case, then the principle of "ensuring a fair presentation" supervenes on GAAP rules. This would mean that GAAP is a more principles-based approach.

We can find a final argument in Rule 203 of the AICPA Code of Conduct.[33] The rule requires that "If such statements or data contain any departure from an accounting principle promulgated by bodies designated by Council to establish such principles that has a material effect on the statements or data taken as a whole ... the member shall not (1) express an opinion or state affirmatively that the financial statements or other financial data of any entity are presented in conformity with generally accepted accounting principles." Thus, the first sentence prohibits accountants from certifying that financial standards are in compliance with GAAP if the statements do not comply with standards designated by the AICPA as authoritative. The first sentence of Rule 203 establishes who (or what institutions) have the authority to determine GAAP. The second sentence is a little unwieldy, but is perhaps more important. It reads as follows:

> If, however, the statements or data contain a departure [from GAAP] and the member can demonstrate that due to unusual circumstances the financial statements or data would otherwise have been misleading, the member can comply with the rule by describing the departure, its approximate effect, if practicable, and the reasons why compliance with the principle would result in a misleading statement.

Thus the second sentence of Rule 203 explicitly permits a departure from GAAP in the unusual case that compliance with GAAP would result in a financial statement that is materially misleading. In an interpretation of Rule 203, AIPCA asserts that while:

> "There is a strong presumption that adherence to officially established accounting principles would in nearly all cases result in financial statements that are

[33] AICPA Code of Ethics, ET Section 203 .01 Accounting Principles.

not misleading,"; it possible that in some circumstances this may not be the case. Therefore, "the rule recognizes that upon occasion there may be unusual circumstances where the literal application of pronouncements on accounting principles would have the effect of rendering financial statements misleading. In such a case, the proper accounting treatment is that which will render the financial statements not misleading."[34]

All of the above is under "02 203 – Departures from Established Accounting Principles. AICPA Code of Ethics."

So, the rule allows for the possibility, however unlikely, that compliance with GAAP may lead to a misleading financial statement. This means that *present fairly* and *in conformity with generally accepted accounting principles* are not synonymous terms. When not complying though, the member cannot simply disregard the rule, but must describe how they are departing from it and why this departure is warranted.

Finally, the text of Rule 203 spells out a prescription. It states that when accountants believe that a literal application of the rules is misleading, "the proper accounting treatment is that which will render the financial statements not misleading."[35]

VIII An Example: The Continental Vending Case

Advocates of the previous interpretation point to a 1969 criminal court case, *United States v. Simon,* which is usually referred to by the corporate audit client at the center of the case, *Continental Vending.* In Continental Vending,[36] a manager and two partners were charged with fraud for certifying a financial statement which they knew to be "false and generally misleading." During the trial, eight defense experts testified that the financial statement submitted by Continental Vending in 1962 was in compliance with GAAP. Two prosecution experts testified that the financial statement was not presented in accordance with GAAP. After trials, the first ending in a hung jury, the defendants were convicted and fined, although they were not sentenced to any jail time.[37]

The significance of the *Continental Vending* case for our purposes is found in the instructions provided to the jury before they deliberated on the verdict.

[34,35] AIPCA Code of Ethics, ET Section 203 .01 Accounting Principles.

[36] *United States v. Simon,* 425 F.2d 796 (1969).

[37] For more information on the Continental Vending case, see David B. Isbell "The Continental Vending Case: Lessons for the Profession," *Journal of Accountancy*, August 1970, p. 34. Isbell notes that the criminal case against the defendants was used as leverage to compel the settling of the $21 million companion civil suit.

The defense asked that the jurors be instructed that the defendants should be acquitted if it was found that the financial statement was submitted in conformity with generally accepted accounting principles. However, the trial court instead instructed jurors that the "critical test was whether the balance sheet fairly presented the financial position without reference to generally accepted accounting principles ... evidence of compliance with generally accepted accounting principles would be very persuasive, but not conclusive."[38] In other words, compliance with rules based GAAP is usually necessary, but not always sufficient to reach the fair presentation standard. The verdict in Continental Vending implies that compliance with GAAP does not exhaust accountants responsibilities to the SEC or investors. It is important to note that the standard established in Continental Vending was the standard of "not misleading." That is similar to the standard established in Rule 203. Some commentators go farther and claim that the Continental Vending case made principles-based accounting the "law of the land."[39]

The accounting industry expressed concern over the verdict of Continental Vending. In 1975, the Auditing Standards Executive Committee (AudSEC) issued *SAS No. 5,* which requires auditors to define "fairness" only within the framework of GAAP. *SAS No. 5* claimed without circumscribing definitions of fairness to those contained with the GAAP framework, it would be impossible to have a uniform standard for judging the presentation of financial position, results of operations, and changes in financial position in financial statements."[40] In 1978, the AICPA was concerned enough over the possible implications of the dual requirements implied by a "present fairly" requirement, that they sought to delete the "present fairly" phrase arguing that fairness "is not a property that can be objectively measured by the auditor." However, after receiving letters of comment from their members, the board reconsidered and "present fairly" remains. The flexibility the use of this phrase provides depends on whether it is possible to distinguish GAAP rules from the GAAP framework and some commentators have complained that this as a distinction without a difference.[41]

---

[38] David B. Isbell, "The Continental Vending Case: Lessons for the Profession," *Journal of Accountancy,* August 1970, p. 35.

[39] Ronald M. Mano, Matthew Mouritsen, and Ryan Pace, "Principles-Based Accounting: Its Not New, Its Not the Rule, It's the Law." *CPA Journal Online* February, 2006.

[40] The Meaning of "Present Fairly in Conformity with Generally Accepted Accounting Principles" in the Independent Auditor's Report, Paragraph 3, cited by Stephen Zeff, "The Primacy of 'Present Fairly' in the Auditor's Report," The Saxe Lectures in Accounting, Rice University, April 10, 2006.

[41] The Auditing Standards Board, "The Auditor's Standards Report", proposed statement on auditing standards, 1980, cited by Stephen Zeff, "The Primacy of 'Present Fairly' in the Auditor's Report," The Saxe Lectures in Accounting, Rice University, April 10, 2006.

IX Recent Developments of "Present Fairly"[42]

Recent events reveal the continuing importance of the concepts of "fair presentation". In an example of history repeating itself, Bernie Ebbers, the former CEO of WorldCom argued that the prosecution had not alleged or proved that WorldCom's accounting was not in compliance with GAAP. Ebbers claimed that, "where a fraud charge is based on improper accounting, the impropriety must be a violation of GAAP, because financials that comply with GAAP must necessarily meet the SEC's disclosure requirements."[43] The Court of Appeals for the Second Circuit explicitly reaffirmed the decision in *Continental Vending* stating that:

> We see no reason to depart from Simon. To be sure, GAAP may have relevance in that defendant's good faith attempt to comply with GAAP or reliance upon an accountant's advice regarding GAAP may negate the government's claim of an intent to deceive … If the government proves that a defendant was responsible for financial reports that intentionally and materially mislead investors the statute [securities fraud] is satisfied. The government is not required in addition to prevail in a battle of expert witnesses over the application of individual GAAP rules.[44]

However, the Court of Appeals ruling was not an unambiguous endorsement of the principles-based approach.[45] The Appeals Court stated that the material misstatements contained in WorldCom's financial reports were a violation of GAAP. In other words, it is not necessary to apply an additional standard, above and beyond GAAP, to demonstrate wrongdoing and establish Ebbers'

---

[42] The requirement to "present fairly" also appears in the Sarbanes–Oxley Act of 2002. Section 302(a)(3) requires both the Chief Executive Officer and the Chief Financial Officer to certify that "the financial statements, and other information included in the report, fairly present in all material respects the financial condition and results of operations of the issuer." In this case, "fairly present" is the only criterion and the explicit separation from "conformity with generally accepted accounting standards" makes it clear that fair presentation requires something beyond mere compliance with accepted rules and standards.

[43,44] *United States v. Ebbers* 458 F. 3d 110, 125 (2nd Circular 2006).

[45] "In a real sense, by alleging and proving that the financial statements were misleading the government did, in fact, allege and prove violations of GAAP according to the AICPAs Codification of Statements on Accounting Standards, AU § 312.04, 'financial statements are materially mis-stated when they contain mis-statements whose effect, individually or in the aggregate, is important enough to cause them not to be presented fairly, in all material respects, in compliance with GAAP.'" *United States v. Ebbers* 458 F. 3d 110, 125 (2nd Circular 2006).

guilt; GAAP is sufficient. Moreover, according to the Court, the AICPA recognizes that, in some instances, compliance with GAAP rules does not ensure the absence of material misstatements or guarantee a fair presentation.[46]

X A Better Question

But have we answered the question of whether being in accordance with generally accepted accounting principles is a principles-based approach. Hardly. As we have seen, the question of whether the United States currently operates under a principles-based or rules-based framework remains an unsettled question. Clearly, the purpose of presenting as useful and accurate a picture as possible overrides the technical application of the rules, according to both the law and common sense. That being the case, part of the difficulty with the first question results from a confusion over the definitions of principles and rules. This confusion results from the fact that rules vary by degrees in terms of their generality, strictness, and rigidity, and principles vary by degrees is terms of their abstractness and inclusiveness. A *hard rule* permits little or no judgment in its application, while a *soft rule* permits some judgment in application within clearly defined limitations. Principles express the same variation; a *general principle* is an abstract injunction, such as the command to "do good and avoid evil." A *narrow principle*, in contrast, contains more clearly defined boundaries, such as the requirement "don't kill."

Given these four categories, it is possible to establish a continuum, with *hard rules* at one end and *general principles* at the other end. The FASB mentions the possibility of developing a continuum. "We characterize accounting standard setting process and its products on a continuum ranging from unequivocally rigid standards on one end to general definitions of economics-based concepts on the other end." The distinction between standards that are rule based and those that are principles based is not well defined and is subject to a variety of interpretations.[47]

While there is little trouble distinguishing between two extremes, there is far more difficulty in defining the prohibitions and requirements that lie near the middle. Considering the lack of clarity of the concepts involved, it is certainly not surprising that there has been substantial disagreement on both

---

[46]"Thus, GAAP itself recognizes that technical compliance with particular GAAP rules may lead to misleading financial statements and imposes an overall requirement that the statements as a whole accurately reflect the financial status of the company."

[47]Bruce Bennett, Michael E. Bradbury, and Helen Prangnell, "Rules, Principles and Judgments in Accounting Standards," *Abacus*, Vol. 42(2), 2006, p. 191.

the merits of either approach and the description of the current standard framework. However, it is perhaps best not to get "bogged down" in semantic quibbles.

One point which is clear is that it is impossible to develop a model that is either entirely principles or rules based. A framework which is purely principles based would be far too abstract to be of frequent and practical use. Consider the example we used above of a general principle; "do good and avoid evil." The injunction seems vague and helpful until we are given specific definitions of "good" and "evil." Beyond these definition, we would want a "roadmap" of how to do good and avoid evil. This roadmap, typically a set of rules, further specifies the general principle. Killing specifies a type of harm. But even that might be too general. Does it include killing mosquitos? A principles-based model is not distinguished by the absence of rules, but rather by the degree of the rules' flexibility (the hardness or softness of the rules) and the priority rules are given within the overall framework, namely, are the rules subordinate to principles or do they stand alone?

It is equally impossible to have an entirely rules-based scheme. This is the case for two reasons; the first is that a set of rules cannot specify every situation. They need to be motivated by a common purpose. In the case of GAAP, the rules are designed in order to promote "decision usefulness." Any rule which violates that is a bad rule. Decision usefulness is the *raison d'être* of the rules and guidelines that govern the accounting profession in the United States. The second reason we need principles is that principles establish coherence among various rules. Principles prevent standard setters from promulgating contradictory rules and also adjudicate between competing rules when conflicts arise. In GAAP, coherence is secured through the principles of relevance, reliability, and comparability.

Thus one can conclude that the real debate is not whether GAAP is a rules-based or principles-based approach; it is whether *decision-usefulness is more likely to be achieved by a framework that places a greater emphasis on rules or a greater emphasis on principles.* It is to this question we now turn.

XI   Argument for a Rules Based Approach

Despite recent enthusiasm for the adoption of a more principles-based approach, proponents of the rule-based approach believe that serious problems may arise and important benefits forgone if FASB and SEC move in this direction. Regardless of the precise definitions of rules and principles, proponents believe the current standard setting framework (perhaps with some adjustments) accomplishes its stated objectives.

Defenders of the rules-based approach argue that it encourages consistency and comparability. "That is, if similar things are accounted for in the same way, either across firms or over time, it becomes possible to assess financial reports of different entities, or the same entity at different points in time, so as to discern the underlying economic events."[48] Supporters of a rules-based framework contend that unless we can place information in context, it is of very little use to us in making decisions. For example, imagine if you were informed that a particular automobile was recently marked-down to $30,000. Should you make the purchase? Before you make a decision it seems reasonable that you would want to know (1) the price of the automobile before the mark-down, i.e. how much has the price been reduced? You might also want to know (2) the prices of similar automobiles currently on the market. Without this information, it would be difficult to determine whether or not $30,000 was a good price. This example points to the importance of *comparability*, in other words, in order to apply the information we need to be able to compare the price of the car over time as well as compare the price of that car with other similar cars on the market.

Further, it is important to have values and prices arrived at through a consistently applied formula or equation. Automobiles sold in the United States are required to prominently disclose their rate of fuel efficiency. In order for this information to be useful to consumers, it is necessary for fuel efficiency rates to be calculated using the same formula. *Consistency* is closely linked to comparability since without being able to depend on the application of a consistent formula, it would be impossible to determine whether cars are becoming more or less fuel-efficient over time or to compare rates of fuel efficiency among several different cars. The concern is that the adoption of a more principles-based framework may make it difficult for end-users of financial information to place the information they receive in context, and without this context, information is, quite simply, not very useful.

A second concern revolves around the difficulties of verifying the accuracy of financial reports and sanctioning enforcement preparers who deviate from the rules. The argument is that a clearly determined rule makes it easier to determine who is and who is not in compliance with the rule. A clearly determined rule will also make it easier to detect and sanction preparers who deviate from the rule. Defenders of a rules-based approach note that this framework has the added benefit of reducing the workload of regulators by limiting the need to determine whether the subjective judgments of auditors and management are in compliance with the standard. A clear and

---

[48] Katherine Schipper, "Principles-Based Accounting Standards," *Accounting Horizons*, Vol. 17, No. 1, March 2003, p. 62.

unambiguous rule may also help auditors resist client pressure for inappropriate accounting treatments.

A third concern is that deviation from a rules-based approach may place a heavier burden on preparers, particularly auditors. Without the benefit of bright line rules, auditors will be forced to interpret the intent of a principles-based guideline. Aristotle's theory of virtue ethics can be viewed as a principles-based framework with the moral and intellectual virtues taking the role of principles. Aristotle clearly states that a student of ethics cannot demand more precision from a science (or body of knowledge) than the subject matter permits. Therefore, Aristotle refuses to give specific rules or a list of actions one must be perform to act virtuously. He argues that "acting virtuously" demands different actions at different times, and what is required depends on the particular circumstances of the situation of the person involved.

So how does the person striving to be virtuous know what to do? Aristotle's theory has been criticized by many for failing to provide more guidance. Aristotle's response is that experience, which he refers to as practical wisdom, enables us to determine how we should act virtuously in a particular situation. Defenders of a rules-based approach fear is that not only will it take a great deal of time and effort for preparers to develop the requisite experience, but also that experience is too subjective and will dangerously diminish consistency and comparability.

Finally, advocates of a rules-based framework express concern over the harmful effects in terms of increased volatility that may result from the adoption of a more principles-based framework. Proponents note that rules become increasingly unwieldy on account of the various exceptions requested by constituents. A principles-based approach will likely eliminate many of these exceptions in an effort to detangle standards from unnecessarily detailed and complex rules. Some of these exceptions were granted in an effort to mitigate volatility in earnings, particularly in cases when the volatility does not signify a change in the underlying economics of the firm or a transaction. Injecting volatility into financial statements increases the overall volatility of the market and this can undermine overall economic stability and diminish growth.

Proponents of a rules-based approach fear that the need (or demand) for exceptions will not disappear even in the transition to a principles-based framework. Exceptions are usually provided for one of three reasons; to prevent volatility, to achieve some specific accounting outcome, or in response to constituent concerns. Without the establishment of detailed rules and guidance, it may not possible for these concerns to be addressed by standard-setters. This lack of detailed guidance may be particularly worrying to preparers in the wake of the Sarbanes–Oxley Act of 2002, which assesses heavy personal penalties for preparers who transgress accounting and regulatory rules. The FASB in *SFAS No. 2* states that, "as more accounting standards are issued, the scope for individual choice inevitably becomes circumscribed."[49] Preparers may appreciate these limitations in the increasingly litigious environment created by Sarbanes–Oxley and a principles-based approach may not harmonize well with the federally mandated rules-regime imposed by Sarbanes–Oxley. A rules-based standard developed to meet the needs of managers and auditors who want a clear answer on every accounting issue will harmonize well with those mandates.

XII What Would a Principles Based Approach Look Like? The True and Fair Override

Proponents of a principles-based approach believe that allowing accounting professionals a wider latitude in which to exercise their best judgment will result in more reliable information. Some suggest the adoption of an overarching standard, such as the "true and fair" override, which serves an important role in the British accounting standards.

> The dominant duty of management with respect to financial reports is that the balance sheet shall give a true and fair view of the affairs of the company at the end of the financial year; and the profit and loss account shall give a true and fair view of the profit and loss and the company for the financial year. (Section 266(2) of the Companies Act 1985.)

The establishment of a principle such as the "true and fair override" would require both corporations and auditors to not follow a standard or rule when the application of that standard or rule would result in financial statements not presenting a true and fair view of the company's financial position. The development of such a principle operates a "supreme standard" against which the judgments of managers and auditors need to be measured. It also serves as a means for adjudicating in situations in which secondary principles and rules are in conflict. Under a model which incorporated a true and fair override or a principle which played a similar role, management and auditors would not be able to seek refuge in the defense of "technical compliance" since "technical compliance" would be neither necessary nor sufficient. This model represents a departure from the current GAAP framework in two

---

[49] Financial Accounting Standards Board, SFAS No. 2, Section 7.

important ways; the first is that under a true and fair override model, technical compliance is necessary, but may not, in some cases, be sufficient. According to proponents, this model would minimize opportunism by preventing opportunistic managers and auditors from merely compiling with the letter, but not the spirit of the law. The second is that the true and fair override applies to the entire financial report, rather than, as in Rule 203, being limited to a particular rule or standard.

XIII Argument for a Principles Based Approach

Supporters of the principles-based framework likewise offer a two-pronged argument in favor of amending the current framework. The first is that the rules-based framework currently undermines the objective of decision usefulness. Their second point is that a principles-based framework will increase the reliability of information without sacrificing comparability and consistency.

The first point is that a rules-based approach leads to the temptation to focus on adherence to the *letter of the rule* rather than compliance with the *intent of the rule*. The susceptibility of a proposed ethical theory to so-called "gaming" is often given as an objection to particular ethical theories. One example of this criticism has been directed at the moral theory of Immanuel Kant, who we met in Chapter 2. Kant believed that an action was morally permissible if it could be made into a universal moral law. That is, if everyone could perform an action without entailing a logical contradiction (as is the case in stealing) or without creating an irrational state of affairs (as is the case if people refuse to offer aid when they are in a position to help), then it is morally permissible for one to perform his or her proposed action.

However, a crafty thinker attempted to find a way around Kant's rule (called the Categorical Imperative) by creating a proposed "maxim" or general rule that would only apply to him. Therefore, he was able to confidently say that it could certainly be a universal law that, for example, "boys named John were allowed to steal a red bicycle from their next-door neighbor's garage at 10:00 am on Sunday, June 1 2009 if the neighbor's name was Ted, the bicycle was a shiny new 10 speed and Ted already had a perfectly good blue bicycle." By crafting the proposed maxim (or rule) in such a way, it appears that John is able to circumvent Kant's injunction to only act according to maxims that could be made in a universal law without contradiction. Thus, John can follow the moral law and steal the coveted bicycle.

Most of us recognize that even if John adhered to the letter of the law, imperative, he certainly did not abide by the spirit of that law. We might say that he got in on a "loophole" and if John's behavior was technically correct, it certainly was not morally right. Kant's defenders argue that they can defeat the "sly universalizer" objection, but the example makes an important point for our purposes here. If Kant's theory is susceptible to this sort of "gaming" of the rules, which is the point "sly universalizer" was trying to make, then this is a serious shortcoming of his moral theory. The problem is that theories which permit individuals to get by with merely following the "form" of the law while disregarding its "substance" create a society of people much like John. Proponents of the principles-based approach to standard setting believe that a greater emphasis on the principles of professional and ethical behavior will prevent those "sly universalizers" from "gaming" the system and doing harm to other people.

A second problem with a rules-based approach is the perceived incentive structure that this framework creates. The SEC refers to the pernicious effects of this incentive structure in the following quote:

> Unfortunately, experience demonstrates that rules-based standards often provide a roadmap to avoidance of the accounting objectives inherent in the standards.
>
> Internal inconsistencies, exceptions, and bright-line tests reward those willing to engineer their way around the intent of the standards. This can result in financial reporting that is not representationally faithful to the underlying economic substance of transactions and events. In a rules-based system, financial reporting may well come to be seen as an act of compliance rather an act of communication.[50]

In 1975, Steven Kerr wrote on "the folly of rewarding A, while hoping for B."[51] Kerr's point is that organizations, and even entire industries, often create incentive structures which reward the very behavior they are hoping to prevent. Proponents of a principles-based approach believe that these types of distorted incentives are created by a rules-based framework. While standard setters painstakingly develop increasingly detailed rules in order to close

---

[50] SEC, "Study Pursuant to Section 108(d) of the Sarbanes-Oxley Act of 2002 on the Adoption by the United States Financial Reporting System of a Principles-Based Accounting System," Office of the Chief Accountant, Office of Economic Analysis, United States Securities and Exchange Commission, July 25, 2003. Cited in George Benson, Michael Bromwich, and Alfred Wagenhofer, "Principles versus Rules-Based Accounting Standards: The FASB's Standard Setting Strategy," *Abacus*, Vol. 42(2), 2006, p. 169.

[51] Steven Kerr, "On the Folly of Rewarding A, While Hoping for B" *Academy of Management Journal*, Vol. 18, No. 4, 1975, 769–783.

"loop-holes", opportunistic auditors and managers work diligently to find exceptions and "game" the system. Opportunists are able to produce financial statements that are technically correct and favorable to their interests, although they may be misleading or misrepresentative of the true economic health of the firm. Opportunistic firms are rewarded by the market, and firms which fail to act opportunistically may be penalized. Technical, rather than substantive, compliance is proven to reap rewards and therefore, companies who were not originally opportunistic may be encouraged to seek the rewards of purely technical compliance.

These distorted incentives place auditors in a difficult position as clients demand more aggressive treatments which violate the intent, but not the letter of the law. As the quote at the beginning of the chapter suggests, the question shifts from "does this treatment, approach, etc., contribute to a fair presentation?" to "show me where in the rules it says we can't do this?". Both corporations and audit firms risk losing market share if they cede the advantages of technical, but not substantive, compliance to the competitors. Therefore, the distorted incentive structures encourages even non-opportunistic actors to act opportunistically. Regulators respond by creating increasingly detailed rules in an effort to curb opportunism and the cycle begins again.

The unfortunate irony, proponents of a more principles-based approach argue, is that no one benefits from this system in the long run. Regulators are over-stretched as they try to anticipate and minimize opportunistic behavior and since all rules are necessarily incomplete, it is impossible to develop a rule that is sufficiently general, while at the same time preventing opportunism. And while technical compliance may allow firms to paint a "rosy picture" of financial good health in the short-term, any serious misrepresentation is almost impossible to maintain in the long term. In short, a rules-based framework creates a "compliance mentality" which encourages participants to view the objective of financial reporting as "showing the firm to its best advantage" within the limits of technical compliance. Since this approach has harmful, and perhaps even dangerous consequences, an alternative must be sought.

A third problem is that a rules-based model sacrifices reliability in order to promote consistency and comparability. If financial statements are not reliable, that is, if they do not provide a fair presentation of the economic substance of a transaction or corporation, the information they present is not useful to consumers. Referring back to the fuel efficiency standard we mentioned earlier, if auto manufacturers are rigging the tests to make their cars appear more fuel efficient then they really are, then whether it is possible to compare the results of one car with another or whether the same formula to calculate fuel efficiency is used over time, is not very relevant. If the presentation fails to correctly represent the underlying phenomena, it is not of much use to the consumer.

Finally, proponents of a more principles-based approach argue that the sort of judgments a principles-based model requires are precisely those an experienced professional should be fully competent to make. Indeed, some have gone further and claimed that the increase in technical accounting belies the claim of accountants to be members of a profession.[52] Advocates of a principles-based approach believe that concerns about the subjectivity of experience are overblown. They believe that auditors, managers, regulators, and the investing public share a common understanding of the concepts and definitions involved in financial reporting, such as "fair presentation" and "not misleading." Moreover, most can sense if a concept is being stretched inappropriately. Concepts are not entirely subjective since we possess a rough, but workable agreement on what should be included and excluded. Consider the term "harm;" while there is certainly disagreement concerning whether certain actions are harmful, there is a wide swath of consensus about these matters as well. For example, almost everyone would agree that to maliciously taunt and tease a disabled child causes harm. That a few misanthropes may disagree does not undermine what the majority believes to be true in this case. Moreover, as we grow in experience our understanding of concepts becomes more nuanced and sophisticated. Simply put, while there may be disagreement around the boundaries of concepts, there is wide-spread consensus which forms the basis for our collective definitions and understanding. Without this agreement, communication of any kind would be virtually impossible.

XIV Conclusion

It is likely that debate over whether FASB and SEC should adopt a more principles-based approach to standard setting will continue. Still, given the commitment to work towards a greater convergence with the more principles-based IFRS, it is possible that a course of action will be selected in the near future. There are three points with which we would like to conclude this chapter. First, this debate reveals the importance of clarity and precision in concepts and definitions. Before it is possible to determine whether a shift towards a more principles focused approach is the best decision, it is necessary to understand what a principles-based approach is and is not. As we have seen, it is impossible to have a purely principles-driven approach to standard setting

---

[52] West, 2003, Cited in Bruce Bennett, Michael E. Bradbury, and Helen Prangnell, "Rules, Principles and Judgments in Accounting Standards," *Abacus*, Vol. 42(2), 2006, p. 189.

and therefore, any change will represent movement on a continuum, rather than a paradigmatic shift. The second point is that this debate, at its center, involves the balancing of values and priorities. The FASB and the SEC will continue to strive to develop a standard which maximizes reliability, relevance, and comparability in order to maximize decision usefulness. This process of trading and prioritizing goods requires not only practical wisdom, but ethical thinking. Third and finally, technical compliance is not the end of the ethical accountant's duties. Ethical practitioners are not only required to adhere to the spirit of the rules and regulations which govern their practice, but they are also obliged to fulfill the letter and the spirit of ethical code that governs their profession. This can be a daunting task, but one which the profession, and the constituents it serves, demands from each of us.

Appendix A:

Summary of Sarbanes–Oxley Act of 2002[1]

Section 3: Commission Rules and Enforcement

A violation of Rules of the Public Company Accounting Oversight Board ("Board") is treated as a violation of the '34 Act, giving rise to the same penalties that may be imposed for violations of that Act.

Section 101: Establishment; Board Membership

The Board will have five financially-literate members, appointed for five-year terms. Two of the members must be or have been certified public accountants, and the remaining three must not be and cannot have been CPAs. The Chair may be held by one of the CPA members, provided that he or she has not been engaged as a practicing CPA for five years.

The Board's members will serve on a full-time basis.

No member may, concurrent with service on the Board, "share in any of the profits of, or receive payments from, a public accounting firm," other than "fixed continuing payments," such as retirement payments.

Members of the Board are appointed by the Commission, "after consultation with" the Chairman of the Federal Reserve Board and the Secretary of the Treasury.

Members may be removed by the Commission "for good cause."

[1]The AICPA is the premier national professional association for CPAs in the United States. © 2005 The American Institute of Certified Public Accountants, ISO 9001 Certified. AICPA, 1211 Avenue of the Americas, New York, NY 10036.

Accounting Ethics, Second Edition. Ronald Duska, Brenda Shay Duska, and Julie Ragatz. © 2011 John Wiley & Sons, Ltd. Published 2011 by John Wiley & Sons, Ltd.

Section 101: Establishment; Duties of the Board

Section 103: Auditing, Quality Control, and Independence Standards and Rules

The Board shall:

(1)   register public accounting firms;
(2)   establish, or adopt, by rule, "auditing, quality control, ethics, independence, and other standards relating to the preparation of audit reports for issuers;"
(3)   conduct inspections of accounting firms;
(4)   conduct investigations and disciplinary proceedings, and impose appropriate sanctions;
(5)   perform such other duties or functions as necessary or appropriate;
(6)   enforce compliance with the Act, the rules of the Board, professional standards, and the securities laws relating to the preparation and issuance of audit reports and the obligations and liabilities of accountants with respect thereto;
(7)   set the budget and manage the operations of the Board and the staff of the Board.

Auditing standards. The Board would be required to "cooperate on an on-going basis" with designated professional groups of accountants and any advisory groups convened in connection with standard-setting, and although the Board can "to the extent that it determines appropriate" adopt standards proposed by those groups, the Board will have authority to amend, modify, repeal, and reject any standards suggested by the groups. The Board must report on its standard-setting activity to the Commission on an annual basis.

The Board must require registered public accounting firms to "prepare, and maintain for a period of not less than 7 years, audit work papers, and other information related to any audit report, in sufficient detail to support the conclusions reached in such report."

The Board must require a 2nd partner review and approval of audit reports registered accounting firms must adopt quality control standards.

The Board must adopt an audit standard to implement the internal control review required by section 404(b). This standard must require the auditor evaluate whether the internal control structure and procedures include records that accurately and fairly reflect the transactions of the issuer, provide reasonable assurance that the transactions are recorded in a manner that will permit the preparation of financial statements in accordance with GAAP, and a description of any material weaknesses in the internal controls.

Section 102(a): Mandatory Registration

Section 102(f): Registration and Annual Fees

Section 109(d): Funding; Annual Accounting Support Fee for the Board

In order to audit a public company, a public accounting firm must register with the Board. The Board shall collect "a registration fee" and "an annual fee" from each registered public accounting firm, in amounts that are "sufficient" to recover the costs of processing and reviewing applications and annual reports.

The Board shall also establish by rule a reasonable "annual accounting support fee" as may be necessary or appropriate to maintain the Board. This fee will be assessed on issuers only.

Section 104: Inspections of Registered Public Accounting Firms

Annual quality reviews (inspections) must be conducted for firms that audit more than 100 issues, all others must be conducted every 3 years. The SEC and/or the Board may order a special inspection of any firm at any time.

Section 105(b)(5): Investigation and Disciplinary Proceedings; Investigations; Use of Documents

Section 105(c)(2): Investigations and Disciplinary Proceedings; Disciplinary Procedures; Public Hearings

Section 105(c)(4): Investigations and Disciplinary Proceedings; Sanctions

Section 105(d): Investigations and Disciplinary Proceedings; Reporting of Sanctions

All documents and information prepared or received by the Board shall be "confidential and privileged as an evidentiary matter (and shall not be subject to civil discovery other legal process) in any proceeding in any Federal or State court or administrative agency, ... unless and until presented in connection with a public proceeding or [otherwise] released" in connection with a disciplinary action. However, all such documents and information can be made available to the SEC, the U.S. Attorney General, and other federal and appropriate state agencies.

Disciplinary hearings will be closed unless the Board orders that they be public, for good cause, and with the consent of the parties.

Sanctions can be imposed by the Board of a firm if it fails to reasonably supervise any associated person with regard to auditing or quality control standards, or otherwise.

No sanctions report will be made available to the public unless and until stays pending appeal have been lifted.

Section 106: Foreign Public Accounting Firms

The bill would subject foreign accounting firms who audit a U.S. company to registrations with the Board. This would include foreign firms that perform some audit work, such as in a foreign subsidiary of a U.S. company, that is relied on by the primary auditor.

Section 107(a): Commission Oversight of the Board; General Oversight Responsibility

Section 107(b): Rules of the Board

Section 107(d): Censure of the Board and Other Sanctions

The SEC shall have "oversight and enforcement authority over the Board." The SEC can, by rule or order, give the Board additional responsibilities. The SEC may require the Board to keep certain records, and it has the power to inspect the Board itself, in the same manner as it can with regard to SROs such as the NASD.

The Board, in its rulemaking process, is to be treated "as if the Board were a 'registered securities association'"-that is, a self-regulatory organization. The Board is required to file proposed rules and proposed rule changes with the SEC. The SEC may approve, reject, or amend such rules.

The Board must notify the SEC of pending investigations involving potential violations of the securities laws, and coordinate its investigation with the SEC Division of Enforcement as necessary to protect an ongoing SEC investigation.

The SEC may, by order, "censure or impose limitations upon the activities, functions, and operations of the Board" if it finds that the Board has violated the Act or the securities laws, or if the Board has failed to ensure the compliance of accounting firms with applicable rules without reasonable justification.

Section 107(c): Commission Review of Disciplinary Action Taken By The Board

The Board must notify the SEC when it imposes "any final sanction" on any accounting firm or associated person. The Board's findings and sanctions are subject to review by the SEC.

The SEC may enhance, modify, cancel, reduce, or require remission of such sanction.

Section 108: Accounting Standards

The SEC is authorized to "recognize, as 'generally accepted' ... any accounting principles" that are established by a standard-setting body that meets the bill's criteria, which include requirements that the body:

(1) be a private entity;
(2) be governed by a board of trustees (or equivalent body), the majority of whom are not or have not been associated persons with a public accounting firm for the past 2 years;
(3) be funded in a manner similar to the Board;
(4) have adopted procedures to ensure prompt consideration of changes to accounting principles by a majority vote;
(5) consider, when adopting standards, the need to keep them current and the extent to which international convergence of standards is necessary or appropriate.

Section 201: Services outside the Scope of Practice of Auditors; Prohibited Activities

It shall be "unlawful" for a registered public accounting firm to provide any non-audit service to an issuer contemporaneously with the audit, including: (1) bookkeeping or other services related to the accounting records or financial statements of the audit client; (2) financial information systems design and implementation; (3) appraisal or valuation services, fairness opinions, or contribution-in-kind reports; (4) actuarial services; (5) internal audit outsourcing services; (6) management functions or human resources; (7) broker or dealer, investment adviser, or investment banking services; (8) legal services and expert services unrelated to the audit; (9) any other service that the Board determines, by regulation, is impermissible. The Board may, on a case-by-case basis, exempt from these prohibitions any person, issuer, public accounting firm, or transaction, subject to review by the Commission.

It will not be unlawful to provide other non-audit services if they are pre-approved by the audit committee in the following manner. The bill allows an accounting firm to "engage in any non-audit service, including tax services," that is not listed above, only if the activity is pre-approved by the audit committee of the issuer. The audit committee will disclose to investors in periodic reports its decision to pre-approve non-audit services. Statutory insurance company regulatory audits are treated as an audit service, and thus do not require pre-approval.

The pre-approval requirement is waived with respect to the provision of non-audit services for an issuer if the aggregate amount of all such non-audit services provided to the issuer constitutes less than 5 % of the total amount of revenues paid by the issuer to its auditor (calculated on the basis of revenues paid by the issuer during the fiscal year when the non-audit services are performed), such services were not recognized by the issuer at the time of the engagement to be non-audit services; and such services are promptly brought to the attention of the audit committee and approved prior to completion of the audit.

The authority to pre-approve services can be delegated to 1 or more members of the audit committee, but any decision by the delegate must be presented to the full audit committee.

Section 203: Audit Partner Rotation

The lead audit or coordinating partner and the reviewing partner must rotate off of the audit every 5 years.

Section 204: Auditor Reports to Audit Committees

The accounting firm must report to the audit committee all "critical accounting policies and practices to be used all alternative treatments of financial information within [GAAP] that have been discussed with management ramifications of the use of such alternative disclosures and treatments, and the treatment preferred" by the firm.

Section 206: Conflicts of Interest

The CEO, Controller, CFO, Chief Accounting Officer or person in an equivalent position cannot have been employed by the company's audit firm during the 1-year period preceding the audit.

Section 207: Study of Mandatory Rotation of Registered Public Accountants

The GAO will do a study on the potential effects of requiring the mandatory rotation of audit firms.

Section 209: Consideration by Appropriate State Regulatory Authorities

State regulators are directed to make an independent determination as to whether the Boards standards shall be applied to small and mid-size non-registered accounting firms.

Section 301: Public Company Audit Committees

Each member of the audit committee shall be a member of the board of directors of the issuer, and shall otherwise be independent.

"Independent" is defined as not receiving, other than for service on the board, any consulting, advisory, or other compensatory fee from the issuer, and as not being an affiliated person of the issuer, or any subsidiary thereof.

The SEC may make exemptions for certain individuals on a case-by-case basis.

The audit committee of an issuer shall be directly responsible for the appointment, compensation, and oversight of the work of any registered public accounting firm employed by that issuer.

The audit committee shall establish procedures for the "receipt, retention, and treatment of complaints" received by the issuer regarding accounting, internal controls, and auditing.

Each audit committee shall have the authority to engage independent counsel or other advisors, as it determines necessary to carry out its duties.

Each issuer shall provide appropriate funding to the audit committee.

Section 302: Corporate Responsibility for Financial Reports

The CEO and CFO of each issuer shall prepare a statement to accompany the audit report to certify the "appropriateness of the financial statements and disclosures contained in the periodic report, and that those financial statements and disclosures fairly present, in all material respects, the operations and financial condition of the issuer." A violation of this section must be knowing and intentional to give rise to liability.

Section 303: Improper Influence on Conduct of Audits

It shall be unlawful for any officer or director of an issuer to take any action to fraudulently influence, coerce, manipulate, or mislead any auditor engaged in the performance of an audit for the purpose of rendering the financial statements materially misleading.

Section 304: Forfeiture of Certain Bonuses and Profits

Section 305: Officer and Director Bars and Penalties; Equitable Relief

If an issuer is required to prepare a restatement due to "material noncompliance" with financial reporting requirements, the chief executive officer and the chief financial officer shall "reimburse the issuer for any bonus or other incentive-based or equity-based compensation received" during the twelve months following the issuance or filing of the non-compliant document and "any profits realized from the sale of securities of the issuer" during that period.

In any action brought by the SEC for violation of the securities laws, federal courts are authorized to "grant any equitable relief that may be appropriate or necessary for the benefit of investors."

Section 305: Officer and Director Bars and Penalties

The SEC may issue an order to prohibit, conditionally or unconditionally, permanently or temporarily, any person who has violated section 10(b) of the 1934 Act from acting as an officer or director of an issuer if the SEC has found that such person's conduct "demonstrates unfitness" to serve as an officer or director of any such issuer.

Section 306: Insider Trades during Pension Fund Black-Out Periods Prohibited

Prohibits the purchase or sale of stock by officers and directors and other insiders during blackout periods. Any profits resulting from sales in violation of this section "shall inure to and be recoverable by the issuer." If the issuer fails to bring suit or prosecute diligently, a suit to recover such profit may be instituted by "the owner of any security of the issuer."

Section 401(a): Disclosures in Periodic Reports; Disclosures Required

Each financial report that is required to be prepared in accordance with GAAP shall "reflect all material correcting adjustments ... that have been identified by a registered accounting firm. ..."

"Each annual and quarterly financial report ... shall disclose all material off-balance sheet transactions" and "other relationships" with "unconsolidated entities" that may have a material current or future effect on the financial condition of the issuer.

The SEC shall issue rules providing that pro forma financial information must be presented so as not to "contain an untrue statement" or omit to state a material fact necessary in order to make the pro forma financial information not misleading.

Section 401 (c): Study and Report on Special Purpose Entities

SEC shall study off-balance sheet disclosures to determine a) extent of off-balance sheet transactions (including assets, liabilities, leases, losses and the use of special purpose entities); and b) whether generally accepted accounting rules result in financial statements of issuers reflecting the economics of such off-balance sheet transactions to investors in a transparent fashion and make a report containing recommendations to the Congress.

Section 402(a): Prohibition on Personal Loans to Executives

Generally, it will be unlawful for an issuer to extend credit to any director or executive officer. Consumer credit companies may make home improvement and consumer credit loans and issue credit cards to its directors and executive officers if it is done in the ordinary course of business on the same terms and conditions made to the general public.

Section 403: Disclosures of Transactions Involving Management and Principal Stockholders

Directors, officers, and 10% owner must report designated transactions by the end of the second business day following the day on which the transaction was executed.

Section 404: Management Assessment of Internal Controls

Requires each annual report of an issuer to contain an "internal control report," which shall:

(1)   state the responsibility of management for establishing and maintaining an adequate internal control structure and procedures for financial reporting; and
(2)   contain an assessment, as of the end of the issuer's fiscal year, of the effectiveness of the internal control structure and procedures of the issuer for financial reporting.

Each issuer's auditor shall attest to, and report on, the assessment made by the management of the issuer. An attestation made under this section shall be in accordance with standards for attestation engagements issued or adopted by the Board. An attestation engagement shall not be the subject of a separate engagement.

The language in the report of the Committee which accompanies the bill to explain the legislative intent states, "– the Committee does not intend that the auditor's evaluation be the subject of a separate engagement or the basis for increased charges or fees."

Directs the SEC to require each issuer to disclose whether it has adopted a code of ethics for its senior financial officers and the contents of that code.

Directs the SEC to revise its regulations concerning prompt disclosure on Form 8-K to require immediate disclosure "of any change in, or waiver of," an issuer's code of ethics.

Section 407: Disclosure of Audit Committee Financial Expert

The SEC shall issue rules to require issuers to disclose whether at least 1 member of its audit committee is a "financial expert."

Section 409: Real Time Disclosure

Issuers must disclose information on material changes in the financial condition or operations of the issuer on a rapid and current basis.

Section 501: Treatment of Securities Analysts by Registered securities Associations

National Securities Exchanges and registered securities associations must adopt conflict of interest rules for research analysts who recommend equities in research reports.

Section 601: SEC Resources and Authority

SEC appropriations for 2003 are increased to $776,000,000. $98 million of the funds shall be used to hire an additional 200 employees to provide enhanced oversight of auditors and audit services required by the Federal securities laws.

Section 602(a): Appearance and Practice before the Commission

The SEC may censure any person, or temporarily bar or deny any person the right to appear or practice before the SEC if the person does not possess the requisite qualifications to represent others, lacks character or integrity, or has willfully violated Federal securities laws.

Section 602(c): Study and Report

SEC is to conduct a study of "securities professionals" (public accountants, public accounting firms, investment bankers, investment advisors, brokers, dealers, attorneys) who have been found to have aided and abetted a violation of Federal securities laws.

Section 602(d): Rules of Professional Responsibility for Attorneys

The SEC shall establish rules setting minimum standards for professional conduct for attorneys practicing before it.

Section 701: GAO Study and Report Regarding Consolidation of Public Accounting Firms

The GAO shall conduct a study regarding the consolidation of public accounting firms since 1989, including the present and future impact of the consolidation, and the solutions to any problems discovered.

Title VIII: Corporate and Criminal Fraud Accountability Act of 2002

It is a felony to "knowingly" destroy or create documents to "impede, obstruct or influence" any existing or contemplated federal investigation.

Auditors are required to maintain "all audit or review work papers" for five years.

The statute of limitations on securities fraud claims is extended to the earlier of five years from the fraud, or two years after the fraud was discovered, from three years and one year, respectively.

Employees of issuers and accounting firms are extended "whistleblower protection" that would prohibit the employer from taking certain actions against employees who lawfully disclose private employer information to, among others, parties in a judicial proceeding involving a fraud claim. Whistle blowers are also granted a remedy of special damages and attorney's fees.

A new crime for securities fraud that has penalties of fines and up to 10 years imprisonment.

Title IX: White Collar Crime Penalty Enhancements

Maximum penalty for mail and wire fraud increased from 5 to 10 years.

Creates a crime for tampering with a record or otherwise impeding any official proceeding.

SEC given authority to seek court freeze of extraordinary payments to directors, offices, partners, controlling persons, agents of employees.

US Sentencing Commission to review sentencing guidelines for securities and accounting fraud.

SEC may prohibit anyone convicted of securities fraud from being an officer or director of any publicly traded company.

Financial Statements filed with the SEC must be certified by the CEO and CFO. The certification must state that the financial statements and disclosures fully comply with provisions of the Securities Exchange Act and that they fairly present, in all material respects, the operations and financial condition of the issuer. Maximum penalties for willful and knowing violations of this section are a fine of not more than $500,000 and/or imprisonment of up to 5 years.

Section 1001: Sense of Congress Regarding Corporate Tax Returns

It is the sense of Congress that the Federal income tax return of a corporation should be signed by the chief executive officer of such corporation.

Section 1102: Tampering With a Record or Otherwise Impeding an Official Proceeding

Makes it a crime for any person to corruptly alter, destroy, mutilate, or conceal any document with the intent to impair the object's integrity or availability for use in an official proceeding or to otherwise obstruct, influence or impede any official proceeding is liable for up to 20 years in prison and a fine.

Section 1103: Temporary Freeze Authority

The SEC is authorized to freeze the payment of an extraordinary payment to any director, officer, partner, controlling person, agent, or employee of a company during an investigation of possible violations of securities laws.

Section 1105: SEC Authority to Prohibit Persons from Serving as Officers or Directors

The SEC may prohibit a person from serving as an officer or director of a public company if the person has committed securities fraud.

Appendix B:
The IMA Code of Conduct for Management Accountants

Practitioners of management accounting and financial management have an obligation to the public, their profession, the organization they serve, and themselves, to maintain the highest standards of ethical conduct. In recognition of this obligation, the Institute of Management Accountants (IMA) has promulgated the following standards of ethical conduct for practitioners of management accounting and financial management. Adherence to these standards internationally is integral to achieving the objective of management accounting.

Competence

Practitioners of management accounting and financial management have a responsibility to:

- Maintain an appropriate level of professional competence by ongoing development of their knowledge and skills.
- Perform their professional duties in accordance with relevant laws, regulations, and technical standards.
- Prepare complete and clear reports and recommendations after appropriate analysis of relevant and reliable information

Confidentiality

Practitioners of management accounting and financial management have a responsibility to:

Accounting Ethics, Second Edition. Ronald Duska, Brenda Shay Duska, and Julie Ragatz.
© 2011 John Wiley & Sons, Ltd. Published 2011 by John Wiley & Sons, Ltd.

- Refrain from disclosing confidential information acquired in the course of their work except when authorized, unless legally obligated to do so.
- Inform subordinates as appropriate regarding the confidentiality of information acquired in the course of their work and monitor their activities to assure the maintenance of that confidentiality.
- Refrain from using or appearing to use confidential information acquired in the course of their work for unethical or illegal advantage either personally or through third parties.

Integrity

Practitioners of management accounting and financial management have a responsibility to:

- Avoid actual or apparent conflicts of interest and advise all appropriate parties of any potential conflict.
- Refrain from engaging in any activity that would prejudice their ability to carry out their duties ethically.
- Refuse any gift, favor, or hospitality that would influence or would appear to influence their actions.
- Refrain from either activity or passively subverting the attainment of the organization's legitimate and ethical objectives.
- Recognize and communicate professional limitations or other constraints that would preclude responsible judgment or successful performance of an activity.
- Communicate unfavorable as well as favorable information and professional judgment or opinion.
- Refrain from engaging [in] or supporting any activity that would discredit the profession.

Objectivity

Practitioners of management accounting and financial management have a responsibility to:

- Communicate information fairly and objectively.
- Disclose fully all relevant information that could reasonably be expected to influence an intended user's understanding of the reports, comments, and recommendations presented.

Resolution of Ethical Conflicts

In applying the standards of ethical conduct, practitioners of management accounting and financial management may encounter problems in identifying unethical behavior or in resolving an ethical conflict. When faced with significant ethical issues practitioners of management accounting and financial management should follow the established policies of the organization bearing on the resolution of such conflict. If these policies do not resolve the ethical conflict, such practitioner should consider the following course of action.

- Discuss such problems with the immediate superior except when it appears that superior is involved, in which case the problem should be presented to the next higher managerial level. If a satisfactory resolution cannot be achieved when the problem is initially presented, submit the issue to the next higher managerial level.
- If the immediate superior is the chief executive officer or equivalent, the acceptable reviewing authority may be a group such as the audit committee, executive committee, board of directors, board of trustees, or owners. Contact with a level above the immediate superior should be initiated only with the superior's knowledge, assuming the superior is not involved. Except where legally prescribed, communication of such problems to authorities or individuals not employed or engaged by the organization is not considered appropriate.
- Clarify relevant ethical issues by confidential discussion with an objective adviser to obtain a better understanding of possible course of action.
- Consult your own attorney as to legal obligations and rights concerning the ethical conflict. If the ethical conflict still exists after exhausting all levels of internal review, there may be no other recourse on significant matters than to resign from the organization and to submit an informative memorandum to an appropriate representative of the organization. After resignation, depending on the nature of the ethical conflict, it may also be appropriate to notify other parties.

Index

Accounting Ethics, Second Edition. Ronald Duska, Brenda Shay Duska, and Julie Ragatz.
© 2011 John Wiley & Sons, Ltd. Published 2011 by John Wiley & Sons, Ltd.